# LABOUR UNIONISM IN THE FINANCIAL SERVICES SECTOR

*To Linda Somerville, senior long-standing finance worker union activist, and socialist, for her continually reasoned and rounded, but always principled positions and actions, on matters of the labour movement over the last two decades.*


*To Fiona Cassidy, my partner, remaining faithful as ever during times when I was again being unfaithful by dedicating myself to the writing of this study.*

# Labour Unionism in the Financial Services Sector

## Fighting for Rights and Representation

GREGOR GALL
*University of Hertfordshire, UK*

# ASHGATE

Published by
Ashgate Publishing Limited
Wey Court East
Union Road
Farnham
Surrey, GU9 7PT
England

Ashgate Publishing Company
Suite 420
101 Cherry Street
Burlington,
VT 05401–4405
USA

www.ashgate.com

**British Library Cataloguing in Publication Data**
Gall, Gregor
  Labour unionism in the financial services sector : fighting
  for rights and representation
  1. Financial services industry - Employees - Labor unions
  2. Financial services industry - Personnel management
  3. Bank employees - Labor unions 4. Banks and banking -
  Personnel management
  I. Title
  331.8'8113321

**Library of Congress Cataloging-in-Publication Data**
Gall, Gregor.
  Labour unionism in the financial services sector : fighting for rights and representation /
by Gregor Gall.
    p. cm.
  Includes bibliographical references and index.
  ISBN 978-0-7546-4223-7
  1. Financial services industry--Employees--Labor unions--Great Britain. I. Title.
  HD6668.F47G35 2008
  331.88'1133210941--dc22

                                                                          2008030726

  ISBN: 978 0 7546 4223 7

**Mixed Sources**
Product group from well-managed
forests and other controlled sources
www.fsc.org Cert no. SGS-COC-2482
© 1996 Forest Stewardship Council
FSC

Printed and bound in Great Britain by
TJ International Ltd, Padstow, Cornwall

# Contents

# List of Tables

# List of Insets

# List of Abbreviations, Acronyms and Organisational Names

| | |
|---|---|
| Accord | the successor to the IUHS |
| AEEU | Amalgamated Electrical and Engineering Union |
| ALGUS | Alliance and Leicester Group Union for Staff |
| AEGIS | AEGIS the Aegon UK Staff Association |
| Amicus | union formed from merger of AEEU and MSF |
| ANGU | Abbey National Group Union |
| APEX | Association of Professional, Executive, Clerical and Computer Staffs |
| ASS | Associated Staff Societies |
| ASTMS | Association of Supervisory, Technical and Managerial Staffs |
| BFSA | Brittannic Field Staff Association |
| BGSA | Barclays Group Staff Association |
| BGSU | Barclays Group Staff Union |
| BIFU | Banking, Insurance and Finance Union |
| BOG | Bank Officers' Guild |
| BoS | Bank of Scotland |
| BSU | Britannia Staff Union |
| CBSSA | Cheshire Building Society Staff Association |
| CBSA | Clydesdale Bank Staff Association |
| CCBSA | Central Council of Banking Staff Associations |
| CCSBSA | Central Council of Scottish Banking Staff Associations |
| CGSA | Cheltenham and Gloucester Staff Association |
| CGUSA | Commercial and General Union Staff Association |
| CGNUSA | Commercial General and Norwich Union Staff Association (company became Aviva) |
| CIR | Commission on Industrial Relations |
| CLB | Company-level Bargaining |
| CWU | Communication Workers' Unions |
| DBSSA | Dunfermline Building Society Staff Association |
| DGSU | Derbyshire Group Staff Union |
| EUO | Employed Union Officer |
| GIO | Guild of Insurance Officers |
| HBoS | Halifax Bank of Scotland |
| HRM | Human Resource Management |
| HSBC | Hong Kong and Shanghai Banking Corporation |
| IDS | Incomes Data Services |

| | |
|---|---|
| IRS | Industrial Relations Services |
| IUHS | Independent Union of Halifax Staff |
| LRD | Labour Research Department |
| LTU | Lloyds Trade Union (also known as LTSBGU – LloydsTSB Group Union – and LGU) |
| MBSA | Midland Bank Staff Association |
| MEB | Multi-employer Bargaining (or industry-wide bargaining) |
| MSF | Manufacturing, Science and Finance union |
| NAG | National Australia Group |
| NEC | National Executive Committee |
| NGSU | Nationwide Group Staff Union |
| NPSA | National and Provincial Staff Association |
| NUBE | National Union of Bank Employees |
| NUIW | National Union of Insurance Workers |
| NWSA | NatWest Staff Association |
| PGSA | Portman Group Staff Association |
| PRP | Performance-related Pay |
| RBS | Royal Bank of Scotland |
| SBA | Scottish Bankers' Associations |
| SSA | Skipton Staff Association |
| STB | Single-table Bargaining |
| STUC | Scottish Trades Union Congress |
| SUWBS | Staff Union West Bromwich Building Society |
| TGWU | Transport and General Workers' Union |
| TUC | Trades Union Congress |
| UBAC | Union for Bradford and Bingley Staff and Associated Companies |
| UFS | Union of Finance Staff |
| UIS | Union of Insurance Staffs |
| Unifi | Merged Finance Union formed from BIFU, NWSA and UNiFI |
| UNiFI | Renamed former BGSU |
| Unite | Merged union formed from Amicus and TGWU |
| USDAW | Union of Shop, Distributive and Allied Workers |
| WISA | Woolwich Independent Staff Association |
| YISA | Yorkshire Independent Staff Association |

# Preface

My interest in studying finance workers resulted from the period of the early 1990s when bank workers seemed to begin to engage in wider strike action and in wider numbers than they had hitherto done before. This phenomenon carried on until 1997. A number of obvious issues were raised. Were bank workers becoming more 'unionate', even 'militant'? Were they, belatedly, joining the ranks of the mainstream labour union movement? And if any off these were the case (and to any significant extent), what explained the sparseness of similar developments in the other sections of the financial services sector? In the background, the perennial issues of class positions and propensity to collectivism and mobilisation for white-collar workers loomed large. This interest was enough to propel me to begin conducting both primary and secondary research of a limited nature. But as the terrain of the inquiry changed, so too did the thrust of the inquiry. By the late 1990s, finance workers, primarily within BIFU and then Unifi, to the extent that they had shown themselves to be otherwise, now seemed to be becalmed by partnership working with employers, union dissolution, renewed employer hostility and organisational dislocation. What explained this apparent turnaround? Was it actually a turnaround or just the manifestation of an overestimation of the extent and nature of the aforementioned developments in 'unionateness'? And was the highpoint of the 1990s actually a highpoint or watershed when viewed in longer historical terms? Thinking through these issues led to a desire to develop a deeper understanding of the historical trajectory of the unionisation of finance workers, and thus provide a more rounded and grounded understanding of the contemporary period. The sum of this thinking is presented in this book.

Alongside this, there is much merit in studying and researching finance workers for the task of the critical mind in the field of employment relations is not just to map out and understand those events and processes which are more interesting and appealing to the researcher – such as strikes and developing union consciousness – but to consider and understand why interesting and appealing events and processes do not happen either as a study in themselves or an aid to understanding how and why these interesting and appealing phenomena might conceivably come about. Thus, in contrast to my study of postal workers (Gall 2003) who can genuinely claim some mantle of 'militancy', this study examines, in particular, the role of employers in influencing and conditioning the existence and nature of the 'moderate' collective organisation of finance workers.

Finally, and while it will come as no great surprise to any mind with a critical faculty, the place of finance workers has not managed to make into the official histories of the banks and financial houses – whether those specially commissioned by those organisations or those given official blessing but written by nominally independent writers. Thus, for example, Cameron (1995), Malcolm (n.d.) and Saville (1996) in their histories of the Bank of Scotland from the point of creation in 1695 to 1945 and 1995 as well as Pugh (1998) on the Halifax – the future merger partner with the Bank of Scotland in 2001 – make only one or two references to issues of staff and staffing. This is something which should strike the reader as remiss because, arguably, banks were the employing organisations *par excellence*, which in a pre-HRM way, heavily subscribed to the notion that 'our staff are our greatest asset'. Therefore, it is an essential task of this study to give full and proper consideration to the workers of the financial services sector, their jobs, functions, roles and struggle for representation of their interests as workers.

# Acknowledgements

I would like to record my gratitude to the officers, activists and members of the various financial services sector unions and staff associations, but particularly those in BIFU and Unifi, for making themselves available to me for conducting the fieldwork and for providing various documentation and materials. Without the help of staff of the BIFU/Unifi research department – particularly, Liz Cairns, David Cowie, John Earls, Pam Monks, John Robinson and Jo Seary – much of the material and data would not have been forthcoming. I would also like to acknowledge the financial support of the Nuffield Foundation (Small Grants Award) and the University of Stirling (Faculty of Management Fund) which allowed much of the later fieldwork to be carried out (see methodology section). To both the universities of Hertfordshire and Stirling, I am indebted for the provision of generous research time to conduct the research and write this study.

## Chapter 1

# Labour Unionism in the Financial Services Sector: Struggling for Rights and Representation

## Introduction

Worker collectivism, defined in terms of attitudes, behaviour and organisation, in the financial services sector has emerged in a significant quantitative way and developed in important qualitative manners since its beginnings in the early part of the twentieth century. This is particularly noteworthy given the greatest and most extensive employer's offensive in Britain against independent labour unionism through fostering the 'peaceful competition' (Bain 1970:131) of staff associations took place in this sector. Yet it is the thesis of this study that despite these advances, (even) independent labour unionism[1] in the sector has been a historically weak form of worker collectivism. Today, collectivism, in terms of both labour unions and staff associations/unions, now stand as a set of significantly neutered and impotent organisations that are in a prolonged crisis, and this itself now constitutes the central component of the acute crisis of worker representation in the financial services sector in Britain. In essence, the fledgling forms of more 'unionate' (Blackburn 1967) collectivism have been overcome by the extent and deleterious nature of the changes enacted by employers, individually and collectively, in the sector. The weak moves towards 'unionateness' by weak forms of worker collectivism have provided no robust defence against the storm forces emanating from employers. The quintessential argument of this study is that the form of labour unionism adopted by independent labour unionism in its battle with dependent unionism forewent the creation of workplace unionism and this

---

1   At this point, it is worth recording that the term 'labour' unionism is used throughout this study because in the contemporary period, and even for a considerable time previous to that, the term 'trade' unionism has been inappropriate. Today, most major unions in Britain are not 'trade' unions but 'general' unions organising 'blue-collar' and 'white-collar' workers across sectors and industries where relatively few members within these unions are organised in any identifiable sense on the basis of a 'trade' (even if the workers still have a 'trade'). Here, and outwith these unions, where something approximates to a 'trade', it is more likely to be an occupation or profession and even here there is an array of different skills involved with individual occupations and professions. And, of course, a particularly salient characteristic of the financial services sector, in historical terms at least, was that banking represented a profession and not a trade. Over time, the strength and persistence of identity, skills and qualifications specific to the financial services sector have become diluted so again the term 'trade' unionism is inappropriate.

led to the inability of independent labour unionism to develop the resources and mobilisation capacities necessary to more forcefully and effectively resist the employers, particularly under a re-ordering of the employment relationship since the 1980s.

But the argument is not just that independent labour unionism has become unstuck in contemporary times. Rather, it is that independent labour unionism has been at a great historical disadvantage compared to labour unionism in general. And, for the moment, the main explanatory variable here is that independent labour unionism developed centralised forms of operation in order to differentiate and protect itself from dependent unionism which was based on an internalist version of mutual gains and reciprocity with employers. This also logically led to the pursuit of industry-wide, multi-employer bargaining rather than company level bargaining. In the combined process, as will be explained, workplace unionism was not developed. So this explanation is argued to be the fundamental, singular reason for the 'undeveloped' nature and general 'underdevelopment'[2] of workplace unionism in the financial services sector as opposed to other factors such as the historically socially conservative composition of the workforce, the historical stability of employment or the paternalistic approach of employers. These latter factors have merely reinforced and concretised the absence of stimuli for the creation of workplace unionism.

Stepping outside the entrenched parameters of competitive unionism to view the totality, the absence of tangible workplace unionism has had significant implications. Foremost, union leaderships have been without independent resource, having no credible counter-weight to employers, and so have been pulled and gravitated towards a particularly close *de facto* partnership and dependent relationship with the employers (which by far predates the formalised partnership agreements of the 1990s and 2000s). This relationship has been based on resources employers have been prepared to give (primarily of facility time) and on a cooperative ideology where labour unions/staff associations have not had recourse to the necessary resources to engage in conflict. The *quid pro quo* has been the granting of necessary resources to run a union where the membership is not the key resource in return for a broadly cooperative agenda and relationship based on the superordination of employer interests. In seeking to provide representation for its members, national organs of worker collective representation have been drawn in and incorporated. Of particular note here is that exclusive engagement with the senior national managements by employed union officers (EUOs) has presented a further impediment to the development of workplace unionism. Even if EUOs and national lay officials wanted to pursue a more 'militant' agenda based on greater membership mobilisation than had been hitherto witnessed, significant obstacles

---

2    The terms undeveloped and underdevelopment are annotated to indicate not an expected trajectory but to contrast this to what passes for 'developed' unionism in other sectors of the economy like engineering.

have existed, namely, overturning the powerful living heritage of past practice and ideology and the inevitable withdrawal of employer support.

*Prima facie*, this might appear as an overly structuralist argument and in line with the school of thought represented by Clegg (1976). It is not, for not only is the division between 'structure' and 'agency' a simplistic and false one where human agencies are the determinants of structure *and* agency but the decision of independent labour unionism to act in this way, for different reasons and from different trajectories in banking (primarily BOG/NUBE/BIFU/Unifi) and insurance (primarily GIO/UIS/NUIW/ASTMS/MSF) represented informed and conscious strategies based on calculations within, and reflecting, an environment of powerful and hostile employers. In banking, the response was to be the antithesis of dependent company unionism, that is, of internalism and staff associations. By some contrast, in insurance, with not all staff associations being employer creatures but having an enterprise affinity, more ground was given by independent unionism to internalism through the adoption of federalised structures for union organisation whereby constituents had considerable autonomy. This debate will be returned to in the concluding chapter.

A key part of the thesis – and central to the analysis of this study – is the concept of 'unionateness', encompassing the notion that a labour union can become a full-blown, full-blooded union to the extent that it declares itself to be a union and is registered as such; regards collective bargaining and the protection of its members' interests (as workers rather than as consumers or citizens) as its main function; is prepared to use all forms of industrial action, including strikes, to pursue these aims; is independent from the employers; and is affiliated to the Trades Union Congress (TUC) and Labour Party (Blackburn 1967:18–19). Accepting Crompton's (1976:422–423) criticism of the assumption implicitly underpinning Blackburn's concept of 'unionateness' – that unionateness represents a continuum where unions are more or less akin to manual unions which thus rules out alternative forms of representation with quite different aims – a number of other cautionary points can be made so that 'unionateness' can still be productively utilised albeit in a tempered manner. First, Kelly's (1996) work on militancy is useful to flesh out what forms mobilisation can take and under which conditions mobilisation may be taken. Second, and following on from this, the distinction of constitutional unionateness and 'actual' unionateness requires making for a union may have the ability to strike without doing so. The former is essentially an internalised 'expression' and the latter an externalised 'action'. Third, affiliation to Labour is not the *sine qua non* that it used to be given the ascendancy of the neo-liberal 'new' Labour project within it. Indeed, there is a case for suggesting that affiliating to Labour since 1997 could be taken as evidence of becoming less unionate. Fourth, Blackburn along with his colleagues (Prandy et al. 1974, 1983) developed the concept of unionateness further by specifying two types, namely, enterprise and societal, where the former concerned the degree of 'militancy' (their term) that would be contemplated in the bargaining relationship with the employer and the latter concerned the extent of identification with, and involvement in, the wider labour union movement. Fifth, the forced diminution of collective bargaining and the use of industrial action to create political and extra-workplace, as opposed to economic, bargaining leverage need to be factored in for contemporary usage. Nonetheless, what is attractive in the fundamental concept of unionateness is its emphasis on members' interests and mobilisation in the pursuit of these as collective agencies and entities without imposing an exacting criterion of a class or sectional consciousness. In later chapters, two elements will be added into unionateness, concerning democracy and union 'form'.

In order to substantiate the key components of the thesis and provide the materials for the accompanying analysis, a schema of quasi-distinct periods is put forward which accords with the notion of 'combined and uneven development' *vis-à-vis* different ideologies and forms of collectivism throughout the financial services sector. Here independent and dependent labour unionism are distinguished from each other on the basis of their ideological complexions from which flow issues of form, structure, *modus operandi* and values.

1918–1969 witnessed the birth of both of independent and dependent labour unionism, while the post-Second World War period saw the establishment of a significant presence of independent labour unionism in the sector. The overall period witnessed successful campaigns which eventually gained the rights of recognition and collective bargaining in banking and insurance. In the pre-Second World War period, a number of employers took the step of creating staff associations or continued their policy of support for staff associations as a means to provide an obstacle to the incursion of independent labour unionism into their operations.

1970–1989 comprised the slow growth and consolidation of both types of labour unionism in terms of membership, organisational presence and influence. The period is characterised by a deep enmity between independent labour unionism and the staff associations, particular in banking, emphasising the competition between the two different types of collective representation. The period also witnessed the fragmentation of relative union cohesion as a result of the decentralisation of collective bargaining from sector to company level. Staff associations begin to question, but not reject, their foundation of 'internalism'.

1990–1999 experienced the growing erosion of traditional terms and conditions of employment following deregulation and the ascendancy of the unitarist human resource management (HRM) practice, with three significant trends consequently set in train, namely, those of a) staff associations becoming more unionate indicated by name changes, affiliations to the TUC and merging with independent unions, indicating a decline in 'internalism', b) a marked, though not extensive, rise in industrial action, and c) significant move towards ending of divided worker representation, epitomised by the creation of Unifi from BIFU, NWSA and UNiFI.

2000–2007 saw labour unionism and the remnants of the staff unions overwhelmed by the challenges of restructuring, reorganisation and downsizing in tandem with a more assertive management approach couched in terms of 'partnership'. Their membership, organisational presence and influence have become severely depleted. The previous advances of 1990–1999 have been overturned by these developments while at the same time the enhanced forms of (still low) levels of collectivism proved unable to resist the employers' initiatives and actions. From a position of weakness, the unions have engaged in partnership agreements and further union merger consolidation.

The chapter structure of this study follows this stylised periodisation of the evolution, development and existence of labour unionism in the financial services sector. Each period forms the basis of a chapter. The final chapter puts the existence and experience of finance workers' collective union organisation into a historical perspective and assesses the prospects for its future. The reason why the periodisation is a stylised one is because it seeks to take what are argued to be the dominant characteristics of the employment relations of certain eras and present them in a manner in which the transition from one period to another is signified by a turning point. However, this is an inexact science. For example, the ending of the first period is premised upon the granting of industry-wide bargaining and creation of ASTMS while the impact of the 'Big Bang' deregulation of 1986 is taken as being one which flowed through the sector in subsequent years and therefore the year of 1986 is not necessarily seen as being a turning point in itself.

The rest of this chapter is concerned with, firstly, laying out the sub-themes that arise from the thesis, and expounding the theoretical perspective underpinning the study. Then a thumbnail sketch of the political economy of the financial services sector in Britain is provided in order to situate the processes and outcomes of employment relations and the research methods used for the study are described.

**Sub-themes Explored**

*Subordinate labour unionism*

Labour unionism is a subordinate social formation *vis-à-vis* employers for employers are 'primary' organisations within the employment relationship (Offe and Wisenthal 1985, *cf.* Muller-Jentsch 1985). Labour unions are then created and built upon the basis of employment having first been created by employers, with the ramifications for the tasks of interest formation and representation by workers. Within this overarching generalisation, labour unionism, nonetheless, represents a challenge to the dominance of the employers but in a diffuse and limited way. The threat is of labour unionism *per se* to managerial prerogative *per se,* or, of labour unionism in the abstract to managerial prerogative in the abstract. In the financial services sector, the actuality has been that of an ineffective challenge to the exercise and effect of managerial prerogative and of the *de facto* subordination of labour unionism to the employer agenda, particularly with regard to resource dependence and incorporation. Financial services sector workers' collective organs of representation (labour unions, staff associations) are a weak form of collectivism that only showed signs of significant developments towards greater unionateness in the period of the late 1980s to late 1990s. They only began to display indications of unionate change (*vis-à-vis* ideology, organisation and resources) as the hegemonic psychological contract, union-employer relationships and material basis of quiescence began to break down. This breaking down gave rise, for the sector, to relatively widespread conflict. However, financial services sector worker collectivism was unable or unwilling to sustain or take further this trajectory *vis-à-vis* mobilisation and ideology. This self-limitation is explicable by several historical factors. In general, of those workplaces that are unionised, they are unionised but not necessarily organised, indicating the inhibition of growth of workplace unionism. This signals the weakness of union presence in qualitative terms, i.e. organisational cohesion and integrity, and activist milieu. In a situation where there are no significant localised structures on the union side, this almost inevitably leads to the domination of the union by the national bodies of the union, company committees, and national executive lay officials, and particularly by EUOs and the general secretary and his/her coterie.

*Turning-points and specific junctures*

In historical terms, there have been several turning points and key junctures that have given a pronounced indication of the dynamics and tensions underlying the employment relationship and employment relations in the financial services sector. So at certain points, the forces behind these tensions become sufficiently strong as to 'breakout' and alter the existing trajectory. These turning points exist in varying degrees of magnitude. With regard to the purpose of developing 'unionateness', and particularly conflictual ideology and power to mobilise, the disorganisation and dislocation of the post-1999 era after the period of the early- to late 1990s is, arguably, the most critical. Other turning points of a lower magnitude are, for example, a) the rise in industrial conflict in the early to late 1990s, precipitating moves towards partnership, the most obvious example being Barclays, b) the tranches of redundancies which have so depleted Unifi membership and ended its ambition to remain an independent union, just four years after coming into existence, and c) the emergence of the call centre as a major means of service delivery with its implications for work organisation, workforce composition and thus union presence and organisation. The notion of turning points in this usage is reflective of a perspective of dialectical materialism and stands in opposition to a perspective of gradual, evolutionary change.

*Crises of representation*

Collectivism of both labour union and staff association types is experiencing a prolonged crisis. As presently constituted, labour unionism can be characterised as a 'busted flush' *vis-à-vis* influence and presence while staff associations, despite substantially transforming themselves, have been overtaken and outmanoeuvred by employer action and changes in labour markets. Critical in explaining these outcomes, employer *paternalism* has been replaced by employer *authoritarianism* cloaked in the form of HRM. The movement from one to the other here reflects the qualitative change in market configuration and employer objective, namely deregulation, new players, and a drive to increase rates of accumulation. The shift from paternalism to authoritarianism has not led to the creation of genuine or effective mechanisms of non-union worker voice. Consequently, a general representation crisis can be talked of, not only in quantitative terms (extent of non-unionism and non-coverage of worker voice mechanisms) but also in qualitative terms (the efficacy of union and non-union mechanisms). Representation is defined here as not merely as access to, and use of, mechanisms but the degree to which these mechanism are able to produce effective consultation and negotiation over issues concerned with terms and conditions of employment and the employment relationship.

*Representation under new work regimes*

The traditional terrain on which the organs of worker collectivism operate has experienced considerable retrenchment. Collective bargaining on annual pay rises has been replaced by individual performance-related pay where the union/staff association role is relegated to trying to influence the size of the total sum available to fund performance related increases and the implementation of the schemes, i.e. assessments. In this regard, and others like the removal or restriction of fringe benefits, the terrain of collective bargaining has been significantly narrowed by a move to unilateral employer determination. The other side to the coin here has been the reassertion of managerial prerogative through partnership agreements. Around thirty have been signed in the financial services sector and none from union positions of strength. Whatever the relevant merits of 'partnership' in general, it is evident that being privy to hitherto unseen company information and being allowed to make inputs into corporate and HR policy at an earlier stage than has been usual has not led the organs of finance workers' collective representation to be any more influential than before. Rather, their weakness has become institutionalised in a mechanism which provides for a symbolic semblance of co-determination and mutual gains.

*Organising new workplaces*

The changed configuration of the financial services sector (e.g., closure of high street branches, transferral of work to call centres, new entrants using call centres, outsourcing of previously internal operations, the establishment of new subsidiaries by established players, new methods of service delivery and so on) has presented the organs of workers' collectivism with major challenges. Whilst some success has been recorded in gaining membership and union recognition in the call centre subsidiaries of established major players and maintaining representational rights in outsourced operations, little success has been achieved in organising many of the smaller operators. More importantly, most of the smaller operators have not even been targeted for recruitment and organising. This situation is explicable by, on the one hand, employer hostility, using strategies of suppression and substitution, and, on the other, paucity of union resources (personnel, financial) where there appear to be identifiable and tangible worker grievances. Consequently, it is not the case that the levels of redundancies *per se* explain falls in union membership. Rather, an inability to repel redundancy and the union-side limitations to recruitment and organising explain membership decline.

*The influence of the wider union malaise in Britain*

Workers' organs of collective representation in the financial services sector have been both influenced by, and been part of, the wider malaise of the union movement. That said, the wider environment, particularly in the private service sectors, has not been conducive to a more unionate form of labour unionism in the sector to develop in (compared to the increasing unionateness of public sector unionism from the 1970s onwards). There has been no ability to 'rise on the coattails' of others. This has accentuated the weakness of relatively weak developments in relatively weak collectivism. Instead, labour unionism in the sector reached its historical apogee at a time when labour unionism was making a general retreat whereby the ascendancy of employer power from the mid-1980s (through such means as HRM) and the whip hand of the labour market represented the both the extension of control and the retaking of initiative.

A significant debate has taken place concerning explanations of the social and class position of financial services sector workers and the presence (or otherwise), and nature, of their labour union behaviour (see, for example, Bain (1970), Blackburn (1967), Lockwood (1958), Prandy et al. (1983)). The main lines of explanations concerned physical and ideological approximation to management, strategic functions workers perform, and internal labour markets. Crompton (1976) characterised this as a debate between 'sociological' versus 'industrial relations' approaches. In the former, the class situation in Weberian terms is the cornerstone of an explanation of the relative underdevelopment of union density and union character. In the latter, this recognised underdevelopment is argued to be a result of trajectories in job regulation and the determination of the employment relationship. By contrast, Crompton (1976) put forward a Marxist analysis which emphasised the heterogeneity and ambiguity of the class positions of those employed within finance with regard to the functions of capital, management and labour and the role of finance within late capitalism. The relative deskilling of tasks and immiseration of working conditions of these functionaries can be detected as a result of rationalisation and reform driven by a regime of competitive accumulation. And while, this in turn has provided the basis for proletarianisation and a potentially enlarged and deepened terrain of labour unionism, this is not an area of inquiry for this study. The reason for this is that the focus is the (actual) organisational and institutional processes and outcomes of labour unionism and industrial relations. And, the justification for this is the desire to understand the ramifications, and variables thereof, of employer policy towards worker collectivism and attendant mobilisation amongst a 'quiescent' workforce. In other words, well-resourced and strategic employer action has been an extremely powerful conditioning force – possibly more so than elsewhere – which necessitates study. Only after doing this can the challenges facing the agency of labour unionism to create collective identity and respond to grievances through recruitment and organising be fully appreciated. The type of argument put forward by Crompton is both one of a certain historical period, and more importantly here, a different level of unit of analysis.

## Intellectual Perspective

The analytical perspective adopted in this study is a form of radical political economy. In terms of the subject matter of the study, this means examining the dynamic, dialectical interplay of 'material' forces (such as the particular structures and processes of capitalist exploitation) and worker agency. In the financial services sector in Britain, this comprises the overall association between two sets of relationships; on the one hand, capital (conditioned by the drive to accumulate under conditions of cartel giving way to a deregulated market where shareholder influence has increased) and labour as the sellers of their labour time and effort, and, on the other, employers and their managements (deploying paternalism, HRM and partnership) and workers and their weak forms of collectivism. In historical terms, the interests of capital and labour are held in the last instance as being diametrically opposed in the abstract by virtue of the exploitation of labour by capital to the disproportionate benefit of capital and the attendant systems of oppression and subordination. However, the articulation of this is subject to the actuality of the balance of power between the two parties, prevailing hegemonic ideologies and the state of workers' collective consciousness, whereby accommodation and compromise are frequently accepted by labour over its exploitation *per se* and the terms for exploitation. Sometimes, particularly in immediate terms, it may appear that the interests of capital and labour can overlap or coincide because of the contingent context of impact of the aforementioned factors (see also Gall (forthcoming) and Gall and Hebdon (2008) for a fuller elaboration). Other aspects to this intellectual perspective are to recognise the ever present tensions between labour as a cost and as an asset as well as those between gaining worker consent and exercising control over workers while viewing change in worker consciousness as an indeterminate process and prioritising the essential need for independent and collective worker representation to defend and advance workers' interests.

**The Changing Political Economy of the Financial Services Sector in Britain**

The financial services sector has traditionally – until the 1980s – been divided into three sub-sectors, namely, banks, building societies and insurance companies, as a result of the nature of the regulatory regime and notions of appropriate market segmentation amongst operators and consumers.[3] This structuration with its sub-sectoral oligopolies provided overall market stability, aided by the concomitant long period of economic growth in the post-war era. A social peace of stability and continuity in employment relations could then be engineered in the form of internalism, paternalism and above market level rates of pay and conditions of employment. For the employers, paternalism was both a conscious strategy and a value system, and operated in the context of labour costs representing 70% of operating costs (Morris 1986a:22). Employers were compelled for market (branch presence) and operational (data processing) reasons to employ high levels of staff relative to their capital investments (buildings, machinery and the like). In order to control pressures on already high labour costs and preserve managerial control, employers were prepared to pay remuneration slightly above market rates as a bulwark against labour unionism with its implications for costs and control. But this was always going to be a balancing act for keeping labour unionism out could also be a recipe for an increasing relative remuneration bill. Yet, the expansion of the capitalisation of financial services employers, particularly amongst the banks, was also facilitated in no small part by peaceful industrial relations and little worker resistance so that in this period the outcome of the balancing act was very favourable towards the employers.

In determining that the industrial relations of the clearing banks until the late 1980s were orderly, peaceful and centralised with employment practices comprising life-time employment, structured careers and paternalistic welfare-orientated personnel policies, Storey's (1995:24) and Morris' (1986a:22–24) characterisation could also be applied in broad measure to building societies and insurance companies (see, for example, Snape et al. (1993)). The organisational culture was conservative and genteel, based on implicit teamwork, risk aversion, hierarchy and bureaucracy, and in the many small workplaces the absence of the development of polarised 'them and us' attitudes existed. Notwithstanding the

---

3    Cowling and Newman (1995), Cressey and Scott (1992), Morgan and Sturdy (2000), Poynter (2000), Regini et al. (1999: chapters 1, 11), Snape et al. (1993), Sparrow (1996), Storey (1995) Storey et al. (1997, 1999) all provided useful overviews on the changes in product markets, regulatory regimes and the human resources (as opposed to industrial relations) implications of these. And in a series of publications, Knights and McCabe (Knights and McCabe 1997, 1998a, 1998b, 1998c, 1998d, 1998e, 2000, McCabe 2000, 2004, 2007, McCabe et al. 1998) examined the tensions in managerial control and objectives within the resultant change programmes from a Foucaudian labour process perspective, highlighting both dysfunction and resistance but without assessing the implications for labour unionism.

highly gendered aspects of employment where women were disproportionately congregated in the lower skilled, lower status and lower paid jobs, workers in the sector also experienced seniority pay, and subsidised money lending.

From the late 1970s onwards, deregulation became pronounced and was accompanied by the introduction of new of information and communication technologies (ICTs), recession, overseas expansion, and the more vigorous articulation of shareholder value. The product market moved towards being highly competitive, turbulent and differentiated. In these circumstances, employers chose to introduce ICTs to take advantage of the opportunities they brought in order to reduce costs, increase control and expand product portfolios. The advances in, and falling relative cost of, ICTs facilitated the entrance of new market players, new products and the reorganisation of operations through centralisation and concentration via regionalisation and specialisation. One result of employers' use of ICTs was that work and employment were restructured whereby some jobs and tasks became redundant while others were created. The creation of jobs in processing and call centres represents just two examples of the latter.[4] Thus, traditional products and delivery mechanisms within the sector have declined (e.g. high-street branches) while significant growth has been experienced in areas such as business finance inter-mediation and personal finance, which are themselves often carried out from new premises (i.e., call centres) via telephony and electronic communication. Often the new products and modes of delivery are provided by recent entrants into the marketplace following the 'Big Bang' deregulation of financial markets of 1986 and the development of more cost-effective means of delivery. The picture painted by many authors (see, for example, Cressey and Scott (1992), Storey et al. (1997), *cf.* Storey (1995)) of change from one form of regulatory and configured regime to another is inevitably a stylised one for within the existing regimes the beginnings of the next are necessarily present. One example is to be found in banking with regard to the process of the concentration of capital through mergers and acquisition which first became evident in the 1960s and 1970s. Thus, in 1967 there were fifteen major banks with ten by 1986 and just six by 2003 despite new market entrants.

Nonetheless, such market and capital restructuring and re-composition within a deregulated and increasingly competitive marketplace have put severe pressure on previously stable and co-operative employment relationships because employers have chosen to respond in a certain manner. Workers became to be seen by employers as a cost as administrators and were required to become a resource as sellers (*Observer* 30 November 1997, Regini et al. 1999), signifying the move from bureaucratic to entrepreneurial modes of operation. This was operationalised through internal competition and communicated to workers through the introduction

---

4    There was also a geographical aspect to the changing political economy of the sector as a result of employing organisations moving some of their operations out of London and the south east of England to cheaper (labour and land) and less unionate areas like south west England (Danford et al. 2003:98).

of contingent pay and employment based on performance measurement which
has replaced automatic incremental and cost-of-living increases (see Smith (1986)
on the case of the building societies). Although the actual and psychological
contractual basis of employment had changed, staffs were also challenged to go
beyond mere minimum contractual compliance where the onus was put on them
(rather than the employers) to retain themselves in their desired employment and
remuneration. Changes to the internalised labour market changes have comprised
staff reductions (voluntary and compulsory redundancies, non-replacement, less
annual recruitment), increase in the use of part-time and casual staff (see *Personnel
Today* 21 August 1997), and segmentation and specialisation with the ending of the
'generalist'. Alongside the move to task specialisation has been the routinisation
and Taylorisation of work, and methods of communication with staff have become
more 'direct', with consultation often replacing negotiation.


**Research Method**

The fieldwork for this study comprises several data sources. First, a series of
interviews with EUOS of the unions and staff associations active in the financial
services sector (BIFU/Unifi, MSF/Amicus-MSF, BGSU/UNiFI, IUHS) as well as
lay activists and members of these unions and staff associations. These interviews
were carried out between 1992–1993, 1995–1999 and 2002–2003. In all, just over
seventy interviews were carried out. For the time and cooperation of these officers,
officials and members, I am again duly grateful. Interviewees were chosen for
their ability to give overviews of their union's activities across the companies in
which the union organised while the lay officials were chosen for their specific
knowledge of, and involvement in, the union's actions in their respective banks.
Second, the gathering of extensive union documentation from all the unions and
staff associations, ranging from policy papers, literature for activists and members,
such as union magazines and newsletters, and press releases. These comprised,
*inter alia*, BIFU's monthly *Report* and *General Secretary's Report to the Annual
Delegate Conference*, Unifi's monthly *Fusion* and fortnightly *e-fusion*, LTU's
more than weekly *Newsletter*, IUHS/Accord's monthly *Accord*, MSF/FSU's bi-
monthly *Finance Update*, Amicus' fortnightly/monthly financial services sector
e-newsletter, UNiFI's monthly *Finance Industry Briefing* and seven other regular
member publications from a number of staff unions like ALGUS and the Brittania
Staff Union. Third, the coverage of relevant issues and developments in the quality
'employment relations' press such as that by *People Management*, *Financial Times*,
*Morning Star*, *Socialist Worker*, *Solidarity*, *Trade Union News*, Incomes Data
Services (*Report*, *Study*), Industrial Relations Services (*Employment Trends*) and
the Involvement and Participation Associations' library of case studies (available

at www.ipa-involve.com).[5] Other 'quality' newspapers were accessed through the Lexis-Nexis electronic database. Lastly, due acknowledgement has to be given to the founding works of Allen and Williams (1960)[6], Blackburn (1967), Checkland (1975), Lockwood (1958), Marsh and Ryan (1980), Morris (1986a, 1986b), Robinson (1969) and Undy et al. (1981) in laying out the empirical groundwork which has been deployed to build the basis of the analysis presented in this study concerning the period prior to the 1990s. These works have been extensively deployed in furtherance of the arguments of the thesis. The strength of the research method is its relative breadth, covering the sub-sectors of the financial services sector (banks, building societies, insurance providers and so on) with longitudinal and extended dimensions. It may be thought that the absence of interviews with employers would constitute a 'hole' in the data. However, the focus of the study is workers and their organs of representation, where the actions of employers and movements in market configuration are of a contextual importance. A more than adequate description and understanding of employers can be gained from the work of other writers and researchers.

## Point of Departure

This study offers a radical historical and longitudinal perspective on labour unionism, employer action and employment relations in the financial services sector. It has been common to examine and understand robust, oppositional worker collectivism for the reason of attempting to tease out lessons for replication and reproduction. This study takes a different tact by approaching the same objective of inquiry but from the opposite 'end' of labour unionism which, while stronger than other labour unionism in the rest of the private services sector, is a much weaker form than that found historically in engineering, manufacturing and printing.

---

5   References to IPA articles from its library are simply denoted by 'IPA' because the articles do not have titles.

6   Allen and Williams' (1960) paper was republished in Allen (1971).

# Chapter 2
# Historical Genesis and Development of Labour Unionism and Staff Associations

## Introduction

This chapter covers the historical genesis and development of independent and dependent labour unionism in the banking and insurance sub-sectors in the quasi-distinct periods of pre-1918, 1919–1945 and 1946–1969. The delineation here is suggestive of the importance of the impact of the world wars on social relations and, in turn in, on industrial relations generally, as well as the reaching of the post-war zenith of labour unionism around the year, 1970. From inauspicious and contested beginnings, by the mid-1960s, some 31% of the 637,000 workers employed in the financial services sector were members of workers' independent or dependent collective organisations, making this the second highest sectoral union density in the private sector at the time (Robinson 1969:19). And of the 157,000 workers employed in the major 'high street' banks, combined independent and dependent union density was 71% (Robinson 1969:19).

Within the aforementioned periodisation, the structure of the chapter is to examine the genesis and development of independent labour unionism in the banking firstly followed by that of their counterparts, the staff associations. The same study is carried out for the insurance sub-sector. The main themes to emerge from the study of the period to 1969 in this chapter are several. The first is that unlike independent labour unionism in other sectors of the economy, independent labour unionism for non-managerial staff in the financial services sector has had to contend in quantitative and qualitative terms with a historically unprecedented offensive from employers to destroy and/or marginalise it. This created the original dual system of employee representation in Britain. Second, despite the scale of resources and determination ploughed into this, in historical terms, independent labour unionism evaded the employers' stranglehold attempted upon it. But in doing so, independent labour unionism remained far from deleteriously unaffected by this sustained employers' offensive. Thus, and thirdly, by the end of the period under consideration, the battle between the forces of independent and dependent labour unionism was an unresolved one – in other words, it was a battle that was between something begun and something not yet ended. Fourth, the manner in which this battle was fought out was not a 'hot' war, being more akin to a 'cold' war based on attrition.

**Formation of Labour Unionism in Banking**

Recognising the dangers of unwarranted historical conflation, the first beginnings of independent collective organs of representation of, and for, bank workers were two events separated by over seventy years distance from each other. The first form of collective staff action was probably the petition of bank clerks against longer opening hours in 1826 (Munn 1982:61). The next reported instance of such collectively orientated action was in 1902 when a bank clerk wrote a book about banks and within this urged unionisation, leading to his dismissal (Blackburn 1967:133). Checkland (1975:512) recorded the next significant phenomenon as the concern of clerks in 1910 over retirement age and pensions while Robinson (1969:19–20) observed that banking was becoming a relatively less exclusive occupation and began taking on the form of bureaucratisation common to many large organisations. Allen and Williams (1960) reported that work intensification was widespread for the remaining bank clerks as a result of enlistment and that inflation was rampant, leading to falling real wages. The first semi-permanent form that collective organisation took was the establishment of the National Association of Bank Clerks (NABC, also known as the National Bank Clerks' Association) as a labour union in England in 1914 with 248 members, and which registered in 1915. Marsh and Ryan (1980:133) reported that the NABC was forced to be a clandestine organisation due to employer hostility. However, this formation was suspended as a result of the imposed social peace arising due to the First World War. Indeed, Blackburn (1967:133) recorded that the union 'died'. However, and in common with other instances of labour unrest as result of the impact of growing social immiseration due to the continuing war, bank workers returned again to the idea of a union before the outbreak of peace. Thus, in December 1917, a meeting of bank clerks in Sheffield resolved to form a 'combination of bank clerks' (BIFU 1992:1, *BIFU Report*, May 1993). Consequently, in 1918 the (National) Bank Officers' Guild (BOG) was established following further agitation over the impacts of the concentration of banks through mergers and acquisitions upon work organisation, work relations and status, and of the First World War upon the cost of living relative to stagnating salaries (Allen and Williams 1960:300, *BIFU Report*, May 1993, Blackburn 1967:133–134, Morris 1986a:27–28). Those who had been active in the NABC were essentially those who re-convened in 1917, with there having been other attempts to form a bank clerks' union since 1900 (Blackburn 1967:134).

This breakthrough of creating a permanent collective organisation was aided by the growth of labour unionism *per se* in the period and the radicalising social impact of the First World War even if the labour unionism of the bank clerks was far from that which was then developing in engineering and manufacturing. With the third spring tide of labour unionism rising, even a labour unionism that eschewed militancy could be a beneficiary because the general trajectory toward labour unionism lifted all and put the employers on the back foot. Indeed, from its inception, the BOG stressed its purpose was representation through conciliation and dialogue of non-clerical bank clerks, avoidance of party politics and promotion and protection of professional standards (Allen and Williams 1960:301, 305, Blackburn 1967:135–136, 139, Lockwood 1958:178–179, 183). Nonetheless, it called itself a labour union and pursued labour union aims through labour union means. It sought registration following its first AGM. Although the term 'national' was seldom used as per the commonly used nomenclature of the 'BOG', the act of the union seeking to be, and being, a national organisation is important for it argued that bank officers' conditions were, in fact, fairly standardised across the banks, many of whom were still regional rather than national banks at this time, and that bank officers held a generic functional position. The other side to being a national organisation – in the context of staff associations – was that of being an independent organisation (see later). In other respects, the Guild was a contradictory organisation in terms of content (policies), composition (members) and (temporal) context.

The response of the employers was swift and decisive by virtue of creating dependent organs of staff representation (see below) and the stone-walling, cold-shouldering and illegitimisation of the BOG. Thus, Allen and Williams (1960:303) recounted that the banks did not victimise BOG activists nor proscribe the organisation at this point. Rather, they refused to meet or speak to it and its officers. In the case of the National Provincial and Union Bank, the employer wilfully ignored the staff's unambiguous preference for the BOG (Allen and Williams 1960:303). Given the resistance of individual employers, essentially the BOG sought both to acknowledge the potency of this and sidestep it by creating a national, inter-employer pay scale through cooperative co-determination via industry-wide collective bargaining (Robinson 1969:20). Thus, in 1919, the BOG applied to the Ministry of Labour and the banks for the Whitley system to be applied to banking (Allen and Williams 1960:307–308, Lockwood 1958:177–178). Although immeasurably strengthened by the reaching of full (armed forces) demobilisation and the return to employment of these radicalised workers, the banks uniformly refused the overture from the BOG and the Ministry of Labour was unwilling to act against this staunch opposition in such a strategic sector of the economy. Undeterred and spurred on, the BOG secured phenomenal growth: Allen and Williams (1960:301) reported that by late 1920, the BOG had organised 27,000 (45%) of the 60,000 bank clerks and Lockwood (1958:147, 177) reported that in 1921 the union had achieved 50% density – having risen from around 10,000 in late 1919 (although Allen and Williams also note that as an aristocracy of labour, the Guild excluded messengers from membership).[1] Some success in gaining the status of a representative agent was recorded when the BOG was admitted to the Banking Insurance Unemployed Council in 1922. However, by 1923, the BOG President was urging a re-evaluation of the moderate and non-political approach because of its sparse return (Blackburn 1967:137, 138–139)

---

1 However, Morris (1986a:27) reported absolute and relative membership being lower (10,000, 35%) in 1921.

despite high union density. Support for such a changed position was evident but was either subsequently overturned or not acted upon. The call for 'militancy' and greater assertion had missed the surge tide of 1919–1921 for it was made on the later ebb tide and amongst a socially conservative elite group of workers. Allen and Williams (1960:305–306) argued that the BOG showed itself to be incapable of understanding that employer resistance could not be overcome by reason and appeals to common interests alone, for industrial force and political pressure were needed to enjoin the employers into granting union recognition and then favourable bargaining outcomes (see also Lockwood (1958:177)). So while the Guild had a strike clause in its constitution, it was widely accepted it was not for actual use, emphasising the limited sense of extant unionateness. This, Allen and Williams (1960) argued resulted from the bank clerks' social conservatism as well as the BOG's own over-estimation of this conservatism. Consequently, various opportunities to work and associate with other workers were rejected (Allen and Williams 1960:312–313). The sense of BOG missing a window of opportunity was manifest when it organised 50% of workers in such a short space of time before falling back (see Table 2.1).

In common with other unions in the period, Guild membership fell further reflecting the impacts of the employers' counter-offensive against labour union *per se* in the conditions of the defeat of the 1926 General Strike, the introduction of the *Trade Disputes Act 1927* and the economic depression and then slump of the 1920s and 1930s. But, it also and more importantly reflected the dashed aspirations of those that joined the BOG and watched as it was unable to develop appropriate and effective *modus operandi* (Allen and Williams 1960). However, the form of the employer counter-offensive in banking took a particular form, seldom so robustly or as extensively found elsewhere, of the creation of staff associations (see below). This counter-offensive played an important part in explaining why, when general union membership began to rise from the mid-1930s, BOG membership did not. Rather, it continued to fall fairly evenly until 1940. A further part of the explanation for this separate trajectory was the growing number of women bank clerks, for although BOG recruited a large number of women, this was not practiced in all regions (Allen and Williams 1960:302). Moreover, and despite, the proportion of BOG members being women increasing, the size of the increase in the number of women bank clerks, and their lower propensity to join (at this point in time) still had a cumulatively negative effect on overall Guild membership (Blackburn 1967:148–149). Across the sector, the BOG had an uneven membership and organisational presence (Blackburn 1967:155–156), reflecting primarily bank policy and attendant actions towards the BOG and the presence and vibrancy of the staff associations. Reflecting its northern strength, seven of its first ten branches were from above the Severn-Wash geographical line. From 17 initial branches in 1919, this increased to 176 in 1921 and to 190 in 1922 (Allen and Williams 1960:302, Blackburn 1967:138).

**Table 2.1    Independent Labour Unionism Membership, 1919–2003**

| BOG/NUBE/BIFU/Unifi Membership | | | | GIO/UIS | NUIW |
|---|---|---|---|---|---|
| Year | Members | % women | Sectoral density | Members | Members (% women) |
| 1919 | 15,000 | – | – | – | – |
| 1920 | 26,522 | – | 45 | – | – |
| 1921 | 29,592 | – | – | 14,551 | – |
| 1922 | 30,137 | 9.1 | 50 | – | – |
| 1923 | 28,088 | 8.0 | – | – | – |
| 1924 | 24,966 | 7.2 | – | – | – |
| 1925 | 24,388 | 6.7 | – | – | – |
| 1926 | 23,319 | 6.1 | – | – | – |
| 1927 | 21,327 | 5.7 | – | – | – |
| 1928 | 19,882 | 5.4 | – | – | – |
| 1929 | 19,293 | 5.5 | 33 | – | – |
| 1930 | 20,426 | 6.4 | – | 13,000 | – |
| 1931 | 21,268 | 7.6 | – | – | – |
| 1932 | 21,473 | 8.6 | – | – | – |
| 1933 | 20,808 | 9.3 | – | – | – |
| 1934 | 20,820 | 10.0 | 33 | – | – |
| 1935 | 20,626 | 10.7 | – | – | – |
| 1936 | 19,586 | 11.0 | – | – | – |
| 1937 | 18,910 | 11.3 | – | – | – |
| 1938 | 18,086 | 11.5 | – | 21,000 | – |
| 1939 | 17,646 | 11.9 | 23 | – | – |
| 1940 | 21,066 | 17.6 | – | – | – |
| 1941 | 25,851 | 22.0 | – | – | – |
| 1942 | 29,316 | 26.9 | 26 | – | – |
| 1943 | 28,830 | 26.6 | – | – | – |
| 1944 | 27,909 | 26.0 | – | – | – |
| 1945 | 27,157 | 24.0 | – | 17,000 | – |
| 1946 | 25,352 | 20.9 | – | – | – |
| 1947 | 25,826 | 21.3 | – | 19,000 | – |
| 1948 | 25,583 | 22.8 | – | – | – |
| 1949 | 29,068 | 23.4 | – | – | – |
| 1950 | 29,622 | 24.0 | – | 16,000 | – |
| 1951 | 34,474 | 24.9 | 35 | 17,000 | – |
| 1952 | 36,879 | 26.2 | – | – | – |
| 1953 | 36,666 | 26.9 | 41 | – | – |
| 1954 | 35,522 | 27.3 | – | – | – |
| 1955 | 47,277 | 29.6 | – | – | – |
| 1956 | 48,647 | 30.2 | 41 | – | – |
| 1957 | 50,147 | 30.8 | – | – | – |
| 1958 | 50,055 | 31.2 | – | – | – |
| 1959 | 50,333 | 31.7 | – | 16,000 | – |

**Table 2.1    continued**

| BOG/NUBE/BIFU/Unifi Membership | | | | GIO/UIS | NUIW |
|---|---|---|---|---|---|
| Year | Members | % women | Sectoral density | Members | Members (% women) |
| 1960 | 52,787 | 32.6 | – | – | – |
| 1961 | 56,458 | 34.6 | – | 17,000 | – |
| 1962 | 59,134 | 35.9 | – | 21,000 | – |
| 1963 | 61,458 | 37.2 | – | – | – |
| 1964 | 56,224 | 35.5 | 38 | – | – |
| 1965 | 58,444 | 37.0 | – | – | – |
| 1966 | 57,862 | – | – | – | – |
| 1967 (June) | 56,700 | – | – | 15,000 | – |
| 1967 (Nov) | 70,600 | 43.0 | – | – | – |
| 1968 | 82,371 | – | – | 15,000 | – |
| 1969 | 87,043 | 45.0 | 50 | – | – |
| 1970 | 89,144 | 48.0 | – | 13,480 | – |
| 1974 | 104,225 | 44.3 | 43 | – | – |
| 1975 | 101,922 | 45.6 | – | – | 25,582 |
| 1977 | 116,730 | 46.6 | – | – | – |
| 1979 | 132,374 | 48.8 | – | – | 20,044 |
| 1980 | 141,042 | 49.1 | – | – | – |
| 1981 | 147,995 | 48.8 | – | – | 19,463 |
| 1982 | 151,985 | 47.7 | – | – | – |
| 1983 | 156,476 | 50.6 | – | – | 18,619 |
| 1984 | 154,579 | 50.9 | – | – | – |
| 1985 | 157,468 | 51.9 | – | – | – |
| 1986 | 158,631 | 52.8 | – | – | – |
| 1987 | 165,839 | 53.7 | – | – | 17,697 (16%) |
| 1988 | 168,408 | 54.5 | – | – | – |
| 1989 | 170,481 | 55.4 | – | – | – |
| 1990 | 170,101 | 55.6 | – | – | – |
| 1991 | 162,429 | 56.4 | – | – | 16,243 (15%) |
| 1992 | 153,562 | 57.1 | – | – | 15,500 (n/a) |
| 1993 | 143,752 | 57.4 | – | – | 10,686 (24%) |
| 1994 | 134,352 | 57.7 | – | – | 10,467 (20%) |
| 1995 | 134,012 | 57.7 | – | – | 10,382 (19%) |
| 1996 | 123,540 | 58.5 | – | – | 10,044 (19%) |
| 1997 | 116,165 | 58.9 | – | – | 10,347 (n/a) |
| 1998 | 112,972 | 59.7 | – | – | 9,704 (n/a) |
| 1999 | 179,544 | 59.3 | – | – | ceased existence |
| 2000 | 171,249 | – | – | – | – |
| 2001 | 160,267 | 59.7 | – | – | – |
| 2002 | 158,733 | 61.1 | – | – | – |
| 2003 | 147,607 | 59.8 | – | – | – |

*Sources:* BIFU (1992, 1995), Blackburn (1967), Crompton (1979), Egan (1982), Lockwood (1958), Morris (1986), TUC Annual Directory (various), and Undy et al. (1981).

*Note*: Missing years and blank spaces indicate there is no available data.

The BOG maintained its recruitment and agitational activity during the late 1920s and 1930s but faced some victimisation, employer anti-union communications to staff, and a culture of fear of the deleterious impact of membership upon employees' promotion prospects (Blackburn 1967:150–153). Nonetheless, BIFU (1992:1) claimed that the BOG secured major successes in 1924 when salary scales were introduced for the first time and when the Cooperative Wholesale Society (CWS) recognised it. This was followed by recognition by the National Bank in 1931. Thus, began the slow and difficult path to gaining institutional-based union recognition amongst the major employing organisations. What made this task even more difficult was that the BOG needed to gain institutional recognition as step towards its goal of industry-wide or multi-employer bargaining (MEB). The tipping point of sufficient institutional recognition to gain MEB was to remain a far off day (in 1968) as individual employers maintained their resistance to independent labour unionism. Blackburn (1967:153) characterised the BOG in the period as 'cautious and defensive' with the staff associations being 'docile and ineffective'. In the mid- to late 1930s, a debate took place amongst BOG activists and officers concerning the desirability and efficacy of the union being more aggressive, more 'unionate' and 'militant', with the result that after movements back and forth, the union affiliated to the STUC in 1939 and the TUC in 1940, and opened up its ranks to non-clerical bank staff in 1941 (Lockwood 1958:182–183). However, NUBE reported its affiliations were strictly 'non-political' and that each year there were moves at conference to disaffiliate from the TUC as a result of outside pressure from the staff associations (Allen 1966:17).

The Second World War was something of a boon for the BOG. Both public policy and public opinion support for labour unionism rose, facilitating the BOG to then rejoin the common upward trajectory in overall union membership and concomitant the relatively higher growth in white-collar unionism. Again though, the picture was not even across the banks (Blackburn 1967:156). The Conditions of Employment and National Arbitration Order (No. 1305) of 1940 was a specific boon. Intended to peacefully resolve industrial disputes during wartime through the Ministry of Labour and the National Arbitration Tribunal, the Order in effect gave BOG union recognition with the banks. By engaging in disagreements with the banks, which if unresolved, the BOG was then entitled to avail itself of the use of binding arbitration. Thus, the BOG gained some degree of recognition should the employers wish to avoid arbitration or a greater degree of leverage through arbitration should they refuse voluntary negotiation. Moreover, the staff associations were not generally qualified to use the machinery because they were deemed to be non-independent. Some did change their constitutions to then be able to use the machinery but none then did so in practice.[2] The employers

---

2    Nonetheless, many began to levy membership subscriptions in order to have the veneer of being independent in order to facilitate possible use of the Order. In the inter-war years, the BOG employed it first union staff while the staff associations continued to use secondees from the banks as their officers.

attempted to take the initiative by establishing a Council of Conciliation in 1941 to which the BOG and the staff associations, through their Central Council of Bank Staff Associations (CCBSA), were invited. In the preparation to establish the Council, the CCBSA worked closely with the banks. The BOG AGM rejected participation for a) fear of loss of autonomy by having to work with the CCBSA, and b) in effect, being required to recognise the legitimacy of the staff associations and to gain their consent before it could talk to the employers. Despite the lack of movement on national bargaining, Barclays recognised the BOG in 1941 as a result of its own internal situation. The bank opposed the conversion of its staff association into a subscription-raising organisation with a different agenda to its own and the BOG had a sizeable membership there (Blackburn 1967:161–162). But Morris (1986a:29), citing an official history of Barclays, suggested that Barclays' miscalculation that the BOG could gain a form of statutory recognition through compulsory arbitration led it to recognise the BOG far before its competitors.

The creation of NUBE in 1946 as a result of the merging of the BOG and Scottish Bankers' Association (SBA) reflected a number of predominant but not uncontested subterranean changes that had been taking place within the BOG *vis-à-vis* unionateness, and particularly assertiveness of demands and appropriate and attendant mobilisations. These meant that union was named the *National Union* of Bank *Employees* as opposed to some configuration of the Bank Officers' *Guild* or the Scottish Bankers' *Association*. Further but small progress towards institutional recognition (and MEB) was made in 1947 when NUBE was recognised by Trustee Savings Bank (TSB) Employer Council, providing for company-level bargaining (CLB) following the recognition of some individual (geographically delimited) TSBs of BOG/NUBE. The following year the Scottish Cooperative Wholesale Bank recognised NUBE. However, the nature of the recognition at the TSB did not satisfy NUBE for it made no provision for arbitration. Arbitration, in NUBE's view, would increase its leverage over the employer and make its leverage less dependent on membership density and mobilisation. Nonetheless, as it remained still shut out by the high street banks (save Barclays), in 1950 NUBE organised a petition in favour of a national minimum salary of some 53,000 out of 90,000 workers when its membership was around 30,000 (Blackburn 1967:166). This facilitated a substantial increase in NUBE membership and an increase in salary grades. But it also led the banks to recognise their staff associations through the fora of establishing some nominal bargaining machinery on wages and conditions (see below). Following the dissolution of the Midland Bank Staff Association (MBSA) in 1950/1951 because of bank negotiating intransigence, NUBE successfully recruited many former MBSA members but was unable to gain recognition. The bank instigated a new staff association to which it awarded rights of arbitration.

Under some external pressure, the CCBSA and NUBE met in 1951 to discuss the machinery for MEB via revisiting the 1941 formula. As NUBE still held the same position, little progress was made until 1954 when it softened its position, whereupon tripartite negotiations under the auspices of the Ministry of Labour took place. By 1956, however, negotiations broke down as a result of the cumulative opposition of individual banks and their staff associations (Blackburn 1967:167–168, Morris 1986a:32). NUBE was then left with the option of trying to return to the unproductive option of attempting to enforce recognition through the compulsory arbitration order or gain it by dint of membership and membership mobilisation. Overall, the immediate post-war period saw some signs of stabilisation and growth in institutional presence of the organ of independent labour unionism.

## Staff Associations in Banking: Origins and Early Years

Blackburn (1967:93) made clear the rationale for, and temporal context of, the creation of the banking staff associations: 'All the staff associations in banking were founded after the Bank Officers' Guild [was established]'. Willman (2005:53) was of the same opinion. Yet the ideology of the staff associations was a more longstanding one of paternalism, commonality of internal employer-staff interests and separation of interests from any external, third party. The *modus operandi* were consultation and compromise. Negotiation was not supposedly needed as a result of the commonality of interests. Even so, not all banks were particularly keen to concede staff representation, even if this was to forestall the BOG, with Blackburn (1967:142–147) recording that all were established with varying degrees of (positive) support and approval. Nonetheless, they all offered a clear alternative to the BOG (Blackburn 1967:140). By 1921, five had been established in the major clearers (Morris 1986a:28). The staff association at Lloyds had its origins in a works council which came into operation in 1918 while the creation of the MBSA in 1919 resulted from a desire to confront the BOG. Staff association were also established in the National Provincial (National Provincial Bank Staff Association), Westminster (the Westminster Bank Guild), and Barclays (Barclays Bank Staff Association) banks in 1919. The Martin's Bank Staff Association was established in the following year. Compared to the BOG, the staff associations were well-funded, facilitated and staffed through employer provision of secondees, offices and access. Indeed, many did not charge individual subscriptions for many years, and in some banks membership was compulsory (BIFU 1992:1). In these and subsequent years, there was evidence that the banks increased salaries and introduced salary scales to rebuff the BOG and appease others from moving towards its 'clutches' (BIFU 1992:1). To support themselves, but in testament to an inherent tension between internalism and externalism via commonality of interests across workforces and inter-organisational cooperation, the staff associations established the CCBSA as early as 1923. The CCBSA acted as quarterly forum of exchange and dialogue, not a negotiating body, where its members retained full autonomy (Blackburn 1967:94–95, Robinson 1969:24).

The staff associations were based on a high, rather than absolute, degree of commonality and compatibility of interests between employees and employer, for their mere existence of separate representation signified that there could not be complete commonality and compatibility of interests (even if this was only predicated on the basis that staff representation is required to prevent misunderstandings and facilitate the recognition of commonality and compatibility). Of course, such a 'concession' by a unitarist-minded set of employers was actually intended to limit the bifurcation of interests by creating an institutional bulwark to this as well as a support for the tight inter-connectedness of interests. Thus, Robinson (1969:23–24) noted that staff associations existed to foster a spirit of mutual cooperation and had no provision for industrial action (or outside political activity). Some of the employer arguments for staff associations concerned the desirability of direct communication, commercial sensitivity and professional status of bank clerks. The material basis of the ideology of internalism was found in the very strong internal labour markets of employing organisations where within lifetime employment and career paths, staff could move from the bottom upwards, and the 'gentleman's agreement' among the banks not to competitively recruit each others' staff or accept into employment staff who had worked for other banks. Ostensibly then, staff in one bank had no commonality of interests with staff in others, and because of the symmetry of interests, no need for industrial action existed and consultation rather than negotiation was appropriate. Blackburn (1967:99–101) critiqued the basis of this materialism to show that it contained a high degree of myth and exaggeration, where virtues were made out of partial actualities, and aspiration and perception were important. He suggested that those who were receptive to its attraction were status conscious and middle-class aspirants. To this extent, staff associations sought to maintain and enhance such an aristocracy of labour. This was helped by the BOG attitude towards the staff associations, which vacillated between attempts at colonisation, cooperation and marginalisation (see also Morris (1986a:31,36,49)). The toing and froing resulted from the failure of different overtures but what stands out is that the BOG members of the various executives of staff associations were pulled towards acting in the interests of the associations and not the BOG (Allen and Williams 1960:309).

In the inter-war years, the staff associations became largely inactive and the banks less supportive of them as they had less need to be – indeed, they instituted salary cuts without consultation (Blackburn 1967:149–150) – given the defeats of the labour union movement and the slack labour market. In this regard, there is similarity to the rise and fall of the use of Joint Industrial Councils. However from 1935, the staff associations begin to come out of hibernation due to tightening labour markets and began to levy their own membership subscriptions. A number of attempts, some successful, some not, were also made to establish further staff associations (Blackburn 1967:159). By the end of the 1940s, most staff associations were levying subscriptions.

Of portent for future developments towards unionateness for both dependent and independent labour unionisms was that the staff associations did not have workplace structures, for members directly elected lay officer bearers who acted on their behalf, and that internalism was as much a pragmatic perspective as an ideological position. Finally, the degree of resistance to labour unionism by the main banks was highlighted by their unwillingness to grant the staff associations anything more than representational rights until the 1960s. But it also testifies to the absence of most of the staff associations asking for such rights because they were seen to be inappropriate - for such a high degree of commonality of interests does not require rights of negotiation (see Morris 1986a:28). From their inception until then, the staff associations had the right to make representation to the directors, not the bank managers, and they did not have rights of information and consultation, much less of collective bargaining. This indicated the degree to which the strategy of 'peaceful competition' (Bain 1970:131) was both forced on the banks by the BOG/NUBE and framed within the wider perspective of limiting any challenges from any staff organ to their managerial prerogative.

### Developments in Scotland

In common with many labour unions which began as regional entities and later became part of national unions, the formation of independent labour unionism for bank workers in Scotland took place on a Scottish basis. According to Munn (1988:182): 'Unrest amongst the staffs of Scottish banks began as early as 1918, in fact as soon as the men came back from the war' with Checkland (1975:582) suggesting this was bound up with the social impact of demobilised troops *vis-à-vis* returning to a civil life of inflation, inadequate housing, economic recession and the like after years of wartime deprivation and sacrifices whilst widespread political radicalisation was taking place and the government promised 'a land fit for heroes'. Thus, in March 1919, the SBA was established as a response to the refusal of the employers to increase salaries. It approached the banks and the Ministry of Labour over union recognition, as well as carrying out a wages survey and suggesting that increases could be paid for by all the banks passing on the costs to customers. Despite prompting from the Government in the post-First World War period, in line with the Whitley Reports of the early post-war period to meet the representatives of staff, the banks in Scotland refused to meet this first labour union organisation, much less recognise it for representational and bargaining purposes. Rather, they established their own staff representative associations and acknowledged the strength of the case the unions were making by issuing concessions (Checkland 1975:582, Munn 1982:63). However, Munn (1982:63) argued that it was unclear whether such advances in terms and conditions of employment resulted from pressure from the SBA or enlightened paternalism on the part of the employers. Of course, both in tandem were possible in the trenchant defence of the managerial prerogative and employer freedom from interference and the point is here that these developments helped maintain non-unionism through substitutionism. Nonetheless, the Bank of Scotland Joint Council of Staff and Directors, established in 1921, was turned into the Bank of Scotland Staff Association a few years later and a staff assurance scheme with a 30% bank contribution was created in 1926 (Cameron 1995:183, Malcolm n.d.: 152, Munn 1988:182). This move was a direct response to the creation of the British Bankers

Association and SBA, the latter's recruitment and activity amongst staff (Cameron 1995:183, Munn 1988:182) and the increasing use of staff petitions on pay by non-aligned groups of bank workers. The Clydesdale Bank Staff Association was established in 1920, although staff joined the MBSA from 1921 because the Midland acquired the Clydesdale in 1919 and the MBSA was seen as being more influential as a result of its greater size. The Clydesdale Bank refused to meet the MBSA although it was prepared to enter into correspondence with it, albeit to no useful outcome for the staff association.

By March 1920, the SBA had 1,000 members and at its first conference, members overturned the Executive's programme of protestation and argued for a plebiscite to decide on strike action after becoming frustrated at the lack of progress in resolving their grievances (Checkland 1975:584). The ballot was won and membership increased to 4,400. The strike was stood down after the Ministry of Labour intervened to conciliate and achieved an agreement from four of the eight banks to meet the SBA. This was reneged on with the movement to strike beginning to dissipate following the demobilisation upon the prospect of meeting with the employers, the perception of bad faith on the part of the leadership, rising wages and falling inflation (Checkland 1975:585–586). Checkland (1975:586–587) argued that the 1920s then became the 'Great Apathy' where the SBA had few members and resources, suffering from the impact of growing unemployment and from a tranche of new entrant workers with no experience or tradition of trade unionism and militancy. Nonetheless, the SBA had sufficient determined activists to maintain itself in these lean years. The SBA threatened strikes without carrying them out until the 1930s in a battle to gain union recognition from individual banks. Behind the scenes, it settled down for a long battle and provided a number of membership services like education courses.

The sense of widespread grievances began to develop with austerity measures in the early 1930s. The SBA undertook campaigning and agitation, leading to two banks granting increases. Campaigning led to the threat of a strike, given that the SBA members sensed susceptibility on the part of the banks. Rather than attempt a Scottish-wide strike, the SBA concentrated on the Union Bank of Scotland where it had 80% density. The strike over pay at the bank (subsequently to become part of the BoS) took place on 30 April 1937 but collapsed by 10am in Glasgow as a result of the harsh company response. The bank threatened to sack strikers and remove their pension entitlement. This created rancour and demoralisation. It sacked also the strike leader. Nonetheless, several immediate outcomes were apparent. First, the Union Bank of Scotland did institute pay increases, and the Scottish Cooperative movement took its business elsewhere in an act of solidarity with the strikers when the bank organised to break the strike. Second, the Bank of Scotland raised its general salary levels and removed its restrictions on when male staff could get married. The SBA continued to be active on the issues of pay, pensions and the marriage restrictions (Checkland 1975:590). It affiliated to the STUC and TUC in 1938–1939. Checkland (1975:591) concluded that prior to 1939, and despite failing to gain union recognition or any direct contact with the banks, it had constituted an important component of relations between the banks and their workforces.

During the Second World War, the SBA experienced several challenges, namely, the effects of retrenchment in employment and the entry of women – with a little experience of labour unionism and a lower propensity to join it – into the workforce. It sought to organise the women workers but, with the legacy of being vanquished in 1937, found this difficult. In response, the SBA steered left. Checkland (1975:597) reported that it turned from: 'pragmatism to ideology. The SBA magazine adopted the Independent Labour Party line, seeking to make socialists out of bankmen [and portraying] the banks … as the crudest of exploiters'. In sum, the SBA argued it would not compromise with internalism. The outcome was that membership dipped even further. To ward against any possibility of the SBA's appeal having a purchase, the banks responded by deploying what would today be referred to as HRM policies and practices, providing better pay and reinvigorating the staff associations. The staff associations were given a tight, more formal structure, often with branch managers as organisers. As a result, the SBA came close to collapse. Nonetheless, the banks recognised the limitations of staff associations and their strategy of internalism, and consented to the creation of the Central Council of the Scottish Bank Staff Associations (CCSBSA) in 1941. It stimulated the establishment of the Federation of Scottish Bank Employers (FSBE) in 1943. With the entry of the Clydesdale Bank to the FSBE, the beginnings of widespread sector-wide co-determination through a Joint Negotiation and Consultative Council (JNCC) with the CCSBSA began. However, a dispute between the CCSBSA and the SBA over the proportionality on the staff side led to the SBA being excluded from the JNCC. The employers refused to have separate negotiations with the SBA. That said the Clydesdale Bank refused to be bound by the outcomes of the JNCC and only recognised the CBSA.

In 1945, the Scottish banks, led by the Bank of Scotland sought to pre-empt expected government pressure to implement a Whitley-type system of sector-wide consultation and bargaining by proposing the establishment of the Associated Staff Societies (ASS). This new body would consist of the CCSBSA and any other staff associations and, critically, the SBA, and would face its counterpart, the FSBE. In 1946, SBA membership was just 1,056 after a lean period comprising declining membership, a strike defeat, exclusion from national bargaining through the JNCC and the absence of domestic recognition with the banks. In such a weak position, it sought support and sustenance through a merger with the BOG in 1946 to form NUBE. At its formation, the SBA's membership constituted just 5% of NUBE's membership (Checkland 1975:650). However, the proposed constitution of the ASS barred NUBE by virtue of excluding its EUOs from being able to represent its members. The constitution allowed for only bank worker representatives to represent bank workers. NUBE refused to accept this and was excluded from the ASS although it had substantial numbers of members in many banks with staff associations and amongst those with no staff associations. As the *de facto* Scottish section of NUBE, the former SBA's membership reached 2,641 in 1952, 4,580 in 1956 and 4,895 in 1959 (Checkland 1975:650, 684).

Although national bargaining machinery was attained in Scotland in 1946, the staff associations did not benefit from its availability in terms of providing benefits for their members. Both the staff associations in the North of Scotland Bank and the BoS held referenda on whether they should continue in existence. Both did, the former on a minority vote; the latter on a majority vote. But in 1955, two other staff associations, the British Linen and RBS, faced similar disenchantment and held referenda, with the result that members voted for their disbandment. NUBE pressed for recognition, presenting a petition signed by over 70% of staff in each case, but without success.

After much lobbying and wrangling, in 1959, and reflecting its growing presence, NUBE was allowed to enter the ASS after its constitution was changed to allow representation by EUOS. Moreover, and as a result of the maintenance of their membership of the employers' federation despite having no staff associations, the British Linen and Royal Bank of Scotland granted NUBE recognition. However, a more united staff side and NUBE's tactic of seeking to take as many disagreements with the banks to the conciliation stage in the disputes procedure (in order to obtain a more favourable outcome to its members through the role of an outside third party), led to resignations from the FSBE by the Clydesdale and National Commercial banks. This precipitated the staff associations in these banks to seek company-level bargaining (CLB). In turn, the employers' federation disbanded leading the CCSBSA to do likewise. Consequently, national bargaining collapsed in 1960. NUBE and the bank staff associations were too weak to compel a change in action. Bargaining, in as much as it existed, reverted to company level, with the RBS and British Linen bargaining directly with NUBE and the other banks (BoS, National Commercial and Clydesdale) dealing only with their staff associations. The former two banks did not attempt revive internalism in an organisational form. Although a bruising experience for NUBE, the staff associations emerged much weakened – their membership fell from 7,281 in 1947 to 5,105 in 1955 and to 4,169 in 1961 (Blackburn 1967:169). Munn (1988:253) wrote of the period: 'Despite relatively low levels of pay for younger staff in the 1950s and 1960s, the level of industrial militancy was low and employment relations in [banks in] Scotland were therefore a rather quiet affair.'

MEB was not re-established in Scotland until 1970, following the stimulus of the creation of such a system for England and Wales in 1968. When it re-emerged, there were just three banks (BoS, RBS and Clydesdale) and NUBE had around 8,500 members (Checkland 1975:685). NUBE and the staff associations agreed to single-table bargaining (STB) to recreate a single staff side. The employers recreated the FSBE. The position of NUBE was strengthened by the vote of the BoS staff association to join NUBE in 1973, bringing its Scottish membership to just under 10,000 (Checkland 1975:686), and by virtue of it having more members than the staff association in RBS. Only in the Clydesdale was NUBE the minority partner to the staff association and in 1974 the CBSA voted to join ASTMS as a result of ASTMS being the sole recognised union in the Midland bank which owned the Clydesdale Bank. Previously, a new CBSA had been established in the 1950s after the first connection with Midland ended. Munn (1998:254) reported in 1960 that most Clydesdale staff belonged to the CBSA (c.1,000) compared to NUBE/BOG (c.630).

## Insurance

The genesis of the main and sustained drive towards unionisation of the insurance sector dates from around the same time as that of banking, whence forth unionisation for office workers – insurance clerks – was separate from the field staff – insurance agents. The former took place through the Guild of Insurance Officials (GIO), formed in 1917–1918, which changed its name to the Union of Insurance Staff (UIS) in 1969, and the latter through the National Federation of Insurance Workers, then renamed the National Union of Insurance Workers (NUIW) after the 1964 merger with the National Amalgamated Union of Life Insurance Workers. The UIS then merged with ASTMS in 1970. The GIO met with a similar response from the employers to that meted out to the BOG, by virtue of experiencing strategies of union substitution and union suppression (Crompton 1979:409). Between 1920 and 1921, five staff associations were established to counter the GIO, these being in the Alliance, Commercial Union, Lancashire, London and Phoenix insurers (Crompton 1979:409). Concomitant, GIO members and activists experienced harassment, intimidation and victimisation: Crompton (1979:409) cited the case of General Accident sacking a GIO member for refusing to give up his or her membership, which provoked a strike by 240 members, which she categorised as 'militant'. The strike was unsuccessful, with the strikers sacked and recognition not gained. Nonetheless, unlike the BOG, the GIO was prepared to ballot its member for strike action and deploy the strike weapon (Allen and Williams 1960:318).

But, unlike in banking, an important and relatively widespread prior stage of unionisation and creation of collective organisations took place from the 1880s onwards in insurance. First, the United Commercial Travellers Association was established in 1883 (eventually joining ASTMS in 1976) and the Royal Liver Employees' Union was established in 1890 (later joining the NUIW in 1974 along with three other Royal Liver staff associations). Second, organisations like the Refuge Assurance Staff Association and Britannic Assurance Company Agent's Association (both established 1906), Refuge Field Staff Association (established 1916) and National Union of Commercial Travellers (established 1918) were founded in the pre-First World War period or during the war itself. Other associations were formed prior to 1914 but folded shortly afterwards or in the immediate post-First World War period like the British Federation of Assurance

Agents which was established in 1902 and dissolved 1907.[3] Third, some friendly societies saw the formation of their own unions in the very early part of twentieth century (Marsh and Ryan 1980), with the National Union of Cooperative Insurance Society Employees (NUCISE) being established later in 1923 and joining the TGWU in 1934. Fourth, the National Life Assurance Agents' Association was established in 1884, followed by the Wesleyn and General Assurance Company Agents' Association in 1907, the Scottish Legal Assurance Agents Association in 1909 and the Scottish Life Agents' Association in 1914. These aforementioned independent unions merged in 1919 to form the National Amalgamated Union of Life Assurance (or Insurance) Workers. Lastly, the National Insurance Clerks' Association was established in 1914.

In the aftermath of the First World War, the National Pearl Federation was established in 1920 and joined with the Pearl Section in 1926 to form the Pearl Federation which later joined the National Amalgamated Union of Life Assurance Workers. At the same time, the National Union of Pearl Assurance Agents was established in 1926 with the London and Manchester Field Staff Association – which later transferred to the NUIW – being established in 1925. The instances of the Pearl workers' labour unions are indicative of a further dissimilarity from those collective organisations of banking whereby not all single employer representative collective organisations were either management-created or management-sponsored. This remained true even if the nomenclature of being a staff association was used. Those at the Royal Guild (established in 1919) and Liverpool Victoria (established in 1907) were also set up independently by the workers there and that at the Royal Guild worked closely with the GIO while the membership of the Pearl and Liverpool Victoria also held GIO membership (Crompton 1979:409). In this general vein, and redolent of the emerging unionateness, it is not particularly surprising to find that the National Amalgamated Union of Life Assurance Workers used strike action to gain union recognition at Pearl Assurance or that an association for managers, the National Association of Liverpool Victoria Managers, was established in 1919.

Common to other independent labour unionisms elsewhere and outside the financial services sector, those in insurance were thus established by means which were localised, either in employing organisations or geographical terms, and in ways were which not necessarily permanent (dissolution by collapse or merger). In essence, birth and rebirth took place over space and time until more permanent forms of more nationwide labour unionisms were established. Part of the dynamic was to create stable and sustainable forms of collective organisation by aggregating resources, which unlike their dependent counterparts, derived wholly from their memberships. In this overall process, insurance workers do not appear to have been entirely immune from the union positive influences of social

---

3   Similarly, some associations founded in the inter-war period folded in the immediate post-Second World War period.

radicalisation and economic immiseration connected with the First World War, Russian Revolution and depression.

Returning to the GIO, its membership increased steadily but not spectacularly to the late 1930s (see Table 2.1), with TUC affiliation being agreed in 1937. The removal of insurance workers to fight in the Second World War saw membership fall. As a result of the Kennett Committee's attempt in 1942 to negotiate the release of workers from the financial services sector where the GIO was the only cross-insurance staff body albeit with minority membership, the committee recommended that the GIO and staff associations establish a joint body. Led by the Alliance Guild, one group of staff associations favoured the creation of a federation of staff associations to negotiate with the GIO, while another group, led by the Royal Guild, favoured finding agreement for merging with the GIO. The former led to the establishment of the Federation of Insurance Staff Associations (FISA) in 1943 while the latter led to four years on on-going talks that did not come to fruition of a merger (Crompton 1979:409). Demobilisation after the Second World War led to a re-absorption of previous union members. A three-year debate over nationalisation between 1948 and 1951 saw the staff associations oppose nationalisation with the GIO adopting a 'non-political' stance which the staff associations took to mean tacit support for nationalisation (Crompton 1979:410). This adversely affected GIO membership levels.

Aggregate membership of the FISA rose to c.6,000 in 1950 as a result of the four original members being joined by another six. Following this and the FISA registering as an independent union, the GIO approached it for merger talks in late 1950. By 1954, these had failed: the FISA continued to favour a loose federation with considerable autonomy for affiliates while the GIO supported a tighter structure to counter the internalism of the staff associations and to solidify the union. The GIO position on the ground was weakened by its inability to significantly increase its membership as the size of the insurance sector workforce expanded from 175,000 in 1951 to 267,000 in 1966 (Crompton 1979:411, Table 2.1) and when general white-collar density was increasing. The UIS organised at several insurance companies but was in a minority in each of these, leading it to incur relatively high administrative costs which prevented it from launching membership drives to secure majority membership (Waddington 1995:169). It was unable to gain recognition using the CIR at General Accident Fire and Life. Meantime, the FISA's membership rose to 8,000 by 1960 and then to 18,000 by 1965 and 34,000 in 1969 as a result of organic growth and the affiliation of previously GIO-friendly staff associations like the Royal and Prudential (Crompton 1979:411).

The NUIW was formed in 1964 following an amalgamation of the National Federation of Insurance Workers with the National Amalgamated Union of Life Insurance Workers. Until 1985, the NUIW was a federation of sections which were constituted as independents unions – a stance adopted to gain constituent parts. In an official history of its predecessors' union badges, Pritchard (2006:20) wrote that 'The national union ... was really a federation of unions relating to a variety of insurance companies with each section retaining their independence to a certain degree'. This structural autonomy, allowing company specific bargaining on the basis of internalism, did not help prevent membership defection and loss (see later). Meantime, the Association of Scientific, Technical and Managerial Staffs (ASTMS) was created in 1969 by the merging of the Association of Supervisory Staff, Executives and Technicians (ASSET), which mainly represented supervisory staff in the metalworking and transport industries, and the Association of Scientific Workers (AScW) whose member comprised technicians and laboratory staff in metalworking, chemicals, universities and the health service. The new merged union was joined by National Union of Commercial Travellers in 1969. To add to the GIO/UIS's woes, ASTMS entered the field, resulting in a complaint by the UIS and NUIW to the TUC against ASTMS under the Bridlington Agreement in early 1970. But the UIS sued for peace and stability by entering into merger talks with ASTMS and these were successfully concluded quickly. The FISA was weakened by the merger of (for it, the large) Prudential and Royal Insurance staff unions with ASTMS (see below) and its inability to offer significant bargaining services because of its low income, leading its affiliates to join the Confederation of Employee Organisations (Waddington 1995:187).

In the post-Second World War period, labour unionism in insurance showed a number of characteristics which would become more pronounced throughout the entire financial services sector towards the end of the twentieth century, these being inter-union cooperation, capital restructuring leading to concentration and centralisation and further unionateness. Thus, the Confederation of Insurance Trade Unions was established in 1947, eventually comprising the NUIW, TGWU, ASTMS, USDAW and NUCISE. The Commercial Union Group (CGU) had deployed staff committees since 1921 as a form of dependent form of representation but when it took over another company, North British and Mercantile, in 1959 (which had longstanding and well established staff association since the 1920s), CGU felt compelled to established a staff association for its whole operation in 1964. Unlike before, membership of the new organisation was voluntary and subscription fees were paid by members. While some aggregation of labour unionism was primarily inspired and driven by the desire to construct viable organisations, this process was also occasioned by the restructuring of capital. Thus, the Guardian Royal Exchange Staff Union was established in 1970 from amalgamation of Guardian Group Staff Association (established 1948) and Royal Exchange Group Guild when the respective two companies merged. In this regard, the creation of the National Union of Cooperative Insurance Agents in 1969 was an aberration and is explicable as a breakaway from USDAW over a dispute over representation on wages.

## Bargaining Strategies and Union Mobilisation in Banking

By the early 1950s, there was increasing dissatisfaction over pay levels and pay structure amongst bank workers, leading employers to strengthen the position of the staff associations by awarding relatively 'large wage settlements' (Taylor 1978:382). However, when the 1952 scales were revised in 1955, NUBE gained a 33% increase in membership because it was, nonetheless apparent, to many bank workers that the gains came as a result of NUBE agitation. NUBE organised a rally in central London on this issue, and according to the Greater London Organiser at the time (interview), bank workers 'were queuing up to join'. But as a result of continuing unsatiated pay demands, employer intransigence and the advance of NUBE here, the staff associations pressed for arbitration mechanisms. The employers were open to this overture because NUBE could potentially use the leverage of the Industrial Disputes Order (No. 1376) of 1951 (which replaced the previous Order 1305) to gain *de facto* recognition. Moreover, the banks recognised the need to strengthen the hand of the staff associations, particularly as they had no constitutional provisions for striking/taking industrial action (Blackburn 1967:107, Morris 1986a:29, 31) albeit the banks did not anticipate the mechanisms would be used. In all the major banks except Barclays, these were gained between 1952 and 1956. Morris (1986a:31) argued not only did the staff associations gain this right on the back of NUBE petitioning action (see above) but that the arbitration mechanisms adopted by banks were specifically designed to exclude NUBE and bolster the staff associations. Again under pressure from NUBE, as a result of its relative strength *and* prevailing marginalisation, the CCBSA agreed a form of national bargaining in 1955 but this was never implemented as a result of employer opposition (Morris 1986a:32). One effect of the granting of recognition to the staff associations was to change NUBE's policy from favouring CLB with superior MEB to favouring just industry-wide bargaining. Despite their existence, the domestic arbitration mechanisms were not used until the 1960s, and in the 1950s there was not much evidence of *bona fide* negotiations between the banks and staff associations (Robinson 1969:27). In a show of relative strength, NUBE declared disputes with the British Line Bank, Midland and RBS and sought to have these dealt with by the Industrial Disputes Tribunal, which the Minister of Labour refused. In response, NUBE organised a lobby of MPs by 3,000 of its members.

As alluded to above, the 1960s saw the first use of arbitration by the staff associations on three separate occasions during 1961–1963 in the Lloyds, Midland and Westminster banks and with success for the staff associations, whereby the other banks implemented the awards as well. The 1960s also saw a new tactic in salary claims: using not just the approach of cost-of-living but also that of productivity given the greater expansion of the banks' activities over its staffing levels, and the growing attention given to productivity-based pay. This was vehemently opposed by the employers. According to a number of government enquiries, staff associations were at least as effective as NUBE in gaining wage increases (Robinson 1969:34) but this was not something Robinson (1969:35–40) found was substantiated. Indeed, in the late 1960s, the sense of wage grievance was added to by government incomes policy. Nonetheless, on a wider range of criteria, Robinson (1969:40–41) concluded that evidence of increasing staff association effectiveness existed. Finally, and with regard to the staff associations, by the mid-1960s, their membership was voluntary and based on subscriptions while a financial subsidy was still paid from the employers in the form of facility time (Robinson 1969:23). At this point in time, staff associations still had no constitutional right to take any form of industrial action. Blackburn (1967:95–97) argued that the staff associations had *de facto* labour union aims and objectives, albeit couched in institutional and not industry-wide terms. One area where staff associations did differ was in their attitudes to NUBE. This reflected, *inter alia*, their relative membership strengths *vis-à-vis* NUBE, their policy positions and employer actions (Blackburn 1967:181, 190, 192). The Lloyds Staff Association was traditionally far stronger than NUBE, allowing and facilitating its greater antagonism with NUBE compared to other staff associations (see Blackburn 1967:150, 164, 167, 181). On an individual institution basis, Blackburn (1967:189, 190, 251, 252) argued that where staff associations were ineffective or less anti-NUBE then NUBE was stronger, whereas NUBE was weaker where staff association were more active, unionate and aggressive (like the Westminster and National Provincial staff associations). Returning to NUBE itself, it had secured some success in its long-running campaign for union recognition. Thus, Lloyds, Westminster and Williams Deacons banks granted NUBE representational rights between 1960 and 1961, with Yorkshire doing similarly in 1965. But representational rights did not include collective bargaining rights and, particularly, collective bargaining on pay. Some small advance towards this was made when Williams Deacon granted full recognition in 1964 as did Westminster in 1969 (see below) but still recognition at the former excluded collective bargaining on pay as this was anticipated to be covered by national collective bargaining (Blackburn 1967:177).

In 1960, at its annual conference, NUBE reformulated its industrial action clause, originally formulated in 1922 under the BOG, to make the possibility of industrial action more feasible following a decade of debate. Previously, a 62.5% plus threshold of all members was required to allow any section of the membership to take industrial action (see Blackburn 1967:89, Lockwood 1958:178–181, Undy et al. 1981:373). Thereafter, any section of the membership could take action if they voted for it in a ballot, achieved a simple majority for action and the executive authorised the action. Following this, NUBE members began to take limited industrial action. In 1960, members undertook an overtime ban at the Derby TSB over a pay rise for managerial salaries. The bank responded by threatening dismissal, leading NUBE to successfully ballot for strike action. This led to further negotiations and a favourable settlement for NUBE. In 1962, NUBE claimed for a 10% pay increase at the TSBs: it was offered 2.5% (Blackburn 1967:170). In response, NUBE reduced its claim to 5% but to no avail. It called for arbitration but the employer imposed the offer, to which NUBE balloted in its strongest areas. The response of low turnout and poor support led to NUBE to accept the pay award. The following year, NUBE undertook a much larger mobilisation in a dispute over pay and the right to arbitration at the TSBs following the imposition of a 3.5% pay award. This began with protest meetings and a strike ballot, leading to a strike for three Saturdays in four branches. From this, NUBE gained a national arbitration clause, the first in banking. NUBE used the arbitration clause to good effect the following year. Moreover, this action led an increase in union membership in the TSB of 16% (Undy et al. 1981:155). Earlier in 1963, NUBE also held a strike at the small foreign bank, Habib Bank of Pakistan, where the employer dismissed some employees during a pay dispute. NUBE's fortnight long strike achieved some limited success here. These actions were characterised by NUBE being in a relatively strong position by virtue of high union density, limited possibility of service substitution and the absence of staff associations (Blackburn 1967:89, Undy et al. 1981). Willman et al. (1993:171) believed that the experience of taking industrial action to gain institutional rights had a positive effect on NUBE: 'greater aggression could be both popular and effective'. However, and compared to the TSB in particular, elsewhere NUBE faced the opposite situation of lower density and the presence of staff associations. In order to try to resolve the results of this situation, namely, the refusal of the major banks to recognise NUBE, NUBE decided in the late 1960s to mobilise for national industrial action to gain recognition. This decision was one which NUBE had been edging towards for sometime (Morris 1986a:36) as the view that it would simply overwhelm the staff associations by dint of numbers began to wane.

Prior to this, NUBE has been involved with the CCBSA in abortive talks on establishing national collective bargaining in 1940 and 1955 (see also Robinson (1969:20–21)) and in this process the MBSA resigned from the CCBSA as it was 'ultra-internalist' (Blackburn 1967:95) while it emerged that the BBSA favoured cooperation with NUBE. In trying to create external leverage on the banks, NUBE invoked the help of International Labour Office to establish a government inquiry (the subsequent Cameron Inquiry of 1963) into anti-union employer actions. Although the report did not find in favour of NUBE's complaints (Robinson 1969:21), it was not altogether without use for NUBE for it helped tip the balance towards those banks that favoured national negotiations (Morris 1986a:35) because it stated that both NUBE and the staff associations, as legitimate staff representative bodies, should have the recourse to national bargaining. This then helped pave the way for NUBE to take part in a joint-working party with employers and staff associations between 1965 and 1967 on developing proposals for national bargaining machinery (see Blackburn (1967:173–174), Morris (1986a:35–36) and Robinson (1969:21–22) for the particular nuances involved here). But this route proved fruitless after the staff associations at the National Provincial and Westminster rejected the proposals and of the big five banks, only two were in any way positive and many of the medium-sized banks were also hostile to domestic recognition of NUBE as well as national bargaining which included NUBE. NUBE then focussed on the areas of its strongest membership density and organisation and mobilised around issues of pay and hours of work which had been the key concerns of discontent among staff, linking these to the necessity of gaining bargaining rights. Morris (1986a:36) characterised this as a 'more militant approach'. Consequently, in late 1967 two days of strikes were held in south Wales, where NUBE organised in excess of 70% of bank workers (Undy et al. 1981:257,373). Morris (1986a:37) suggested the 1967 campaign and strike increased NUBE membership by 30% while Undy et al. (1981:155) reported it was more like 40% (see also Table 2.1). With a further two days of strikes to be held in Yorkshire by 6,000 members, a 3,000 strong demonstration in London and after intervention of a concerned Ministry of Labour, the banks agreed to union recognition, particularly as they faced the prospect of their end of year auditing being delayed and of government intervention.

On the basis of the progress made in the previous talks, this led to the creation of the Joint Negotiating Committee in English Clearing Banks, comprised of NUBE, the staff associations and the employers' body, the Federation of London Clearing Bank Employers in 1968. Two banks – Midlands and Coutts – declined to be involved but subsequently the recalcitrant Midland fell in. However, Morris (1986a:41,32–34,35,39) noted that the conceding of national bargaining by the banks, in part, represented their realisation that coordinated bargaining met their objectives. This pertained to avoiding pay leapfrogging between companies, taking wages out of competition between banks, preventing a union-inspired link between pay and productivity, and directing the focus of NUBE away from the workplace[4], as well as their specific difficulty of dealing with the staff associations' claims in a competitive situation with NUBE and within the environment of a tightening labour market. Moreover, creating the national machinery helped establish a line between what were negotiable (pay, conditions) and non-negotiable (staffing, performance, performance measurement, task allocation etc) issues at this level as well what areas management exercised unilateral control over at the company level. In turn, both bolstered protection of the managerial prerogative, particularly where the narrowed scope of joint-determination took place at one step removed from arena of where management decisions were made (Morris 1986a:45). It should also be recalled that the banks ceded MEB when other sectors were going in the opposite direction (encouraged by the Donovan Report), and that the spur was not the prevalence of wage drift through unofficial bargaining as was the case when MEB was established elsewhere. In these senses, there was no basis to an attempt to regain of control through the sharing of control as the Alan Flanders' (1970:172) dictum has it.

NUBE secured a major advance in gaining its objective of MEB, for this allowed it to aggregate and concentrate its extant forces and resources in a way which made them more than the sum of their parts. These bargaining rights (and those at company-level by 1971) were gained as a result of political and quasi-political pressures being exerted at industry and national levels, rather than as a

---

4  Indeed, when the banks came under pressure from the National Board of Prices and Incomes in the late 1960s to engage in CLB on pay as a way to relate pay to productivity, the banks resisted this because it would undermine their plan for coordinated pay bargaining (Morris 1986a:46).

result of workplace industrial mobilisation.[5] But the configuration of MEB was such that the staff associations were also part of the machinery and, within this set up, they maintained their institutional support from employers, which, in turn, made them more stable propositions. The staff associations showed themselves to be particularly flexible and pragmatic given that MEB undermined the internalism they were based upon. So the boon was not as extensive and deep-seated as NUBE expected, for the gains made in pay and conditions were not its alone (Taylor 1978:383). The impact of MEB at this point in time, where NUBE had developed little workplace unionism to speak of, was to reinforce this absence of workplace unionism for pay and conditions were set at the extra-workplace levels (company and super-company). The accession by the banks to full domestic bargaining rights was structured in a way that both emphasised the separation of company and industry-level bargaining and the centralised nature of individual banks. The former was willingly accepted by NUBE, again with deleterious consequence for developing workplace unionism. Storey (1995:34), therefore, claimed '[n]ational level pay bargaining divorced the union from domestic job regulation'. For the staff associations, who were also granted CLB rights, this did not matter for they did not seek to develop workplace unionism (of any sort) but it did for NUBE because without workplace unionism it was more likely to be unable to pose a strong threat to the staff associations. An intriguing aspect of the granting of full recognition at the industry and company levels within banking was that both mechanisms contained provision for unilateral, binding arbitration. Pay and conditions were to be dealt with at the industry level and matters of staffing and employment at the centralised company level. The existence of the mechanisms was a *de facto* form of no-strike agreement which suited both sides but at the potential cost of allowing either party to impose its will on the other through referral to arbitration (albeit not of the pendulum variety). The MEB mechanism strengthened the staff associations' leverage, in particular, given they had shown no propensity to take industrial action for grievance resolution. It gave them a cost-free mechanism which they could free ride off. For NUBE, it represented the results of limited but aggressive mobilisation of its membership to get a 'seat at the table' from which subsequent membership mobilisation was seen as then unnecessary and superfluous, this chiming with both some attested reality of membership and union values and perceptions (see also Morris (1986a:110) of bank workers as the 'aristocracy' of labourers and clerks. On banks' part, the *de facto* no-strike agreement was vital to ward against the effects of competitive labour unionism as well as control NUBE in its own right.

---

5    As emphasised later on, the move to bargaining rights at centralised levels and in the way this was achieved meant that local and workplace unionism was not likely to develop in a strong manner. It is interesting to note that the new bargaining structures made no provision for, or acknowledgement of, local top-up bargaining, for  NUBE was not in a position to move in this direction had it so wished because of the absence of workplace unionism.

Given that NUBE favoured MEB over CLB and gained the former before the latter in three of four main banks, it sought to undermine the domestic bargaining as a further move against internalism. The problem here was that by prioritising MEB, and despite industry norms and standards, NUBE necessarily limited the remit of the machinery to issues which were common to all the banks (i.e., pay and conditions of employment), thus bolstering the importance of CLB on issues like staffing levels and workloads. And, NUBE's bargaining strategy to subvert domestic negotiations by moving the issues they covered to the MEB was not successful (Undy et al. 1981:302). Indeed, CLB was subsequently widened by the onset of job evaluation. Finally, Morris (1986a:45) noted that the complexion of the MEB did not allow for job regulation (at any level) and CLB was not concerned with interpreting industry-wide agreements. Consequently, a potential spur or boost to workplace unionism was not present as was sometimes found elsewhere.

A further half-day strike in 1969 was held to successfully compel the banks to pay the first negotiated pay award after the National Board for Prices and Incomes had recommended it be delayed by a year. This was the first of three occasions when NUBE negotiated pay awards were referred to the NBPI, creating discontent (see Undy et al. 1981:258). Such a token action resulted from the ballot result – although the majority was clearly for strike action, the turnout was less than 50%. But the pay award was implemented and backdated. Full recognition amongst the individual banks was not gained until 1969 and would appear to be related to NUBE's new found willingness to at last deploy industrial action to attain it. NatWest granted full bargaining rights in 1969 to NUBE as did Barclays, National and Deacons (with Midlands and Lloyds doing so in 1970). Prior to this, both NUBE and the staff associations had the representational rights – the right to meet, but not negotiate, with the directors. Just before the new decade, the various staff associations of the National and Provincial Banks (NPSA, National Provincial Bank Ladies' Guild (established 1936), District Bank Staff Association (established 1940)) merged with the Westminster Bank Guild to form National Westminster Staff Association (NWSA), with 23,502 members, following the merger of the respective banks. NUBE also organised two days of strikes at the Edinburgh, Nottingham, Liverpool and Sheffield TSBs in early 1969 over the TSB Employers' Council decision not to negotiate on its pay claim. The action resolved the dispute to NUBE's satisfaction. By contrast, selective strike action to resolve a dispute with the Cooperative Bank in 1973 was unsuccessful and stood down. This precipitated a debate at NUBE's annual conference, where the National Executive was criticised for not paying the strikers full strike pay, this being held to have undermined the strikers' determination and resilience (Undy et al. 1981:257).

## Union Density, Unionateness and Mobilising Capacity

By the mid-1960s, as Table 2.2 shows for the largest six banks, the staff associations were in the dominant position with regard to density in four of these, with the position being reversed in Barclays and TSB. The consequence of this was that NUBE was still hemmed in by the combination of dependent labour unionism and internalism. However, the cases of the TSB and Barclays provided important exemplars for NUBE. The case of TSB was believed to show that with an open field, NUBE would reign supreme, in turn, justifying the attempt to kill the staff associations. Meantime, the case Barclays, where the BOG/NUBE had had recognition since 1941 and was on a level playing field with the BBSA, was also believed to show

**Table 2.2    NUBE and Staff Association Membership, 1964**

| Bank | Numbers Employed | NUBE (density) | Staff Associations (density) |
|---|---|---|---|
| Barclays | 30,000 | 14,631 (49%) | 11,366 (38%) |
| Coutts | 785 | 180 (23%) | 0 (0%) |
| District | 4,710 | 1,375 (29%) | 2,458 (52%) |
| Glyn Mills | 947 | 30 (3%) | 537 (57%) |
| Lloyds | 25,000 | 5,931 (24%) | 16,190 (65%) |
| Martins | 6,344 | 2,298 (36%) | 2,750 (43%) |
| Midland | 27,000 | 7,842 (29%) | 10,975 (41%) |
| National | 606 | 530 (87%) | 0 (0%) |
| National Provincial | 18,190 | 3,046 (17%) | 10,306 (57%) |
| Westminster | 19,000 | 4,328 (23%) | 14,469 (76%) |
| William Deacons | 2,300 | 1,599 (70%) | 0 (0%) |
| Bank of Scotland | 3,036 | 1,061 (35%) | 1,200 (40%) |
| British Linen | 1,766 | 1,062 (60%) | 0 (0%) |
| Clydesdale | 2,750 | 874 (32%) | 1,254 (46%) |
| National Commercial | 3,739 | 723 (19%) | 2,046 (55%) |
| Royal Bank of Scotland | 2,371 | 1,214 (51%) | 0 (0%) |
| Yorkshire | 1,486 | 617 (42%) | 600 (40%) |
| CWS/SCWS | 847 | 847 (100%) | 0 (0%) |
| Lewis' | 182 | 6 (3%) | 155 (88%) |
| TSBs | 7,500 | 5,645 (75%) | 0 (0%) |
| Foreign/Overseas Banks | 9,000 | 2,376 (26%) | 169 (2%) |
| Bank of England | 7,000 | 9 (0%) | 0 (0%) |
| Total | 174,559 | 56,224 (32%) | 74,475 (43%) |

*Source:* Blackburn (1967:273–274) with permission.

that NUBE could outflank internalism. But the attainment of MEB and CLB with their single-table bargaining (STB) procedures deepened tensions within NUBE between its pragmatists and traditonalists. The former believed that cooperation with the staff associations in these bodies was essential for pragmatic reasons. The latter believed that cooperation was wrong and unnecessary as NUBE would soon assume superiority as a result of greater membership growth because – as in the case of Barclays – superior effectiveness would be demonstrated and validated so that NUBE would similarly prevail.

In the post-Second World War period of 1949 to 1963, NUBE recorded uninterrupted growth of 111% in membership as a result of 'the impact of inflation on their relatively fixed incomes' (Allen 1966:15). Overall, the level of union density in the sector rose from 38.9% in 1948 to 42.9% in 1968 and because of the absolute growth in employment by 66% in the period this represented an 83% growth in the numbers of members (Bain and Price 1983:15). Clearly, the banks were not 'non-unionised until [the] late 1960s' (Storey 1995:27). According to Undy et al. (1981:63), NUBE organised 37.6% of bank workers in 1964, 49.6% in 1969 and 43.1% in 1974 (although calculations from Morris (1986a:38, 10) suggest the figure of 39.6% for 1970). NUBE's membership showed a marked geographical dimension. Blackburn (1967:117–120) reported that membership densities varied from 28% in the southern region to 82% in south Wales, with nine regions having in excess of 50% density and eight less than 50%. Blackburn attributed this variation to the presence and absence of staff associations, the traditions of regional political dominance and the regionalised nature of many banks. This spatial dimension was often reflected and reinforced by the strategic choice of NUBE to stage strike action in its strongest areas of support, that is, its northern areas.

Within this framework, Blackburn (1967:187–188) argued that in the period of the 1950s to the mid-1960s NUBE increased its density more than the staff associations while the staff associations increased their unionateness more than NUBE. However, he argued this assessment had to be viewed in the context where a) the staff associations had less opportunity to increase their density and more opportunity to increase their unionateness, and b) increasing density was a bigger relative achievement for NUBE while increasing unionateness was a more significant development for the staff associations. Despite the increasing unionateness of staff associations, the employers still preferred to support them in opposition to NUBE. For the banks, it was a price worth paying albeit one that would subsequently unravel in ways that did not support the banks' interests (see following chapters). To these points can be added a number of others concerning the relationship between dependent and independent labour unionism. Thus, staff associations were not in any significant measure independent of the employers but they were arguably (relatively) more effective than NUBE in representing workers' material interests because of the willingness of the employers to satiate some of their demands in order to close down opportunities for the bigger and more worrying threat, namely, NUBE. Indeed, the employers were prepared-cum-forced to accede to slightly more robust and effective staff associations. Meantime, NUBE was independent but, directly, less effective for representing members' collective interests. One of the particular challenges facing the BOG/ NUBE was that its appeal to bank workers was potentially lessened the more that the staff associations became unionate, whereby the basis of the BOG/NUBE's criticisms were vindicated but then subsequently undermined because of the unionate changes. In turn, this potentially reduced the distinctive appeal of the BOG/NUBE, as it were, stealing its thunder. Indeed, for the BOG/NUBE to retain a distinctive appeal, it had to become more unionate itself as the ground on which it worked *vis-à-vis* the staff associations changed. But in doing so, the BOG/NUBE had to manage the tension of being ahead of the staff associations but not too far ahead of them in terms of unionateness lest it marginalised itself from the more conservative elements of bank workers (non-members, staff association members) which it sought to win over. And within this, some opinion in the BOG/NUBE favoured being more robust so that the divergence between it, on the one hand, and on the other hand, those BOG/NUBE members prepared to wait for some catching up (in terms of unionateness) of the staff association members alongside those conservative members of the BOG/NUBE (Blackburn 1967:240) was one that could not be resolved.

Another aspect of this challenge was the 'Catch 22' situation facing the BOG/ NUBE until the late 1960s. Less bank workers joined it because it was not recognised by employers and so had no representational or bargaining rights; arguably, it was not recognised because it had not been sufficiently robust or unionate enough to force recognition from employers; part of this inability to be robust resulted from lack of numerical support and strategically seeking to be respectable; the danger it faced was that being 'too' robust or unionate could weaken not strengthen itself because this might make it lose any credibility or respectability, particularly if the chosen robust methods did not gain union recognition and it looked weaker as a result of taking action (where strength is one aspect of both credibility and respect); but in not testing out this it would never find out whether this was actually the case. Furthermore, in not being robust the BOG/NUBE could end up being too like the staff associations and the market for that brand was saturated already. In terms of NUBE's aspiration of national collective bargaining to aid itself in the context of the staff associations and undermine their internalism, the irony was that the staff associations were also in favour of MEB in as much as this was likely to keep NUBE out of their patches – the individual banks – because MEB focuses on inter-, not intra-, bank employment relations. Indeed, national bargaining would again help the staff associations develop their unionateness and, thus, help counter their force of their critic's case.

**Union Politics**

Although NUBE/BIFU became known as a 'rightwing'-cum-'non-political' union (see next chapter), this was not a forgone conclusion since its creation as the BOG. By 1950, there were four Communist Party NEC members and around twenty EUOs and senior lay officials that were also members including positions like the vice-president. The communists worked in tandem with a similar sized milieu of Labour left members. Collectively, they were able to achieve such positions of influence as a result of their advocacy of emphasis on wage agitation (see before). Because of the 'cold war', the communists did not operate openly as communists, and as a result of security service infiltration passing information to the right-wing Labour caucus which dominated the national leadership, the communists were forced out in the early 1960s on the pain of be 'outed' and/or sacked. This set the left back until the early 1980s (see next chapter). With the left forced out, the right ceased to organise as a caucus because it then completely dominated the union and, thus, had no need to.

**Conclusion**

The actions of financial services sector workers constituted a momentum towards creating their own collective, primarily inter- rather than intra-workplace, organisations, where they were subject to the impact of wider societal changes *vis-à-vis* radicalisation and proletarianisation. However, to paraphrase Marx, they did not do so in circumstances of their own choosing. Initially, they contended with suppression but this soon shifted to substitution. The causation is clear – once viable independent labour unionism was established, employers moved to substitutionism. This aspect of employer response found parallels elsewhere but suggested that whilst the sector and its workers were subject to general forces, their specific articulation and expression was far from mainstream. The establishing and development of independent unionism in qualitative and quantitative terms within a dynamic and changing environment meant that it could be both an attraction and a repulsion for a relatively heterogeneous workforce which was influenced by past and present tendencies in socialisation. In other words, and remembering the initial and explosive growth of the BOG and SBA, in a period of general radicalisation, independent labour unionism in the sector could be a draw – to extent that it represented the aspiration of those that were radicalised towards labour unionism and to the extent that it kept in tune with those that were already labour unionists. In itself, this was a difficult balancing act, being testament to labour unionism constituting shifting alliances of views about method and aim based upon coherence around the principle of independent worker collectivism in the workplace. But in a period when radicalisation was in reverse, the maintenance of radicalism ceases to become the draw it once was and likely helped reinforce the salience of internalism because it becomes a self-evidently weakened force and does not fit with the predominant worldview amongst the workforce of what is both possible and desirable. So whilst independent labour unionism survived and prospered in qualified terms, it nonetheless remained a relatively fragile phenomenon. It was still out-resourced and out-legitimatised by the organs of internalism and it displayed a low level of unionateness. Indeed, its future was not assured but the same could be said of the staff associations. Consequently, this was a battle that was between something begun and something not yet ended.

Indeed, by the close of the 1960s, NUBE had triumphed in as much as it was still in existence and was a sizeable force despite being a weak form of labour unionism. Although it had not resolved the following problems, it had not been defeated by them either: a) gaining of concessions from employers was both a spur and setback to union presence for it constituted substitutionism as well as demonstration effect; b) without increased membership it was difficult to compel union recognition from employers and without union recognition it was difficult to gain increased union membership because membership is based on perceived effectiveness; c) in criticising the staff associations for not being sufficiently assertive, the logic of this was to establish the agenda of reform and not abolition of the associations; and d) in compelling concessions from employers, force was necessary to be used even though the use of force was often seen as distasteful by its own members. In this last regard, Blackburn (1967:90) argued that in the 1960s: 'members [were] willing to support such militancy under what they felt to be extreme provocation, although it would be wrong to assume that the general attitude towards strikes [was] sympathetic'. Indeed, NUBE was prepared to use strike action to obtain bargaining mechanisms that obviated the need for strike action. Both membership of, and recognition, for white-collar unions have been argued by Bain (1970) to be largely predicated on employment concentration, employer policy and government action. Without discounting the influence of these, the campaigning activity of independent labour unionism to create leverage over employers appears to be at least equally important, either it its own right or as a way of taking advantage of the configuration of these three other factors.

Alongside these aforementioned tensions, for the first forty years of the BOG/ NUBE's existence, there was no formal collective bargaining to speak of and little *de facto* either (*cf.* Clegg's (1976) argument). This was clearly an impediment – although not the only one – to developing workplace unionism. In this situation, most union activists' effort was spent on recruitment and retention of members. For example, 5,496 members were struck off in 1960, representing just over 10% of total membership, for reasons of leaving the sector, death, resignation and lapsing (Blackburn 1967:91), so running to stand still, let alone advance, took considerable effort. In not attempting to develop workplace unionism, the BOG/NUBE was not alone. Moreover, the staff associations had no demonstrable local organisation, branches or conference either until the mid-1960s with its office bearers elected by subordinate levels. This reflected the situation where there membership was not the source of bargaining power. Nonetheless, the staff associations had, as the BOG/ NUBE did, correspondents in workplaces to recruit and distribute materials.

Although the trajectory of independent labour unionism in insurance has significant differences with that in banking, it too faced the challenge of internalism and staff associations. But its relationship to these bodies was different because they were less beholden to internalism and because independent enterprise unions existed. Nonetheless, this still resulted in a weak form of national independent unionism which was compelled to seek defensive merger much earlier than that in banking.

Of portent for the future was that staff associations constituted a form of labour unionism, albeit a dependent and internalist one, because their existence intrinsically and fundamentally testified to the objective differentiation between labour and capital, workers and employers, and thus the demand for separate forms of interest representation. In this sense, staff associations – dependent upon contingent processes – could become an embryo for the development of more conventional labour unionism. Such turning points did occur through the creation of the CCBBSA and the establishment of MEB, thus eroding internalism. Equally well, it could be argued, as Allen and Williams (1960) did, that the BOG missed a historic opportunity to kill off the staff associations so that other turning points were not created. Related to this is that the BOG/NUBE arguably showed insufficient collective assertiveness at many key moments prior to the late 1960s.[6] Thus, the force of historical legacy, both positive and negative, was alive and well for independent labour unionism. In a hostile environment, the repercussions of missed or not taken opportunities and employer counter-attack for a subordinate body rippled down the years. So while subsequent dynamism and agency existed, they did so on the foundation of the processes and outcomes of previous years. Consequently, the relative lack of unionateness of the staff associations and their organisational strength held back the attempts of the BOG/NUBE to maintain and developments its own unionateness (and density or completeness on this basis). In practice, for the BOG/NUBE to advance, it had to not only develop itself but have a favourable knock-on impact upon internalism to bring it towards itself. To this extent, NUBE was vindicated but also marginalised. Its criticisms of internalism were valid but also vindicated in as much as the organs of internalism responded by mutation in a relatively more unionate direction, which then reduced the 'brand appeal' of NUBE.

---

6    Although the condition of the labour market and body politic was less favourable in the 1950s, one can still reasonably pose the issue of why NUBE did not take the kind of action it took in the 1960s in the 1950s.

# Chapter 3
# Development of Labour Union Presence and Organisation, 1970–1989

## Introduction

The beginning of the 1970s represented a further historical turning point for labour unionism in the financial services sector by virtue of, firstly, many staff associations succumbing to independent labour unionism, secondly, a tranche of new dependent unionisms being established following significant changes in industrial relations law under the *Industrial Relations Act 1971*, and thirdly, the granting of union recognition agreements to NUBE. What partially united the first two developments was that the newly created union, ASTMS, pursued an aggressive policy of amalgamations of staff associations, and this expanding labour unionism acted as a further spur for many employers to establish staff associations in their operations in the light of the *Industrial Relations Act 1971*. The phenomenon of ASTMS was a marriage of strategy and circumstance, whereby it sought to take advantage of an opening for self-expansion. In the background, class polarisation and radicalisation were taking place, occasioning the then Conservative government of 1970–1974 to legislate for the *Industrial Relations Act 1971*, and producing a groundswell for labour unionism. But, as before, this was a double-edged sword for independent labour unionism in the sector for such an environment where labour unionism was identified with radicalism constituted both a force for attraction and repulsion for a relatively heterogeneous workforce who were influenced by past and present socialisation trajectories. In the background, other subterranean processes were also taking place. For example, by 1970 women had become the majority of the financial services sector workforce – a phenomenon which was subsequently extended and never reversed (Morris 1986a:91), and, meantime, NUBE/BIFU developed its bargaining agenda and tactics, although it did not become 'militant'[1], and was already experiencing financial difficulties (Buchanan 1981:46) as a result of its particular *modus operandi*.

---

1   In Morris's (1986a:36, 54, 64) survey of NUBE, he often referred to as NUBE/ BIFU becoming more 'militant' but did so in such a relativist way as to undermine the specificity of the term he was using. (See concluding chapter discussion of the presence and absence of militancy.)

The structure of this chapter is to begin by examining the extension and development of NUBE's institutional presence in banking and its overall growth strategy. This is followed by assessing the outcomes of bargaining in banking and the nature of industrial action activity in the sector before considering the growth of ASTMS in insurance and the development of dependent unionism in the building societies. Finally, the issues of union political complexion and the prospects for union merger are analysed.

## Banking – The Extension and Development of NUBE/BIFU's Institutional Presence

NatWest granted full domestic bargaining rights in 1969 to NUBE as did Barclays with Midlands and Lloyds doing so in 1970. Those agreements, which did not cover non-clerical staff, were subsequently extended to those staff after one or two years after the initial granting of recognition. The same was broadly true for national bargaining – initially granted in 1968 and extended in 1970. In Scotland, this extension happened too in 1971. All this was achieved without the use or threat of industrial action. The nature of the recognition agreements was that co-determination of job regulation was not part of their remit (see, for example, Terry and Newell (1996) on the Midland). What is important to note is that by 1971, NUBE had gained union recognition for eighty bargaining groups (rather than eighty different employers). Whilst a considerable achievement in itself, it also represented a considerable challenge to union resources given the way that NUBE carried out its representative activities through 'servicing' via EUOs. Post-entry closed shops were established in 1972 by NUBE at the Cooperative, Scottish Cooperative Wholesale, TSB and Yorkshire banks under the influence of the *Industrial Relations Act 1971* (Weekes et al. 1975:51) while recognition was gained or extended for NUBE through establishing procedural agreements at the ten foreign banks (Baroda, Central Bank of India, Cyprus, Greece, India, Nedbank, New Zealand, Pakistan, State Bank of India, Tokyo), seven specialist banks (Credit Factoring, Lloyds and BOLSA, United Dominions Trust, Joint Credit Card Company, Centre File, BACS, United Commercial) and several smaller banks (Airdrie, Clydesdale, Lewis, Standard and Chartered) and the Stock Exchange between 1971 and 1976. Weekes et al. (1975:51) reported that the post-entry closed shops at the Yorkshire Bank increased membership from 600 to 2,400, and at the TSB from 9,000 to 11,000. In 1973, procedural agreements were signed at four further specialist banks. In 1974, NUBE gained recognition for managers at the Midland and at Barclays Bank International, and for staff at Scottish Finance, Lombard North Central and Eurocom Data. Even at this stage, NUBE/BIFU's growth in its institutional presence and rights was not all one-way traffic (see next chapter) for BIFU experienced recognition disputes at the Midland Montague, Narody Moscow and Tokyo banks in 1985 and it was refused extension of recognition to the NatWest Investment Bank (as was the LGU at Lloyds Merchant Bank).[2]

In tune with the dominant trajectory at the time following the Donovan Report (1968), some banks made moves to formalisation of industrial relations by promoting lay representation between 1971 and 1973 (Morris 1986a:51, Storey 1995:35, Undy et al. 1981: 302). Following a Commission on Industrial Relations report on the Williams and Glyns bank which embarrassed NUBE by highlighting that the staff association there had a superior form of lay representation to NUBE, NUBE adopted the policy of having office reps. Together, this led to the slow process of creation of facility time and resources as well seconded reps and then accredited office reps systems over the next decade. NUBE found itself in a difficult position in as much as it was not a wealthy organisation and was, therefore, keen to gain a 'cost-free' resource. But it was acutely aware that in doing so, it could become reliant upon employers and have the representatives becoming *de facto* company advocates under the pull of internalism. Moreover, the seconded representatives were charged with dealing with individual grievances and rather than being union organisers or negotiators. Meantime, the staff associations continued to receive subsidised office rent and equipment and pension contributions of employed association officers (Morris 1986a:51). So while sanctioned lay representation increased markedly, it did not lead to the creation of negotiation on staffing, task determination or work measurement in the workplace.

**NUBE/BIFU Growth Strategies**

NUBE's increase in membership after the gaining of MEB and CLB recognition in the banks was far less than it expected despite growing employment levels there, suggesting that it was not simply lack of recognition that held its numerical potential back. Bargaining effectiveness was the missing component whereby NUBE could not fully take advantage of its newly gained representational rights because of its subordinate position to the staff associations. Between 1969 and 1984, its membership in the banks rose from c.63,000 to c.75,000 whilst for the staff associations the figures were c.69,000 to c.99,000 – in spite of losing some 10,000 members through the MBSA (Morris 1986a:102). In terms of density, NUBE/BIFU membership fell from 35.3% in 1969 to 27.8% by 1975 whilst that of the staff associations rose slightly from 40.5% to 41.7% (Morris 1986a:101). Indeed, between 1971 and 1985, NUBE/BIFU decisively lost its membership superiority over the BBSA and its weakness *vis-à-vis* both LGSU and NWSA was deepened (Morris 1986a:109). Given that the membership surge did not occur, NUBE/BIFU sought both organic and inorganic growth outside the main clearing banks as it continued to be hemmed in, outgunned and outmanoeuvred by the bank

---

2   In 1989, the Midland derecognised MSF so that BIFU became the sole recognised union.

staff associations. One particular aspect that was central to NUBE's calculations for the need for growth was that its income per member was restrained in that the level of subscription it could levy was related to those charged by the staff associations (which continued to be subsidised by their relevant employers through secondees and facilities). Indeed, NUBE's expenditure exceeded its income and its assets and reserves were minimal.

Table 3.1 shows the fruits of this inorganic growth. This began in 1970 following the approach of a number of insurance staff associations to NUBE for amalgamation and then NUBE changing its constitution to allow this in 1971 (Buchanan 1981:46). But compared to ASTMS (see below), this was poor fare. By 1974, only 5% of its members where outside banking (Undy et al. 1981:73), with the only obvious organic gain being obtaining recognition at Ecclesiastical Insurance in 1972. Indeed in 1979, BIFU was talking to 22 staff associations about amalgamation (Willman et al. 1993:181) but it is clear that not much came of these discussions in the 1980s. In the building societies, NUBE/BIFU made some advances but these were relatively costly exercises (see below). The one clear benefit of the transfers of the staff associations of the two Scottish clearing banks was to early on remove competition to NUBE/BIFU and allow the progression to a high level of density, paving the way for Scotland to become a union stronghold (given the situation already in the Clydesdale and TSB).

In the context of the *Industrial Relations Act 1971*, NUBE registered in order to provide a bulwark against incursions by bank staff associations who had already registered and to facilitate its own expansion into new areas but, in doing so, was obliged to leave the TUC through expulsion for the period 1973–1975 for breaking TUC policy.[3] Thus, it opened up itself to possible membership poaching by TUC-affiliated unions, APEX and ASTMS. While Coates and Topham (1988:21) castigated NUBE for registering and thus breaking TUC policy, it should also be recalled that the National Graphical Association (NGA) and some other unions did likewise for similar reasons to NUBE. Before the *Industrial Relations Act 1971* was repealed, NUBE made more applications for Section 45 (sole and exclusive) recognition, numbering seventeen of the fifty-four, than any other union (Weekes et al.1975:131, see also Kessler and Palmer (1996:48)). These covered 27,000 workers. Successes were recorded in insurance at Commercial Union, Norwich Union and General Accident but these represented small beer. Nonetheless, the strategy NUBE embarked upon recorded some success in that the percentage of its membership in the high street banks declined from 77% in 1970 to 58% by 1975, 51% by 1980 and 48% by 1985 (Morris 1986a:103,110) while overall membership was growing. The culmination of this was the change of name to BIFU in 1979. Financially, its problems were eased not erased.

---

3   For the same period of time, NUBE lapsed its affiliation to the STUC (BIFU 1992:5).

**Table 3.1     Transfers of Staff Associations to NUBE/BIFU by Year, 1968–1989**

| |
|---|
| 1989 Northern Rock |
| 1987 Bank of England Staff Organisation (with 3,000 members, and established in 1973) |
| 1984 Coventry Building Society, Chelsea Building Society |
| 1982 Royal Liver and Composite |
| 1981 Eagle Star (with c.6,000 members but lost union recognition as a result) |
| 1979 Phoenix Staff Union |
| 1978 Guardian Royal Exchange Staff Union (with c.5,500 members) |
| 1974 Royal Bank of Scotland |
| 1973 Bank of Scotland |
| 1972 Williams and Glynn (with 600 members, as bought by RBS) |
| 1968 Yorkshire Bank |

*Notes*: All transfers were from staff associations unless stated otherwise. The Williams and Glyn staff association merged with NUBE on the recommendation of CIR after it failed to gain a certificate of independence.

**Staff Associations**

Indicative of the continuing war of attrition in the 1970s, NUBE attempted to get the staff associations outlawed as dependent organisations under the *Industrial Relations Act 1971* and *Trade Union and Labour Relations Act* (1974, 1976) (Morris 1986a:102, 105, Willman et al. 1993:182). This failed because staff associations had developed, and continued to develop, some unionateness and the legislative criteria were based on financial, not 'industrial', independence. In banking itself, the three staff associations formed the Clearing Bank Staff Association (CBSA) in the early 1970s following the rationalisation of the banks through mergers in the late 1960s (Crompton and Jones 1984:262) for the purposes of information exchange and coordination of bargaining at the industry level. The CBSA, the successor of the CCBSA, became the Clearing Bank Union (CBU) in 1977 following the failure of merger talks with NUBE (see below). It performed the same functions as the CBSA but represented another small departure by virtue of the change in nomenclature. Outside the banks, and spurred on by legislative requirements, most staff associations in insurance began to charge membership subscriptions by the mid-1970s (Waddington 1995:186).

**Bargaining Outcomes in Banking**

One of the first tangible outcomes of the national machinery was a new task-related pay structure based on job evaluation in 1970. The rise of job evaluation systems from the late 1960s – as broad exercises in forms of productivity and work measurement – stimulated workplace unionism in many industries. But again, this was not the case in banking. Morris (1986a:48) argued that the agreement met the banks' interests and reinforced their commitment to the national machinery because of the flexibility entertained between the company and industry levels of bargaining. Institutionally, workplace job regulation was, thus, unlikely to potentially arise in these conditions, and coupled with the ramifications of the internal labour markets (based on secure jobs with seniority pay), the standardisation of operations and the absence of a craft mentality, this was all the more so. Thus, Morris (1986a:58) commented that management maintained its unilateral control over performance management, work practices and work organisation. Wage settlements in England and Wales were often lower than in Scotland under MEB (BIFU 1992), suggesting that the absence of staff associations was a key factor in determining NUBE's greater bargaining effectiveness there. More generally, increases in holiday entitlement and territorial allowances, and a reduction in the length of the working week were gained through negotiation and arbitration.

There were relatively few references to arbitration between 1969 and 1977 at MEB (nine) or CLB (sixteen) levels in spite of the rigidity of the prior stages procedures. The majority were in the earlier years and arose from a backlog of issues to be dealt with and the desire to standardise conditions across the banks (Morris 1986a:54–55). Nearly all were referred by the staff side. The hold of internalism was further eroded by the use of the mechanisms to establish the principle of inter-bank comparability. Meanwhile, the banks became rather annoyed by the staff side trying to establish precedents because it reduced their scope for future manoeuvre particularly where precedent was set by the act of arbitration. NUBE, in particular, sought to move as many issues dealt at CLB to MEB in order to take them into an arena where it had relatively more influence and thereby create tensions between the employers and their staff associations. For such reasons, the MEB arbitration mechanism was rescinded when the joint-staff side collapsed after the withdrawal of NUBE in 1977, occasioning the banks to reaffirm their support for arbitration albeit without any immediate substantive outcome (Morris 1986a:61–62). That MEB did not end after NUBE's withdrawal from the single-staff side arose because of the employers' need to control wage claims, particularly during a period of incomes policy.[4] Consequently, the banks conceded separate bargaining rights to NUBE/BIFU at industry and company levels. Of course, this did not mean the banks were not able to play and benefit from 'divide and rule'. Frequently, they agreed a pay deal with one side and imposed it on the other as well as being able to introduce Saturday working. But at the same time, they were subject to inter-union competition which stimulated pay leapfrogging with BIFU using its IT/data processing members to spearhead action in 1979 and 1980, and the use of domestic arbitration by NUBE to undermine the national agreements that the CBU signed with the employers and imposed upon NUBE in 1981. This further convinced

---

4   In the early 1980s, for example, staff costs represented three-quarters of operating costs (see, for example, MacInnes (1988:130)).

the banks of the need for arbitration. However, the wider economic and political climates were also changing, with a recession, large employer bad lending debts and a new hard-right Tory government in operation (Morris 1986a:62–63). Thus, employers removed the arbitration clauses in 1981 because of the rising proportion of operating costs accounted for by labour costs, as product market competition intensified leading them to believe that the necessity of controlling of labour costs outweighed the prospect of industrial action (Morris 1986b:134). In their place, conciliation clauses were introduced following the example of the Midland.

The consequence of the ending of STB and the arbitration clauses and more acute competitive unionism as merger talks failed (see below) was a marked move towards relatively greater conflict, which was expressed on some occasions as open conflict, that is, industrial action. For example, BIFU balloted frequently for industrial action on pay, and most action was of a localised nature (see below). But, there was little evidence of BIFU winning the war of attrition against the staff associations by demonstrating its superior bargaining outcomes. In either relative or absolute terms, BIFU membership in the banks fell in relation to the staff associations. BIFU faced a 'Catch-22' situation of needing more members which could be then mobilised in order to demonstrate its bargaining superiority but it needed to demonstrate its bargaining superiority in order to gain more members. To this extent, the staff associations did not need to become particularly more unionate from 1978 to the mid-1980s, and as with the 'reverse' of BIFU's brand, they needed to maintain their distinctive brand image, which was still based around partnership and cooperation. These two facets concerning NUBE and the staff associations were in spite, and because, of the ability of the banks to 'agree' lower real value MEB settlements with the CBU and then impose them upon BIFU from 1981. Here, the first offer was also the last offer, and conciliation eschewed. Recession 'compelled'[5] toughness, whereby unemployment allowed more talk of the ability to pay than to pay the cost-of-living. Increasing competition in changing market conditions then 'compelled' market differentiation and, thus, a greater focus upon the company level through the diminution of the scope of MEB. For reasons of wanting the ability to respond in a differentially internalised and competitive manner, Midland left the employers' federation and thus the system of MEB in 1986. NatWest followed a year, precipitating the end of MEB and the employers' federation as competition for staff increased and the pressure of industrial action was beginning to take a toll (even though the ending of MEB was ostensibly about London Weighting Allowance). The ending of MEB was essentially a reflection of growing divergence between the banks on performance and profits in context of deregulation allowing the entrance of new players and new products (Storey 1995: 34–35, Storey et al. 1997:26,41). Thereafter, the LGSU pulled out of CBU in 1987. In Scotland, MEB was suspended in 1983 as the employers ended the

---

5    This is expressed in this way to denote that despite the coercive environment of accumulation, employers still exercise choice in terms of how to react and respond, even if this is a limited choice.

arbitration clause and then ended in 1986 after the Clydesdale left the employers' federation, precipitating its demise.

## New Technology

The decade of 1980s saw some of the most extensive technological advances in the organisation of the processing of data in the financial services sector, and banking in particular, having considerable ramifications for the organisation of work and workers' conditions of employment (Morris 1986a, Willman 1986). While NUBE/BIFU was fully cognisant of these ramifications in terms of redundancies and workloads (see, for example, BIFU (1982)), and did try to widen its bargaining agenda to take account of this, success was not forthcoming and resistance and overt conflict were absent (Morris 1986a:81). This has been attributed to its weak bargaining power *vis-à-vis* the staff associations and its own density and mobilising capacity, whereby it was unable to successfully press for the implementation of its proposed job security agreements (Terry and Newell 1996, Willman 1986:242–243), as well as the subsequent post-implementation absence of redundancies because of overall growth in employment (MacInnes 1988).[6] Moreover, the banks were only prepared to go as far as engaging in consultation on this new agenda, and in this there were aided by the limited demands of the CBU (Morris 1986a:114). Thus, new technology as a central component of innovation and investment was never allowed to be a subject of negotiation and this continued[7] even when the 1980s witnessed far-reaching wider economic recession, and the introduction of the far more potent micro-processing technologies (Willman 1986) with labour shedding implications. As the banks were unwilling at this stage to contemplate the disruption for work commitment and paternalism arising from widespread redundancies, much redeployment was used in the early to mid-1980s so the most obvious reason for a crisis in relations was avoided. Indeed, some of this was possible because some new technologies facilitated increased amounts of work as customers were offered new services using these new technologies.

Whilst Morris (1986a:83) noted that using consultation blunted possible resistance without ceding power and led the focus of attention to be concerned with execution not conception, BIFU, nonetheless, attempted to outflank and undermine the staff associations by talking up the threat of job losses as well as using the benefit of consultation to develop a bargaining relationship with the

---

6    This stands in relation to the period of the 1960s and 1970s when NUBE did not seek such agreements because of growth in employment and output, whereby compulsory redundancies were extremely unlikely, and no strikes were recorded against the implementation of new technology (Morris 1986a, Willman 1986:216).

7    Interestingly, BIFU and the employers' federation favoured a national new technology deal but the individual employers resisted this. Midland and NatWest subsequently agreed to institutional consultation arrangements on new technology.

growing personnel departments in the banks. The reaction of BIFU to its failure to gain new technology agreements was to harden its policy but again without addressing the attendant issue of mobilisation to achieve implementation (see also Terry and Newell (1996)). In only three localised cases concerning individual banks – Jersey, Blackpool and City of London – did BIFU gain anything approximating to its demands and this arose as a result of industrial action (Morris 1986a:84). What is striking about Wilman's (1986) study of the introduction of new technology into the TSB in the early 1980s is that BIFU was unable and unwilling to compel the employer to reach an accommodation given its near 100% density – following a closed shop agreement in 1976 – and the absence of any staff association. In essence, new technology in TSB remained an issue for consultation and not negotiation, and union influence was both marginal and on the margins (Willman 1986:242). The same points can be made about Terry and Newell's (1996) and Morris's (1986a:82) studies of the Midland where BIFU had 80% density and the situations at the Cooperative Bank (see Marginson 1999) and Guardian Royal Exchange (Batstone et al. 1987) with similarly high union densities.

**Industrial Action**

Historically-speaking, Britain experienced its highest period of strike activity in the 1970s when judged by number of strikes, days not worked and workers involved. Most of this action was taken by manual workers in both the private and public sectors. Therefore, the obvious issue then to examine is what took place in the financial services sector in this period. The gaining of union recognition had been NUBE's main priority in order that it would then have the institutional platform upon which to then pursue improved terms and conditions of employment for its members without deploying industrial action given its belief that it would be unable to mobilise its members (Morris 1986a:63, 64), it was in a minority position (*vis-à-vis* the staff associations) and that organising either single company or industry-wide industrial action would have been, at this stage, pressing the 'nuclear button' which the union was unwillingly to do. Consequently, the 1970s saw very little industrial action of any kind in banking. This was reinforced by the success of NUBE pressing for both the extension of union recognition to non-clerical grades where recognition was already held and union recognition in hitherto unrecognised employing organisations without using industrial action.[8] Thus, Gall (1993:67–68) recorded only eight cases of industrial action – mostly

---

8    The ramifications of this was both positive and negative; positive in that NUBE was a sufficiently strong and credible bargaining opponent to warrant union recognition but negative in that no force was exerted to better the terms of the union recognition and cement the connection between membership participation through mobilisation and gaining union advances.

strikes in individual companies but involving relatively small numbers of staff – in the banking sector in the 1970s. These included strikes and an overtime ban at the Cooperative bank in 1973/1974 and industrial action at Lloyds against extended opening hours. Storey (1995:35) commented that 'the 1970s were relatively strike free' and MacInnes (1988:131) noted that: 'collective industrial conflict was rarely threatened and almost never used' while Edwards (1983) and Hyman (1989:32) were correct to record of this period the historically low level of strikes in the sector.

The period of the early 1980s (1980–1983) witnessed a very limited number of relatively small strikes by specialist or specific groups of bank workers. This was despite the ending of the MEB and CLB arbitration clauses, and contrary to the expectations of the employers (Morris 1986a:63). These five actions of the period included those by BIFU NatWest messenger staff in 1980 which gained sympathetic action from workers in other banks in a dispute over differentials, a one-day strike in 1981 by BIFU Midland computer members on pay, and a three-week long strike by 98 BIFU Midland Bank Heathrow members (out of the 158 staff there) in 1983 over unilateral changes to shift patterns and the suspension of five members for refusing to accept these. Larger instances of action included selective regional industrial action by BIFU members in the clearing banks on pay in 1981 and a half-day strike by 50,000 BIFU members in 1983 in the clearing banks over Christmas working arrangements. The industrial action secured some advance but the strike did not as BIFU members represented just 33% of staff and CBU members crossed BIFU picketlines. The pattern of specialist groups of BIFU members taking industrial action was becoming marked as in 1985 its NatWest maintenance staff members took strike action against job losses, its Midland computer members struck over retirement packages and its Lloyds computer worker members also struck for a day over shift pay. This reflected both their strategic power and that the employers had separated these groups of specialist workers from their generalist colleagues after the former's use as the 'shock troops' of industrial action after 1978.

The first move towards industrial action by the staff associations, through the CBU, took place in 1985 when all three member constituents voted for an overtime and cooperation ban on pay. No action ensued as the majorities were insufficient according to NWSA and LGSU constitutional rules to trigger a mandate, and an improved offer was made. For the BGSU, this represented its first ever vote for industrial action. The CBU ballot followed the rejection by the employers of the CBU's demand for unilateral binding arbitration. BIFU members rejected strike action (71%:29%) on this improved offer but narrowly supported (51%:49%) an overtime ban which was not implemented. Meantime, BIFU members in the Clydesdale, BoS and RBS voted 76%:24% for an overtime ban to improve their pay offer. Whereupon this resulted in no improvement after being implemented, a ballot was held for an overtime ban and selective strike action. Thus resulted in a 59%:41% vote for – representing the first Scottish bank strike vote – but the action was not escalated and was ended as the BIFU leadership believed the vote for to be too small when the turnout was taken into account. The offer on the table was then accepted. In 1986, BIFU's recommendation to its Barclays, Lloyds and NatWest members to take strike action over pay was narrowly rejected by 52%:48% while the LGSU recommendation for an overtime ban was also rejected. In the same year, BIFU Midland computer members took strike action over shift pay while BIFU members at seven Indian banks successfully threatened strike action over job losses, leading to improved severance terms. In 1987, both BIFU and CBU members voted on industrial action on an imposed pay rise. BIFU members voted 64%:36% for an overtime ban but against strike action (52%:48%) while the NWSA voted 53%:47% for the ban as did the LGSU and BGSU on similar votes. This led to cooperation between BIFU and the CBU on the implementation of the ban but the LGSU broke ranks when it accepted an improved pay offer from Lloyds. In turn, this led to a further ballot on industrial action, including strike action and a work-to-rule, at the Midland and Barclays banks which resulted in rejection of strike action but industrial action short of a strike for sixteen weeks. But BGSU members called off their industrial action, leading BIFU members at the Midland to do so too. NatWest made an improved off so that no industrial action resulted although both NWSA and BIFU voted for an overtime ban. Whilst the industrial action brought some 2,000 new members to BIFU, its facilities were reduced by the Midland as a consequence. Meantime, BIFU TSB members instituted an indefinite overtime ban against increased workloads. In 1988, Clydesdale BIFU members balloted for industrial action on a pay offer, whence an improved offer was accepted after the overtime ban was implemented while BIFU members rejected industrial action in a ballot (80%:20%) over longer opening hours at Standard Charter. In 1988 and 1989, overtime bans were voted for by BIFU Lloyds members on margins of 3:1 on opening hours and pay (in conjunction with LGSU members) while in two banks (Barclays and Lloyds), BIFU members took three days of strike action in computing over pay and one-day strikes in Cambridge and Birmingham over local allowances. Finally, in 1989 BIFU members in NatWest voted against an overtime ban on pay while fellow members in Lloyds did similarly, BIFU members in TSB Trust Company struck for half a day on pay, and BIFU Barclays data processing members twice struck for 1–2 hour periods over holidays and pay.

In the insurance sub-sector, only five instances of industrial action are known of in the 1970s (strikes at Cooperative Insurance Service in 1973/1974 and at the Prudential Assurance Company in 1975 and industrial action at Scottish Legal, the Refuge, and Royal Liver (Undy et al 1981:258)) and there were only six instances of industrial action in the period 1980 to 1989; a work-to-rule by ASTMS members at Legal and General over pay, a strike by 14,000 NUIW members at the Prudential against changes to their terms and conditions in 1983, a one-day strike by ASTMS members at Zurich Insurance in 1986, two one-day strikes by ASTMS members at both Pearl Assurance over job cuts and at Legal and General over union rights in 1987, and, finally, a work-to-rule by BIFU members at Eagle Star over derecognition and the setting up of a staff association in 1988. In Legal and General, a move to decentralise collective bargaining led to a 77%:23% vote for an overtime ban. When instituted, the employer suspended some members, leading to the strike. Despite this paucity, Undy et al. (1981:257) talked erroneously (sic) of a 'growth of militancy [by ASTMS] in its traditionally quiescent areas such as ... insurance, banking and finance'. This contrasted with the view of EUOs at the time that most insurance workers preferred legal and procedural *modus operandi* rather than industrial action (see Melling 2004:79, 86, 101).

Whilst taking on board that workers respond to extant rather than abstract grievances and that 'contented' workers do not take industrial action, an assessment of the industrial action still highlights that the greatest advances towards robust and active collectivism were made amongst bank workers. So the period of the 1980s, prior to 1988, was not quite one of disputes being 'few and far between' (Storey et al 1999:149). Nonetheless, the new found direction was based on action short of a strike, votes for action and action of a tentative nature. Consequently, Leif Mills, then BIFU general secretary could still state: 'to take industrial action is a regret that it is necessary [at all]' (*BIFU Report*, September 1989). Insurance workers were a pale imitation and action of any kind by building society workers did not register at all. So the period of the 1980s represented a considerable advance on the 1970s for bank workers, with BIFU more to the fore. Initially, specialist groups of BIFU members were the vanguard. In an earlier analysis (Gall 1993:69–70), the contours of industrial action in the banks were analysed in terms of voting patterns, negotiating outcomes and worker attitudes. These showed progress towards unionateness but limitations were also stressed in regards of staff associations undermining relatively more robust action by BIFU or its desire to be relatively more robust, and the superior organising potential of computer workers (greater concentration of numbers, less personalised managerial relations and greater strategic leverage). It should also be recalled that the late 1980s was a period of the 'Lawson boom' whereby the tightening labour market was a factor in a slight revival in overall strike activity.

## Insurance

The early 1970s saw what could be described as the rise of 'new' staff internalism – or certainly its second wave – following the creation of many new staff associations in insurance, and the building societies (see below), for reasons of the challenge to non-unionism from labour unionism and a changed legislative environment.[9] In insurance, the pattern of development was markedly different from that in the building societies, not least because of the tradition of independent unionism and the presence of ASTMS in the former. In 1970, the Staff Association of General Accident (SAGA[10], which subsequently joined APEX in 1974 after a battle with

---

9   The Excess Insurance Group Staff Association was a partial exception in that it was established in late 1960s.

10   The CIR found SAGA to be heavily influenced by management (Weekes et al. 1975:143) and this played a part in its subsequent merger with APEX.

ASTMS), Royal London Mutual Staff Association (which joined ASMTS in 1972) and Eagle Star Staff Association were established. In 1971, Norwich Union Group Staff Association was established to supersede the company's Salaries Advisory Committee, spurred on by the *Industrial Relations Act 1971*, but its members then joined ASTMS after it failed to gain union recognition for ASTMS had union recognition (see Waddington 1995:170) whilst 1972 saw the creation of the Sun Life Staff Association, and 1974 the formation of the Legal and General Staff Association. ASTMS pursued a vigorous and 'aggressive' strategy of transfers of engagement in order to grow more widely and increase its presence and bargaining power in the sector (Undy et al. 1981). By 1980, it claimed some 75,000 members in the sector (Eaton and Gill 1981:131), up from 35,000 in 1974 (Undy et al. 1981:148). These transfers of engagement provided ASTMS with around 44,000 additional members (Undy et al. 1981:203). Following this, eleven other staff associations, largely located in insurance joined ASTMS between 1975 and 1986 (Maksymiw et al. 1990:175, see also Jenkins (1990:113–116)). Table 3.2 below gives a full list of the transfers of engagements.

**Table 3.2     Transfers to ASTMS by Year, 1970–1989**

| | |
|---|---|
| 1989 | Lloyds Register Staff Association |
| 1986 | Sun Alliance and London Staff Association |
| 1985 | Bank of New Zealand Staff Association |
| 1980 | Australia and New Zealand Banking Group Staff Association |
| 1979 | Colonial Mutual Life Assurance Society |
| 1978 | Excess Insurance Group Staff Association, Pearl Federation (NUIW section), Refuge Section (NUIW section) |
| 1976 | United Commercial Travellers Association, Liverpool and Victoria Managers Association |
| 1975 | London and Manchester (NUIW section) and Midland Bank Technical Services Association |
| 1974 | Midland Bank Staff Association, Clydesdale Bank Staff Association and National Union of Pearl Assurance Agents transferred (having left the NUIW over the Industrial Relations Act 1971) |
| 1973 | Assurance Representatives' Organisation (Ireland), Stamford Mutual Staff Association |
| 1971 | Royal Group Staff Guild |
| 1970 | Prudential Clerical Staff Association, Prudential Male Staff Association, Prudential Ladies' Staff Welfare Staff Association (in total 5,000–6,000 members), National Farmers' Union Insurance Society, Union of Insurance Staffs (17,000 members) and Royal Insurance Group Union (6,000 members) |

Freeman (1984:243–244) observed that at its establishment ASTMS had less than 80,000 members but six year later it had more than 300,000 members largely as a result of 'appealing to employees in insurance, banking and building societies who had traditionally resisted white collar unionism ... [through] a series of mergers and amalgamations with staff associations ... becoming a federation of company unions'. Later, Jenkins (1990:116) reported that these transfers brought 80,000 members into ASTMS over the subsequent years. Moreover, some of the appeal of ASTMS for employers was that it offered to help manage staff expectations in job evaluation exercises that many employing organisations were implementing in return for union recognition. This could be seen as another form of partnership before 'partnership'. Amicus (n.d), the merged successor to ASTMS through MSF, recorded that: 'ASTMS grew phenomenally, expanding rapidly into new areas of industry and services. A particularly significant development began with the merger of the Prudential Assurance Staff Associations. This was followed by other staff organisations in the insurance industry including the Union of Insurance Staffs. During its existence, over thirty different organisations merged with ASTMS'. This growth in a socially conservative area of the labour movement sat rather uneasily with the public personae of ASTMS as a left-wing union by dint of its national leadership in the form of Clive Jenkins (Eaton and Gill 1981:130–131) but it was managed by the federal structure, the maintenance of the constituent component's previous constitutions and the opting out of paying the political levy (Waddington 1995:188).

The motivation on the part of those transferring was defensive. They concluded that they were too small and resource poor to be able to provide the bargaining power and professional skills needed to facilitate effective representation in a situation where employment regulation and work organisation were becoming more formally rule bound and juridified. Furthermore, the defensive rationale included not merging with rival NUBE – which would have been perceived by staff associations as tantamount to submission and defeat – and wishing to prevent NUBE from achieving further consolidation. If merger with NUBE took place, the staff associations believed that the bargaining rights and influence accorded to their type of labour unionism would be lost forever. The case of the MBSA is apposite here. It faced membership decline and thus general decline, from 14,000 in 1968 to 10,000 in 1974 (Undy et al. 1981:206). However, Dickens (1975:39) showed the context of the MBSA joining ASTMS was driven by more than just membership decline – put another way, there was a specific context to a declining membership which was unable to meet several perceived challenges (see also Morris (1986a:52–53)). Thus, the MBSA was also acutely aware that NUBE members now had both company-level and sector-level bargaining rights in its bank, undermining the specific purchase of staff association internalism. Indeed, at the time of merger, there was the possibility of being swamped by NUBE as a result of NUBE merging with other bank staff associations. So, according to Morris (1986a:52) and Undy et al. (1981:210–212), the MBSA transferred to ASTMS, and not NUBE, because it needed greater independence but had animosity toward NUBE and NUBE would not concede the internal autonomy it desired. The *realpolitik* of ASTMS agreeing to the status of internal autonomy for the transferees was crucial, for under this arrangement, the newly joined sections of ASTMS would be allowed to maintain organisational and bargaining autonomy (Undy et al. 1981:211–212). Moreover, and although ASTMS was affiliated to the Labour Party, it operated within the financial services sector as an apolitical organisation, seeking to prevent alienation from members and potential members who were judged to be politically conservative, and being more concerned with 'bread and butter' labour unionism (see Undy et al. 1981:154, 212). The downside of ASTMS strategy was that where it acquired membership through the UIS where staff associations also existed, it could not then increase this organically and gain recognition so it ended up with the costly task of servicing minority memberships without employer support (as at Commercial Union, and Sun Life). The cost implications were exacerbated by taking on the former unions and associations' staffs.

However, ASTMS also sought to grow organically by undermining the membership basis of staff associations. At Norwich Union, ASTMS gained recognition as result of former UIS membership while the company refused to recognise the Norwich Union Group Staff Association because it favoured single union representation and the staff association was not helped in its establishment by company (Waddington 1995:170). Consequently, NUGSA membership fell from 2,488 in 1973 to 266 by 1975 (Waddington 1995:170). ASTMS was not successful in doing similarly at the Commercial Union and Sun Life because the employers supported their staff associations and recognised them. Elsewhere, employers at Prudential, Cooperative Insurance and Royal Liver strenuously opposed ASTMS's presence (Jenkins 1990:115, Melling 2004:86). However, it did gain recognition at Scottish Widows in 1975, and at Legal and General in 1979 (Haynes and Allen 2001).

Until 1985, the NUIW was a federation of sections which were constituted as independents unions with their own general secretaries, finances and the like. The NUIW's main purpose was to allow affiliation to the TUC and Confederation of Insurance Trade Unions. This structural autonomy allowing company specific bargaining on the basis of internalism did not help prevent membership defection and loss. The Britannic Field Staff Association moved to full independence in 1987 while four sections (e.g., the Royal Liver, and the Pearl) merged with ASTMS between 1974 and 1978 because ASTMS had recognition for the non-field staff grades, could provide wider bargaining and representational services and ASTMS offered sectional autonomy and exemption from paying the political fund (Waddington 1995:188–189). Unable to remain viable, the Royal Liver and Composite Section with 850 members joined BIFU in 1982 after a 4:1 voted in favour. The employers welcomed such moves as they constituted a turn towards to single union representation. The three largest and remaining sections (Liverpool Victoria, Prudential and Royal London) attempted a rearguard action by becoming a single, centralised union and increasing recruitment activities in companies like the Nationwide estate agency arm. Ultimately, these proved incapable of stemming the decline, such that the NUIW merged with the successor to ASTMS, MSF, in 1999. However, it is interesting to note that the Prudential section was affiliated to Labour and the Liverpool Victoria section had a political fund (Eaton and Gill 1981:299). Subsequent to becoming a centralised union in 1985, the NUIW established a political fund in 1988 on a 74% majority on a 51% turnout (Maksymiw et al. 1990:246). Prior to the *Trade Union Act 1984*, the NUIW did not elect its senior office bearers.

Alongside the decline of the NUIW, ASTMS merged with the Technical, Administrative and Supervisory Staffs (TASS) to form the Manufacturing, Finance and Science union (MSF) in 1988 and APEX merged into the GMB in 1989. Although the insurance and building society members in these two salient merging unions were not the majorities of their memberships and were not in commanding positions, these mergers do, nonetheless, suggest that the labour unionism that these unions represented in the financial services sector was far from healthy and viable, and that expansionary projects in both the financial services and other sectors had failed. For example, by the 1980s a number of employers, for which ASTMS had 'inherited' union recognition (after staff associations transfers) derecognised ASTMS (Freeman 1984:244) and the 'servicing' approach of EUO domination and elite lay participation with a paternalist *modus operandi* (see, for example, Batstone et al. (1987: chapter 5) and Fosh and Cohen (1990:123)) did not augur well for an changed era of employer hostility. In a survey on participative democracy across five workplaces spread across the economy, Fosh and Cohen (1990:109, 114–15) ranked their insurance company workplace as scoring the lowest on representativeness, accountability and membership involvement where branch committee and membership meetings were held monthly and branch mass meetings were held irregularly with no workplace meetings. They attributed this largely to the incorporation and bureaucratisation of the key leaders (company secondees) and stewards. Similar patterns and trajectories can be identified in Batstone et al.'s (1987) study of an insurance company in the early 1980s. So while employers had previously supported a labour unionism – based on a 'servicing' approach – for reasons of providing a controlled and manageable union presence, with the consequence that this tended to lock the labour unionism into a relationship of undue dependence, come the change to a harsher environment, the labour unionism here was ill-prepared to respond where it faced reduced facilities and legitimacy. This, in turn, emphasised increased union weakness to an instrumentally inclined union membership and increased the costs of servicing a widely dispersed patchwork of relatively small groups of members.

In terms of BIFU's presence in insurance, it gained transfers from the associations and unions at Royal Liver and Composite, Eagle Star, Phoenix Staff and Guardian Royal Exchange (see Table 3.1). This created tensions with ASTMS (*Financial Times* 4 January 1982). The Phoenix Staff Union choose to merge with BIFU in 1979 to gain wide ranging bargaining support services because it was put off by ASTMS's political profile and activity even though ASTMS had 500 members at the company. However, BIFU was derecognised in favour of the Sun

Alliance and London Staff Association (SALSA) by Sun Alliance when it acquired Phoenix Assurance. But as the result of the holding of a management ballot, staff indicated majority support for BIFU over SALSA or SALSA as part of ASTMS (with whom SALSA had built up a close relationship). SALSA then conducted its own membership ballot on merging with ASTMS which favoured doing so. Whereupon it merged with ASTMS, it was also derecognised. Campaigning by both ASTMS and BIFU to re-obtain recognition was not fruitful while a Sun Alliance Staff Union was established by ex-SALSA members. It gained recognition while ASTMS and BIFU had their check-off facilities withdrawn leading to dwindling memberships (Waddington 1995:172). This type of ASTMS-BIFU competition was earlier paralleled by BIFU's 'acquisition' of the Guardian Royal Exchange Staff Union in 1979, and the failed attempt by the TUC to establish agreement on spheres of influence to prevent competitive activities (Waddington 1995:180). In 1986, BIFU was derecognised by Eagle Star so that its staff association existed as

---

**INSET 3.1 Royal Insurance**

The staff association, which had existed since the 1920s, decided to join ASTMS in 1970 because it faced the prospect of being unable to respond adequately to the challenges it faced vis-à-vis job redesign, changes in remuneration and computerisation. Its options were either to raise membership subscriptions in order to provide the resource needed to employ specialist staff to allow it negotiate on these issues or join a body like ASTMS which had this resource and expertise to hand already. In 'buying in' the negotiating expertise as an arms length move, when the staff association entered ASTMS, it also maintained a large degree of autonomy as a company section with its own annual conference and executive committee. The employer provided the facilities for two full-time seconded reps, office accommodation and equipment. It supported union membership, which had been maintained at a 75% density, and provided the facilities on the basis that '[t]he objective is to have a broadly representative union led by capable people who have a good understanding of our businesses'. The involvement of ASTMS national officials was relatively minor. Royal Insurance began to devolve personnel management responsibilities to its constituent parts prior to the 1980s as well as introduce employee involvement mechanisms. Two salient points emerge here. First, the option of developing the lay expertise to deal with the challenges did not appear to be considered. And second, because the union at the company level was quite centralised, it was not well prepared for the devolution of management responsibility.

*Source*: Mick Marchington interviewed Bob Bell, employee relations manager, Royal Insurance, Employee Relations, 1984, 6/1:17–21.

---

the sole recognised body. In 1988, this body became the Union of Finance Staff (but now simply 'UFS') after takeover by the Zurich Financial Services group. It is a non-TUC affiliated union which, constitutionally, is open to all workers but has its core members in the financial services sector, where it stresses it operates on the basis of seeking partnership with employers, and has a section for managers, the Finance Managers' Association.

## Staff Associations in Building Societies

The growth of the building societies' market presence and share of the expanding financial services sector up to the early 1980s is sometimes forgotten because of the relatively late, but now dominant, presence of banks into the mortgage market. With this competition, the deregulation of financial services product markets and the ability of building societies to demutualise and convert into banks under the *Building Societies Act 1986*, the numbers of building societies fell from 504 to 225 between 1969 and 1983 (Purcell 1984:7). The rapid process of concentration continued thereafter although the total number of branches grew considerably at the same time (Wilkinson et al. 1998:45–46). Prior to 1970, there existed only one staff association amongst building societies and the presence of independent labour unionism was non-existent (Swabe and Price 1984, Winterton and Winteron 1982). So while the terrain was not particularly hospitable (see below), it was nonetheless an open one (see Swabe and Price 1984b:8). In 1971, NUBE changed its constitution to permit it to recruit outside its traditional banking constituency. This was partially carried out with a view to beginning recruitment and organisation in building societies, hitherto essentially ignored by NUBE. This, and the influence of the *Industrial Relations Act 1971* and *Trade Union and Labour Relations Act 1974* in giving attention to the desirability of organised employee representation and strengthening the method by which union recognition could be gained, provided the stimulus for the building societies to begin the process of creating staff associations. Nonetheless, Swabe and Price (1984a:199) also noted that staff demand for fuller collective representation was evident, suggesting that the hitherto existing consultative committees or councils had become (or remained) unsatisfying within a continuing context of benevolent paternalism and high introspection. So by 1974, seven staff associations had been established, rising to 23 by 1982 and 24 by 1984, although some 251 building societies existed (Purcell 1984:5, Swabe and Price 1984a:195). Purcell (1984:5) reported that by 1984 nineteen of the top twenty five societies ranked by assets had staff associations. Yet, except for the Nationwide, staff associations had not been established at the big five building societies (Swabe and Price 1984b:8). The building societies with the twenty-three staff associations in 1980 had a collective workforce of 38,534, in which the average staff association density was 73%, the lowest being 57% and highest 86% (Swabe and Price 1984a:196). By 1981, the majority of the staff associations had become listed as unions with certificates of independence, covering around 25,000 workers (Winterton and Winterton 1982:12), with this figure being 67% by 1984 (Purcell 1984:5). In twenty three building societies which had staff associations listed as unions there was no rival labour union activity (Swabe and Price 1984b:8).

The staff associations were suspicious of, if not hostile to, independent labour unionism. Their high membership densities provided a good bulwark against NUBE quite apart from the related support they received from their employers. Alongside this, building societies were culturally distinct, of a small size and practiced above market level paternalism, aiding the sense that its workers did not perceive the need of mainstream labour unionism (Swabe and Price 1984a:199). As with banking and insurance, the employers in this sub-sector welcomed, encouraged and facilitated their creation and development. Indeed, the longstanding Building Societies' Association (BSA) played a role in encouraging internalism of a union or non-union kind (Danford et al. 2003:99, Purcell 1984:5, Swabe and Price 1984b:8). With the introduction of the *Industrial Relations Act 1971* and then *Trade Union and Labour Relations Act 1974*, Winterton and Winterton (1982:12, 13) argued the BSA and Federation of Building Society Staff Associations specifically encouraged the establishment of staff associations that could pass muster. That said, there is very little evidence of direct funding from employers in these conditions, aided by staff associations raising subscriptions from members. Subsidies were in kind – offices and equipment at non-commercial rates (see, for example, Purcell (1984:6)). Reports of the bargaining and representational activities of the staff associations suggest they were neither sham nor robust exercises, partly because a perceived overwhelming commonality of interests was underpinned by right of redress to unilateral arbitration in many cases (see Purcell 1984, Swabe and Price 1984a, 1984b). The irony for the employers of introducing unilateral arbitration to limit any threat from independent labour unionism or possibly more unionate staff associations was that it prevented the likelihood of industrial action at the price that concessions could also be wrenched out of them. Subsequently, the employers changed the terms of referral to arbitration from unilateral to bilateral. This undermined the staff associations as they were (and remained) extremely unlikely to use industrial action (*cf.* Purcell 1984:6). Now they have to rely only on force of argument and creating political and market leverage.

Given the small size of most of the staff associations, representation and collective bargaining were carried out by paid external experts, with varying degrees of effectiveness (Purcell 1984:6, Swabe and Price 1984a:200–202). However, some of the large staff associations at the Abbey and Halifax had small numbers of EUOs. Both suggested a centralised structure to the staff associations – which was the case – in facing the employer who also operated in a centralised manner. Consequently, there was no sense in which workplace (dependent) unionism developed by dint of bargaining structures (or other social influences). Indeed, Wilkinson et al. (1998) highlighted that the exchange between the associations and their employers was a highly formalised and structured one based on centralised forums. The composition of officers of staff associations, despite the overwhelming majority of building society staff, and thus staff association members, being women and from clerical grades, comprised male, junior managers. And while the constitutional possibility of industrial action existed, the rubric of the salient clauses in the staff associations alone – quite apart from the points made above – made this high unlikely. Collectively, the staff associations banded together under a Federation of Building Society Staff Associations from 1974, again an uneasy expression of the tension between internalism and externalism (albeit the Halifax, and Bradford and Bingley staff associations were the only major ones not to join). This organisation carried out research for comparability on pay and conditions and encouraged the creation of staff associations in other building societies but did not carry out any bargaining role like the CBU.

Nonetheless, there were some incursions from independent unionism. NUBE gained sole bargaining rights at the Dewsbury and West Riding, Colne, Barnsley, and Northampton and Midland building societies in 1972, followed by another five in 1973, four in 1974, one in 1975, and one in 1976. While a significant achievement, only two of these societies had more 100 staff and the significant associations at the Abbey and Halifax remained untouched so penetration was limited and excluded the large societies (Swabe and Price 1984b:6–7, see also Winterton and Winterton (1982:12)). Moreover, NUBE had unrecognised membership in another nine. Although NUBE had left the TUC to be able to use the CIR to gain union recognition, it experienced limited success in doing so. It was successful in only a tiny handful of cases: at the Hastings and Thanet, recognition was gained voluntarily after withdrawal of the application while at the Bridgwater Building Society in 1974 and Coventry Economic Building Society in 1973[11], recognition was gained after both staff associations failed to gain certificates of independence. However, in the latter, NUBE was derecognised in 1977 after the staff association gained a certificate of independence. Moreover, recognition was withdrawn from NUBE from the Town and Country and Sussex building societies in favour of staff associations in this period. And at the Anglia, Temperance and West Bromwich building societies, employer help for staff associations and resistance to independent labour unionism resulted in NUBE being unable to gain recognition (Winterton and Winterton 1982:12). Both ASTMS and APEX were even less successful at gaining recognition during these years and by using the statutory mechanisms. Thus, ASTMS won recognition only at the Liverpool, lost a ballot for recognition under the CIR mechanism at the Bedfordshire and mounted a failed recruitment exercise at the Bradford and Bingley. That said, it was clear that neither ASTMS nor APEX prioritised organising in this sub-sector (Swabe and Price 1984b, Winterton and Winterton 1982:12).

---

11    The CIR found a combination of undue influenced exerted by senior management in terms of the staff association's establishment, holding officer positions and member recruitment, and the associations having no paid officials or independent outside help (Weekes et al. 1975:140), prevented independence.

Swabe and Price (1984b:10) found the dominant perception of NUBE in building societies was one of poor internal communications, local organisation and specialist knowledge at the company level which, by default, emphasised the virtues of the special relationship of internalism. This coupled with a lack of organising capacity, leading to failed Section 11 statutory recognition applications by NUBE, ASTMS and APEX at Northern Rock, West Bromwich and Nationwide, meant that the dominant strategy deployed by NUBE, and ASTMS, was growth through acquisition via convincing the staff associations to recommend merger (Swabe and Price 1984b:10). Indeed, this was a strategy recommended by the CIR given the hostility of employers and the inadequacy of dependent staff representation (Swabe and Price 1984b:9). The main merits of the amalgamation strategy were that it had lower costs than starting organising from scratch where competition existed (particularly for resource poor NUBE/BIFU), and by offering to retain autonomy within the labour union the staff associations could maintain much of their character and policies. Yet by the end of the decade, NUBE/BIFU had no more than a toehold in the building societies, and one where small memberships were gained a high cost because of the lack of economies of scale and the financial implications of granting sectional autonomy in terms of EUOs and structures.[12] Moreover, the lack of assimilation of new members meant that they did not help increase overall unionateness or strength. If anything, such transfers could be seen to dilute the relative unionateness of BIFU and ASTMS and not challenge and overcome the legacy and living embodiment of internalism. And despite having to adapt to a more stringent legal environment, staff associations remained largely unchallenged. Indeed, the compulsion of the legal framework helped sustain this form of dependent unionism by giving it an air of independence. Finally, as a result of building society mergers, staff associations merged with each other following this (for example, Burnley and Provincial in 1983 and Birmingham and Bridgwater in 1986).

---

12 For example, BIFU gained transfers from the Chelsea and Coventry staff associations in 1984, bringing in just 478 members (Swabe and Price 1984b:11). This became a costlier one when both employers refused to recognise BIFU. Moreover, Redman et al. (1997) and Snape et al. (1993) found managerial staff in the Northern Rock in the late 1980s increasingly favoured BIFU as a more robust and effective body than the staff association due to changes in their jobs. Consequently, the staff association transferred to BIFU, but membership remained here as the buying in of a service as opposed to including a degree of active self-representation. Later, in 1989, BIFU gained recognition at the Bradford Pennine.

**Democracy, Participation, Government and Politics**

NUBE operated as centralised union for a number of historical and continuing reasons.[13] Competition with, and opposition to, the strong bank staff associations meant that NUBE prized and promoted independence from the employers, and because of this, favoured MEB. (By contrast, ASTMS' strategy was based on incorporating existing staff associations within a system of decentralised collective bargaining where there were no other rival collective associations of dependent unionism and dependent unionism elsewhere was far less strong.) This general trajectory led NUBE/BIFU to use EUOs to a degree that was unusual for a union with such a low income – derived from a low level of subscription rate as a result of competition with staff associations which received employer subsidy – and organise on a non-company basis in order to avoid the pull of *de facto* company or enterprise unionism. The rationale for the heavy reliance on EUOs lay in the prospect of victimisation of activists and the non-existence of workplace bargaining in the absence of workplace union recognition (see Undy et al. (1981:85, 303)). Activists were left to be micro-union level administrators, dealing with issues of recruitment, communication and individual grievances (Weekes et al. 1975), which suited an administrative and bureaucratically-minded union machine.[14] For the above reasons, and others outlined elsewhere, the BOG/ NUBE created multi-institutional, geographical branches and sections in order to emphasis this independence from the banks and difference from the staff associations as well as bringing together the few activists it had (see also Blackburn (1967:84–85, 91)). While wanting to be different from the staff associations, their

---

13    This trajectory was reinforced, not changed, by the gaining of CLB and MEB for NUBE chose to continue to operate as before because little had fundamentally changed *vis-à-vis* the battle against internalism. One indication of the centralisation was the move by BIFU to have its subscriptions paid by direct debit, rather than through check-off – this being far in advance of all other unions who did so because of legislative change in the 1990s or who now do so of their own volition (see Morris and Willman (1994:103)). In terms of wider unionism, NUBE was not dissimilar to how a number of other white-collar, professional unions operated (see Undy et al. 1981).

14    Even where there were office representatives charged with these functions, not all positions were filled (see, for example, Batstone et al. (1987:189) where only 69% were filled). And, in the Midland bank in the late 1980s, for example, BIFU had the opportunity for 176 local reps for its 16,000 members as per its recognition agreement (Terry and Newell 1996:54). This would have represented one rep for every 90 members – quite a high ratio – but only 66 places were taken (Terry and Newell 1996:54), giving a ratio of 1:242 (see also Batstone et al. (1987)). Whether representatives were active is another matter. Both filling positions and obtaining activity were held back, *inter alia*, by the absence of a bargaining function.

existence as significant bodies also represented a pull, whereby their non-use of workplace unionism and its attendant structures meant that with a relatively socially conservative workforce, NUBE found another material reason not to develop workplace unionism. Workplace unionism or workplace branches did not therefore exist in any meaningful sense. Job regulation was, thus, also absent. The historical importance of this will be addressed more fully in the concluding chapter but for now it is sufficient to recognise that the absence of workplace unionism helped establish a certain kind of union form.

Following on from this, NUBE came under pressure from members from the early 1970s to form institutionally-based branches and occupationally-based sections, and this pressure was ceded to by the mid- to late 1970s (Eaton and Gill 1981:290, Egan 1982:28, Maksymiw et al. 1990:84, Undy et al. 1981:302, 309, Willman et al. 1993:170). This arose because of the disjuncture between the forms of internal union representation and members' specific material interests, particularly where extant union structures had been dominated by the interests of membership of the four main clearing banks (Barclays, Lloyds, Midland and NatWest). Whilst an accommodation, this compromise also created new tensions along vertical and horizontal, and centripetal and centrifugal, axes within what aspired to be a singular, national union. In doing so, NUBE aped some aspects of the staff associations and supported qualified notions of internalism and sectionalism. Ironically, this move towards federalisation also made the amalgamation of smaller associations into NUBE/BIFU easier because the formers' autonomy on their immediate industrial relations issues was preserved, and it fitted with the later return to CLB elsewhere in the sector. So whilst the move towards greater internal sectionalism resulted in the creation of section conferences in 1981, BIFU also established in 1980 a Clearing Bank Union section within itself to give formal representation to its largest membership section (BIFU 1992:7, 8). In total, and by 1988, BIFU had 366 branches and sections, compared with 252 in 1980 (Egan 1982:28, Maksymiw et al. 1990:84), of which the majority were institutional by the mid-1980s (Morris 1986b:137). Nonetheless, underneath this, workplace unionism was still largely absent, particularly because the new sectional organisation became very institutionalised, formalised and hierarchical by way of its company committee structure and its rule bound ways of working (see, for example, Batstone et al. (1987) and MacInnes (1988:133)). A further important outcome of the relative structural decentralisation was that, with the increase in branches and sections, NUBE could not afford to hire further EUOs to 'service' their needs. Consequently, it negotiated seconded rep positions, imitating the facilities that staff associations had long enjoyed (Undy et al. 1981:302–303).

*Prima facie*, BIFU was quite a democratic union by virtue of its extensive use of regular membership newsletters (general and sectional) and of ballots on employer pay offers throughout the bargaining units it had union recognition for. But in the absence of any significant workplace unionism, this was an exercise in atomised and low level individualised involvement (rather than participation) as well as inactive collectivism. In turn, this fed a predominant attitude of 'so what has the union done for me?'. Moreover, in other measures, NUBE/BIFU was not particularly democratic where democracy is taken to be the rule by the many. For example, the general secretary and EUOs were appointed as were seconded representatives (Eaton and Gill 1981, Maksymiw et al. 1990). In this regard, Kelly and Heery (1994:54) noted that BIFU had a low adherence to representative principles in the selection of officers. This picture did not change until the 1980s and as a result of legislation like the *Trade Union Act 1984* (see Undy et al. 1996). NEC members were elected annually by ballots of Area Council delegates who were themselves selected by branches (Weekes et al.1975:89) and other senior positions like president and vice-president were elected by conference delegates (Eaton and Gill 1981:290) rather than by direct membership ballots. Furthermore, the c.5,000 office representatives (Eaton and Gill 1981:290) – as opposed to shop stewards – that existed by the early 1980s since their creation in 1972 had no *de facto* or *de jure* position of authority in the overall union structure. The creation of an office reps system was spurred on by a CIR report highlighting the lack of workplace representation in NUBE's structure. The BOG/NUBE had been unwilling to develop such a representative layer to its structure because it believed they would be colonised by a pro-company mentality, which only EUOs could resist (Undy et al. 1981:303), even though the staff associations in banking had deployed such a system for many years. Indeed, the staff associations were much better organised at the workplace level although this was not used to contest managerial authority. But it took until later in the 1980s for BIFU to develop this rep system, even in Scotland where staff associations were absent (see, for example, MacInnes (1988:133)).

In BIFU, activists reported that Leif Mills regularly ignored conference decisions while the union and national executive were dominated by the position of the general secretary (even though the former appointed the latter). This phenomenon is indicative of not just the domination of 'superordinates' but also the deference of 'subordinates'. And whilst in all unions under capitalism, there is often deference to the experience and expertise of career EUOs who are also often better educated and more articulate than members, there was an additional factor at work in BIFU. Thus, the sense of deference and hierarchy of the employing institutions, along with the relative social conservatism of the workers themselves, was forcefully carried into labour unionism (especially where members had no countervailing power base such as workplace unionism). So, the issue concerns the social reasons of why members accepted their leaders' leadership, and why they did not hold them more accountable and impose their own agendas.

Politically, BIFU (and its predecessors) became known as a respectable and moderate union (see, for example, Crompton (1989:145), Crompton and Jones (1984:179), *Financial Times* (25 October 1982, 24 September 1984, 1 June 1987), Lockwood (1958:176, 178–179) and Morris (1986b:139)). Sometimes, this was couched in terms of being 'non-political' (Eaton and Gill 1981:289), 'non-militant'

(Lockwood 1958:178, Lumley 1973:33, Morris 1986a:28)[15] or as 'be[ing] on the right-wing of the trade union movement' (Maksymiw et al. 1990:83). Here, the promotion of significant individual membership financial services was seen as being a touchstone of this, covering work *and* non-work professional, legal and insurance services. BIFU, as with NUBE and the BOG before it, straddled an uneasy divide. It was an independent union but not a particularly unionate one given the competition it faced, unlike most other unions, of staff associations/ unions on its 'right' and ASTMS/MSF on its 'left'. For example, it opposed nationalisation of financial institutions in 1977 at the TUC (BIFU 1992:7)[16], it did not vote on 'political' motions at the TUC (before 1973 and after it re-affiliation in 1975) because the basis of its affiliation was industrial and it did not have policy on political issues, it abstained at the TUC Congress in 1984 on whether to support the striking miners, its own conference voted to reject setting up a political ballot in 1986, and it maintained its position of employing an MP from each of the two main political parties (Conservative, Labour) as parliamentary consultants. Yet, it supported the creation of worker directors in evidence to the Bullock Commission of 1975 and in the Commission's subsequent report of 1977, it revised its stringent rules on the threshold needed for strike action, set up strike fund and a Broad Left was established in 1981 with the backing of three of the thirty NEC members and membership of 30–40 delegates at the 1982 annual conference of 500 delegates (Eaton and Gill 1981:293). Often conferences decisions were taken against the advice of the NEC. The Broad Left campaigned for positions to be adopted and implemented on more robust responses to employers, the election of EUOs and allowing political discussions in the union (on issues like apartheid). Those of the Broad Left and those entering BIFU with experience of other unions often characterised BIFU as a union in name only – the reality being closer to a staff association.

In terms of gender politics, and assuming that women finance sector workers have additional rather than separate interests to their male counterparts, NUBE did not represent in proportional terms the numerical domination of women. In 1970, women comprised for the first time the majority of the banking workforce and in 1983, the majority of BIFU members. By 1985, women comprised 59% of the workforce and 51.9% of BIFU membership. Yet despite a 47% female membership in 1977, NUBE was male dominated: its NEC was 87% male, its EUOs were 90% male and its TUC delegates were 100% male (Taylor 1978:188). In 1980, the percentages were 87.5% and 89% and by 1989 80% and 81%, for the first two categories respectively (Eaton and Gill 1981:291, Maksymiw et al. 1990:84). Egan (1982:29) also reported that BIFU activists, office holders and conference delegates were disproportionately male. And, by the time of Heery and Kelly's (1989:197) study of union officers in 1986, the situation in this regard

---

15   Lumley (1973:55–56) attributes some of NUBE 'non-militancy' to the impact of its vertical organising scope where higher grades and managers were members.

16   ASTMS did likewise, fearing job losses upon rationalisation (Melling 2004:99).

had not changed. Thus, both Eaton and Gill (1981:291) and Maksymiw et al. (1990:84) noted that, despite the creation of a Women's Equality Working Party in 1975 – which was upgraded in 1980 to an Equal Opportunities Committee – and the adoption of certain policies on gender discrimination by employers, 'there is plenty of scope for further [progress]'. This stands rather awkwardly with NUBE having adopted equal pay policy in 1967 (Crompton 1989:148), and suggests that adopting formal policy was easier to achieve than more wide-ranging and deep-seated internal change.

When turning to the issue of membership attitudes towards union participation, Crompton and Jones' (1984:198–199, 262–263) study of a bank and an insurance company between 1979 and 1981 indicated that, unprompted by a specific question, only 5% of BIFU members thought BIFU was 'too militant', yet amongst staff association members, this was 33% and amongst non-union members 10%. Meantime, the corresponding figures for ASTMS being 'too militant' were 10% for ASTMS members and 8% amongst non-members. This suggests there was a yet to be tried and potentially tapped reservoir of members willing to at least consider further or more assertive collective action. Of course, whether members would take such action would have been influenced by the nature of their orientation towards their union. Crompton and Jones (1984:199) also found that 43% of ASTMS and 37% of BIFU members joined for reasons of instrumental protection of an individualised nature and Batstone et al. (1987:191–195) also identified insurance orientated and passive motivations for joining at the Guardian Royal Exchange. Indeed, as late as the early 1970s, free membership was conferred on insurance workers in some companies. Thus, if a move towards greater collective assertiveness was made, a tension for some members between their desires and their preparedness would have had to be brooked. This is no to discount the continuing favourable disposition of some BIFU activists towards their employers as a result of a mutual gains perspective (see MacInnes (1988:133)). For BIFU here, one additional dimension was although it had a smaller proportion of senior staff in membership than the staff associations (Crompton and Jones 1984:197, Morris 1986a:112, 1986b:133), it had to contend with the ramifications of a membership that in 1985 was 84% comprised of ABC1 social categories (Sherman 1986:95).

**Inter-union Relations**

In much of the post-war period, NUBE/BIFU primarily regarded the staff associations not as rival unions but as the main part of employer strategy to keep labour unionism out of the sector. Consequently, it believed it was in a 'kill or be killed' situation. This tension pervaded the creation of industry-wide and domestic bargaining in banking and rose to the surface when in 1977 NUBE pulled out of the single staff side – a form of STB – that the employers forced upon it. Between 1968 and 1977, NUBE believed it could outflank the staff associations within these bargaining arrangements as the only legitimate (and independent) form of labour unionism but as the minority body, hemmed in by two other hostile players, this proved not to be the case, hence its withdrawal. In BIFU's (1992:7) words, NUBE withdrew 'as a result of many years' frustration due to the restrictive policies of the staff associations'. Morris (1986a:105) explained the situation rather differently. After the failure of the merger talks (see below), NUBE decided that it needed to return to its strategy of burying the staff associations through membership growth and that required withdrawing from joint-working in order to show that it was more effective in bargaining. The opportunity arose when the CBU submitted a pay claim which broke the then pay norm – so NUBE stated it could not support this as the claim broke TUC policy. Morris (1986a:105) pointed out the irony of NUBE, the longstanding critic of staff association moderation, using this as the pretext. This was a potentially dangerous move for it was by no means certain that NUBE would maintain its MEB rights, that MEB itself would continue and that CLB would not be strengthened. Outside the constraints of STB, NUBE/BIFU hoped to be able to show that it was the more effective body and that the decision of individual union membership would be predicated on this issue of efficacy (Morris 1986b:132–133). Whilst BIFU did increase its absolute membership level and at a faster relative rate than the CBU between 1977 and 1984, it still remained in a minority (albeit from a ratio of 41:59 in 1977 to 44:56 (calculated from Morris (1986b:133)). Therefore, NUBE/BIFU was forced to accentuate the difference through policies rather than action or results (Morris 1986b:133), territory on which the CBU could both easily compete and look unionate on. As Morris (1986b:133–134) noted, this competition was skilfully exploited by the employers, leading to the intensification and extensification of the wage-effort bargain, and the exacerbation of NUBE/BIFU's financial weakness.

Organisationally, and under the first era of MEB with STB, NUBE and the staff associations held off-on merger talks from 1973 on the creation of an Association of Banking and Finance Unions (ABFU). However, they were initially as much influenced the *realpolitik* that NUBE was not powerful enough to 'kill' the staff associations no matter how much it detested them as well as the consequences of NUBE's expulsion from the TUC for registering under the *Industrial Relations Act 1971*. With regard to the former, NUBE membership fell between 1970 and 1973 (Morris 1986a:103). With regard to the latter, expulsion entailed losing the protection of the TUC's Bridlington Rules against incursions from other affiliated-unions, which became a distinct possibility with the emergence of the aggressive ASTMS and the MBSA joining it in 1974. So whilst, NUBE and the staff associations could not agree on issues of structure, subscription destination and locus of EUOs (Morris 1986a:104), reflecting their different perspectives and politics – NUBE favouring centralisation based on geographical branches, the staff associations decentralisation based on companies – some of the compulsion for merging was taken off by NUBE's re-admittance into the TUC in 1975 following the repeal of the Act, its improving financial position (Morris 1986a:104) and its withdrawal from the MEB STB in 1977. Finally, ASTMS did not make any breakthrough from its bridgehead at the Midland. Following the breakdown of the ABFU talks, the three staff associations formed the CBU in 1977. It operated as a coordinating body and continued until 1988 when MEB ended. Nonetheless, the pressures towards merging remained so that attempts were made between 1978 and 1980, and 1982 and 1985. The former talks deployed an independent arbitrator and despite considerable progress, BIFU came under pressure from its activists to refuse the proposed union structure, because it ceded ground to the staff associations, which then limited BIFU's room for accommodation (Morris 1986a:106, 1986b:135). But another reason for the elusive breakthrough was that BIFU was not derecognised after leaving the MEB staff side because the banks believed coordinated bargaining was necessary to stop pay leapfrogging (following the ending of the incomes policy in 1979 after the Conservatives' election to office). In other words, BIFU found itself in a position of resilience. The latter talks were rather disingenuous on the part of the CBU for it put forward preconditions that BIFU could not agree to (Morris 1986b:136). Again issues of structure reflected issues of power and perspectives, namely, loose federation of company unions versus centralised union and where subscriptions were to be paid to, where officials would be employed, branch structure, and TUC affiliation (Morris 1986b:136–137). The difficulties, *in toto*, were indicative of the limited developments towards unionateness on the staff associations' part as well as the cost and dynamics needed to justify and operationalise separate existence accentuating differences and inter-union competition. It is also of interest to note that the employers in banking had no clear view of whether the staff associations should merge together themselves or whether they should merge with NUBE. Whilst they benefited from supporting a dependent form of unionism and from the effect of 'divide and rule', they also experienced competitive bargaining, and increased industrial relations instability and uncertainty. The fear of unknown and, in particular whether NUBE might colonise the staff associations, is likely to have prevented the banks from taking any long-term position and action (*cf.* Morris 1986a:104, 107).

## Conclusion

The dominant strategy of employers in the sector continued to be predicated upon moulding their workers' collective representation through competition and pacification with limited rights rather than confrontation and exclusion. This was because their priority was to maintain industrial relations stability and the managerial prerogative so they could 'get on' with 'business'. Structured and internalised paternalism still reigned while performance management had yet to become a major objective. Partnership before partnership thus existed in banks, insurance and building societies. But as the decade of the 1980s unfolded, and increasing competition emerged, then more staff cooperation was sought to respond to this. But as this occurred precisely at the time that job security and career progression were being eroded, the banks began to introduce what were to become hallmarks of early HRM (quality circles, briefing groups, employee involvement). Open industrial conflict became the progeny of this, representing a turning point in regard of a key aspect of growing unionateness.

The level of union density in the sector rose from 42.9% in 1968 to 54.8% in 1979 and, because of the absolute employment growth of 24% in this period, this represented a 58% growth in the numbers of members (Bain and Price 1983:15). The death knell of staff associations was far from sounded by this point. Despite much of the hidden subsidy from employers ending in the 1970s with the introduction of legislation on independence, union effectiveness and formalisation, and the transfer of staff associations to, and organic expansion of, independent labour unionism, in 1979 staff associations still maintained a 65% density in banking, 75% in insurance and 76% in building societies (Waddington 1995:186). Thus, for example, Lumley's (1973:111) prediction of a merger between NUBE and the banking staff associations, on the basis that because the staff associations were not as effective as NUBE they would lose members, was profoundly mistaken. In all three sub-sectors, the existence of dependent unionism placed severe restraints on independent unionism being able to grow organically – that being the critical task to achieve for long-term viability.

Historically, NUBE/BIFU has been a relatively poor union with low subscription rates, a high dependence on subscriptions and high reliance on (costly) EUOs (Willman et al. 1993:170–171, 175). Low or non-existent staff association subscriptions kept those of the BOG/NUBE low as well (see Taylor 1978:66) while its brand of labour unionism was reliant upon independence from the employers and so employed (rather than seconded) officers were necessary. In 1991, BIFU had fifty EUOs, giving it an average officer-to-member ratio *vis-à-vis other* unions (Kelly and Heery 1994:50). This level of EUOs for servicing a middle-sized membership but on relatively low membership subscriptions was difficult to maintain for the growth of BIFU membership in a period of an expanding workforce was not sufficiently great to weather the subsequent downturn because it was still held back by competition with the staff associations. NUBE/BIFU never made its target of financial viability of 200,000 members (see Maksymiw et al. 1990:83) despite honing its particular 'brand' appeal to the wider body of finance workers, namely, that of moderate, non-political but effective independent labour unionism in contradistinction to the staff associations and ASTMS. In banking, the three staff associations won the growth battle and their growth was entirely organic whereas BIFU was both organic and inorganic. The cases of the non-competition in the Midland and Scottish clearing banks show what may have been possible in Barclays, Lloyds and NatWest if the same situation had prevailed. But NUBE/BIFU's essential problem in waging a war of attrition and obliteration against the staff associations was that they adapted to these criticisms by becoming more unionate and these moves were reluctantly accepted by employers as 'better unionate dependent labour unionism than even more unionate independent labour unionism'. Without workplace unionism, and compared to the relative ease of organising in, and the facility subsidy from, the large banks (despite the competition with staff associations), NUBE/BIFU membership in the international banks, insurance companies and building societies was expensive to service because the total membership was small, fragmented and without employer subsidy. Indeed, to NUBE this reinforced the validity of its centralised operation but in doing so this again had high cost implications.

The battle against internalism in insurance was also lost by both the GIO/UIS and NUIW. Despite adopting structures that catered towards the needs of single company unionism, both never were able to grow organically and encroach upon the staff associations. In aping a version of internalism here, the labour unionisms were caught between a rock and a hard place of simultaneously trying to be both like and different from the staff associations. But the structure of federalism obviated against both pattern or standardised bargaining and the building up of the direction and resources to facilitate centrally-led and enforced expansive organising within existing companies (let alone new ones). If it were not for ASTMS and its policy, there would have been no other 'white knight' waiting in the wings. When a number of NUIW members joined ASTMS, a synergy was affected in as much these added agent members to the clerical members derived from the former UIS (Waddington 1995:188). But in the long-term, the ASTMS federal structural also reproduced these debilitating weaknesses, and ultimately the model of ASTMS was not a viable one either.

# Chapter 4

# Weathering Storms: Stimuli, Opportunities and Challenges, 1990–1999

## Introduction

The central focus of this chapter is the argument that a trajectory towards oppositionalism amongst the labour unionism of the financial services sector can be identified, and this was, in turn, part of, and a response to, the move towards adversarialism in the wider employment relations of the sector between 1990 and 1999 (cf. IRS 2004:21). Adversarialism can be conceived of as a paradigm where tendencies, defined as intentions, processes and outcomes, towards conflict and antagonism in the relationships between employers and unions, and within employers and unions, predominate over those towards pragmatic or ideological co-operation and partnership. Oppositionalism on the part of labour unionism entails tendencies towards more ambitious demands and intransigence in obtaining these along with constituent mobilisation, through the fora of collective bargaining, and un-commonality of interests with employers. These tendencies may emerge from different parts of a union such as EUOs, activists or members (or an amalgam of the three) in conscious and deliberate ways or in a relatively unplanned building up of a 'head of steam', and be predicated on relative increases in organisational power bases, centred on union density, membership participation, and collective cohesiveness. Increasing organisational bargaining power would thus be deployed under adversarialism in a manner that is more 'unionate' (Blackburn 1967). Adversarialism, in regard of both parties, is thus a relationship and phenomenon of perspective, attitude and practice, where management's right to manage is both increasingly asserted but also questioned and challenged. The salient turning points are a building up of strike activity to an apex in 1997 but with no strikes subsequently recorded for 1999.

In this chapter, the use of the term 'staff associations' is replaced by that of 'staff unions' in most cases to acknowledge the significant moves taken by most of these bodies towards greater unionateness in this period. This recognises more than just their own change in nomenclature but also their association with other labour unionisms, engagement in inter-union bargaining activities and the decline in their cooperative internalism. Whether all staff unions are entitled to go as far to call themselves independent unions like the UFS (from 1988) or ANGU (from 2001) will be explored. The subject of employer-union partnerships will be largely dealt with in the following chapter. For now, it is worth observing that amongst the employers with staff unions, there was partnership before 'partnership' by dint of the prevalence of 'internalism' which far predated the developments of the mid-1990s onwards.[1] Following from this, there was no need for formal partnerships as were practiced later on. But for another reason, formal partnership has not been entertained by staff unions. Thus, partnership was gaining ground precisely at the juncture when the staff unions were trying to establish some distance and independence from their employers. They would have only been in a position to establish partnership once this formative task had been completed. Thus, only six of the partnership agreements listed in Table 5.5 (Chapter 5) are with staff unions. By contrast, the independent labour unions lacked influence, not independence, and were keener to consider partnership deals.

The structure of chapter is to firstly examine the salient environmental factors (employer behaviour, employment contraction) before moving to consider the evidence of moves towards oppositionalism (industrial action, organisational representations of unionateness, membership attitudes). Following from this, an explanation for these moves towards adversarialism is presented. The final part of the chapter assesses the organisational presence of labour unionism and reduction in the scope of bargaining.

**Employer Strategy Behaviour**

The decade of the 1990s saw increasingly clear evidence that employers throughout the sector were only prepared to countenance union presence and involvement over certain issues within their operations so long as they deemed it constructive and not obstructive. This took the form of less negotiation and more consultation (see, for example, Wilkinson (1995)) over a smaller array of issues and both paved the way for the move towards partnership. Marginalisation through cooption, rather than outright exclusion through union derecognition and removal of, and reductions in, facilities was the primary *modus operandi*. Wilkinson and Holden's (2001) case study of the Cooperative Bank is an exemplar here for the bargaining agenda was narrowed, consultation predominated over negotiation, and agreements were re-interpreted. Of course, this did not mean some union derecognition did not happen (see below), or that facilities were not reduced as at the Cooperative, or that employers willingly conceded union recognition in new or extant non-recognised operations (so that 'double breasting' did occur). It did not also mean that many

---

1    Just one small, more contemporary but pre-partnership wave example of this is the IUHS which declared in its members' magazine, *Accord* (issues 29, 1997 and 14, 1996 respectively): 'We recognise that it is in our interests to support the business but it is not in our interests to do so on the backs of our members … [and we have] never take[n] strike action and if this did happen it would be a failure of both the union and employer'. Here, the IUHS was articulating a position of critical but unconditional *de facto* partnership. It is not incongruous that the employer did then institute a partnership agreement in 2007 for the Halifax merged with Bank of Scotland to form HBoS, bringing with it Unifi/Amicus.

employers were not hardnosed in doing this. Barclays, HSBC, NAG and RBS behaved this way while, by contrast, NatWest was relatively constructive. Indeed, the NAG developed a strategy to move from 'strong employee/union links' of the past to 'strong employee/employer links' of the future where the union's role was to be changed from an 'advocate' to an 'employee insurance [scheme]' (in LRD 1997:8, see also *Herald* 27 June 1994). And from the mid-1990s onwards, HSBC remained the hard nut in banking. Alongside this institutional framework, the ending of MEB led the banks to an increasing concentration on company-level HRM (Wilkinson 1995:103–104, 106). Under this, unions were cut out from substantive influence by the consequent devolution of managerial responsibility because of the weakness of labour unionism at the workplace level – with the main focus before having been the company and industry levels – and the introduction of employee involvement methods. This was also true of the insurance sector (see, for example, Poynter (2000) and Upchurch and Danford (2001)).

So while not necessarily instituted with the foremost purpose of union marginalisation in mind, various new management techniques such as suggestion schemes and employee share ownership plans were introduced at employing organisations like AXA, LloydsTSB, Halifax and NatWest from the 1990s. These techniques created new, non-union means of communication which solidified direct employee-manager links. The 1998 *Workplace Employee Relations Survey* recorded high levels of employee involvement techniques in the sector compared to others (Cully et al. 1999:68, 70). For employers, their primary purpose has been to

---

**INSET 4.1 Human Resource Management**

HRM practice has been seen to be antagonistic towards labour unionism because it often seeks to decollectivise and individualise the relationships between workers as well as the relationship between workers and employers/managers. Whilst this is true, it should not be lost sight of that HRM also deploys collective mechanisms to mediate and structure the relationships between superordinates and subordinates where workers are either atomised from each other (rather than individualised from each other for individualisation necessarily implies difference) or put together in managerially defined and created groups like team briefings, teamworking and quality circles. This suggests that the defining feature of HRM is not individualism *per se* but the use of many and various means by which employers can act unilaterally and in a unitarist manner (under which they achieve worker subscription to their worldview). In other words, it is to remove the recourse that workers have to accessing or creating independent collective resources by which to try to defend and advance their interests. And part of this orientation has also been to bypass and marginalise extant labour unions and labour union-influenced institutions by establishing new forms of communication and consultation (but not negotiation).

sensitise workers in a fragmented and atomised manner to the interplay of company objectives and the marketplace. The techniques chimed with the devolution of managerial responsibility as increasingly lower level sub-units of workforces were targeted for the HRM treatment. And here, probably the most important of all these has been the rise of teamworking throughout the sector (see Stuart and Martinez Lucio 2008, Upchurch and Danford 2001). Under teamworking, a new focus of (managerially determined) sub-workplace level collectivism has been established. The impact of some of these policies and actions will be returned to at the end of this chapter. Finally, it is again worth recalling the influence of the wider context in which the employers operated in. The late 1980s-early 1990s saw a tightening labour market under the 'Lawson boom' (of the then Conservative Chancellor of the Exchequer). One indication of this was that in London, the Midland established a workplace crèche-cum-nursery with 130 places. Equally indicative of the subsequent slackening of the labour market from the early to mid-1990s was that Midland shelved its nursery/crèche after 1992.

**Employment Contraction and Job Losses**

The estimates and reports of job losses in the sector are many and varied but they all have one thing in common, namely, their extensive nature. For example, Unifi estimated in 2001 that between c.150,000 and c.200,000 jobs overall had been shed in the sector in the previous decade. Earlier, it suggested the figure for banking was c.100,000 between 1990 and 2000 (Unifi press release 20 May 2000) while Ed Sweeney, BIFU general secretary, reported the figure was c.130,000 between 1989 and 1997 and BIFU estimated that 110,000 jobs were lost between 1991 and 1995 (with 70,000 between 1990 and 1993) and 130,000 jobs were lost between 1990 and 1998. According to the British Bankers' Association, clearing bank employment rose from 307,000 in 1986 to 348,800 in 1990 before falling back to 272,000 in 1997, whilst IRS (1995c) reported that employment in the main high street banks rose from 273,700 in 1983 to 355,700 in 1989 before falling to 300,100 in 1993. Meantime, MSF (1999) estimated that 15,000 jobs were lost in insurance between 1996 and 1999 as a result of mergers, with employment there having peaked in 1991 with a workforce of 249,000 staff, whereupon between 1991 and 1995, 37,500 job were shed (Poynter 2001:120). In terms of the shrinkage in the sector's 'high street' presence, branch numbers fell from c.17,000 in 1995 to c.12,000 in 1999, with 4,000 less existing in 2001 than in 1991. Between 1990 and 1993, 1,000 branches were closed, 2,800 between 1989 and 1995, and 3,000 between 1990 and 1998. Using other data, a significant branch closure programme of c.40% of offices between 1990 and 2006 took place (computed from Campaign for Community Banking Services figures [www.communitybanking.org.uk]). Within banks alone, the numbers of branches fell from 10,436 in 1986 to 8,005 in

1994 (Storey et al. 1999:130).[2] The emphasis on job losses and branch closures is explicable by virtue of labour costs accounting for two-thirds of total operating costs and branches are expensive units of operation (Storey et al. 1999:131) within the framework of the drive to accumulate.

The implications of these job losses and contraction were not necessarily as straightforward as might seem. Compared to the outsourcing and offshoring of a decade later (see next chapter), the closure of branch offices and the transferral of much administration previously undertaken there to regional processing centres concentrated strategic power into a small number of operating units (Storey 1995, Storey et al. 1997, 1999), potentially serving as a boon to an assertive labour unionism which was willing to act strategically.[3] Secondly, while BIFU membership declined from 1990, its membership at the beginning of the wave of redundancies in the early 1990s in the banks (where most of BIFU membership was concentrated) was unaffected in as much as it continued to grow until 1992/1993 and in these banks union density overall continued to rise until 1995 (see later, and Gall (1999:126)). Therefore, there is a certain degree of irony in that whilst BIFU had appropriate policy for combating redundancies and job losses through advocating job security agreements involving reduced working weeks, it did not appear to have to hand, or be prepared to develop, the means by which to enforce them in this sub-sector. The one, partial exception was in 1997 when BIFU obtained the extension of the TSB job security agreement to LloydsTSB. Instead, it condemned the job losses, sought to expose their rationale of ratcheting up profits, pointed out they were bad for staff morale and customers, and where negotiations took place, focused upon the numbers to be cut, increasing severance terms and no compulsory redundancies. Underlying these tactics was the perspective held by BIFU/Unifi (see, for example, leaflet February 1995, press release 20 May 1999) and other staff unions like IUHS/Accord (see, for example, its newsletters 9 (1996), 17 (1997) and 29 (2000)) that redundancies could not be stopped because of competitive pressures with profits being essential for employment provision in a market system. What remained, they believed, was that the numbers could be moderated and the process mediated. For BIFU, this saw a change in the use of tactics, whereby more emphasis was placed on political and public lobbying. Of note, however, was that concession bargaining did not develop, reflecting the lack of power of the unions to give ground on pay and conditions given their increasingly unilateral determination.

---

2   It should be noted that the number of branches rose to a peak in 1968 and declined steadily thereafter (Morris 1986a:17, Storey 1995:28, Storey et al. 1999:130).

3   However, the ability to do this depends not just on willingness to act but capability to act *vis-à-vis* union density and workplace unionism. Whether by design or default with regard to union mobilisation, the employment of workers from without the sector who had no occupational or sectoral affinity and in contingent manners through temporary and part-time contracts (along with Taylorist means of work organisation) meant this was a considerable challenge.

**Moving Towards Oppositionalism**

The argument presented here is that a trajectory towards oppositionalism – limited, uneven and fragile – but a trajectory nonetheless can be identified for labour unionism in the sector between 1990 and 1999. The evidence to support this will be reviewed through considering the areas of a) industrial action activity, b) organisational representations of unionateness, c) membership attitudes, and d) political developments.

*Industrial action activity*

The 1990s saw a considerable increase in the deployment of collective industrial action by bank workers. The year, 1997, represented a high point for a quarter of a century. In this sense, the *Financial Times* (9 May 1995) was shown for a time be incorrect when it stated '[s]trikes in banking [today] remain rare'. The growing unionateness recorded in the previous chapter would have been brought into doubt or thrown into reverse if this increased use of collective industrial action and other parallel manifestations had not occurred for the 1990s saw a much tougher employer-led climate of first compulsory redundancies in the 1990s (e.g., 1992 – Bank of England, 1993 – Barclays, NatWest, and Cooperative, 1999 – NatWest and Woolwich), imposed pay offers (see below), pay rises becoming contingent upon performance and the first pay freezes (e.g., Barclays managers 1993, NatWest 1995). All these breached longstanding traditions and expectations of secure jobs, incremental progression and rising real wages. Indeed, and based on their study (Cressey and Scott 1992), Cressey and Scott suggested resistance would continue and increase in response to changes centred around job security (*Personnel Today* 29 September 1992, 25 September 1994). But what was also marked is that there was little sense in which the threat of job losses lessened the prospects of industrial action as was often found elsewhere at the time. Certainly, the language and rhetoric of BIFU and then the staff unions reflected the anticipated trajectory of Cressey and Scott, in the process becoming more like other labour unions. Press releases and reports abounded with unions considering industrial action over some issues and issuing threats to ballot for action on others (like anticipated compulsory job losses at NatWest in 1999). This section provides a detailed account of the salient developments before moving to an assessment of them. The decade began with a predominant diet of rejections of industrial action, majorities being deemed too small for action to proceed on and slight concessions being argued by negotiators to be capable of defusing the head of steam built up.[4] That said industrial action

---

4   Of course, there were also instances where industrial action mandates were not implemented due to sufficient concessions being gained like the cases of TSB data processing workers in 1992, and RBS IT workers voting in 1993 by 72% for strike action on a 54% turnout – the bank responded by threatening an application for an injunction but BIFU ignored this and won dispute without striking.

ballots continued to be cemented into the repertoire of labour unionism compared to their absence prior to the mid- to late 1980s.

In 1990, NatWest BIFU members voted for industrial action short of a strike (52:48 on a 38% turnout) to increase their pay off but their union leadership deemed the majority too slim to proceed with, especially as the NWSA was not taking similar action. In 1991, BIFU NatWest members again voted for similar industrial action on their pay offer but no action was forthcoming whilst BIFU Cooperative Bank members voted 56%:44% against striking, Lloyds LTU members voted similarly by 53%:47% as did Midland BIFU members by 56%:43% on their pay offers. In 1992, Midland BIFU members voted 51%:49% against industrial action on pay and BIFU TSB members voted 77%:23% for their first ever national strike on pay, compulsory redundancies but minor concessions resulted in no action being taken. Also in 1992, NWSA voted for industrial action on their pay offer but the majority was deemed to small to proceed with while likewise Barclays BIFU members voted for their first ever national strike on a below inflation pay offer and PRP but the majority was deemed to be too small (53:47 on a 40% turnout) to proceed with where BGSU members were not balloted on action. BIFU members rejected striking at Lloyds in 1993 and again NWSA voted for industrial action on their pay offer but the majority was deemed to small to proceed with while BIFU Midland members voted narrowly not to take their first ever national strike action on pay. Finally, in 1993, BIFU computer members at the Midland voted against strike action on the issue of redundancies. In 1994, BIFU TSB voted 50% for striking on a 42% turnout on pay but the mandate was not used as further talks were offered. But after no progress was made, a two-hour strike was organised but then called off and the pay award accepted. Also in 1994, BIFU members at the Midland voted for strike action on pay but the turnout meant that a majority was not in favour of striking while a similar situation prevailed with BGSU members at Barclays over redundancies. BIFU members at the Bank of England rejected strike action over job cuts.

However, some of the signs of the coming unrest were seen to be emerging even at this point. BIFU members at Lloyds voted to strike by 63%:37% in 1991 against new pay structures which it was believed would end collective bargaining and see the introduction of PRP. This led to a one-day action, which while being 'the best supported action in a major clearing bank for twenty years' (BIFU in LRD 1992) was also ineffective as a result of LTU members, who outnumbered BIFU members by 3:2, crossing the picketlines. In turn, this led to particular acrimony between BIFU and LTU, where the latter's accused BIFU of being too hasty in rejecting the initial offer, balloting and voting for a one-day strike action. In 1991, Barclays BIFU data processing members in Nantwich, Northampton and Manchester took industrial action – a mixture of work-to-rule, overtime, strikes, picketing and flying pickets – for seven weeks against employer attempts to end national bargaining, and introduce PRP (Gall 1993:68). Meanwhile in 1992, TSB BIFU members in IT/computing in Manchester and Milton Keynes walked out for 1½ days in their first ever strike (Gall 1993:68–89), NatWest BIFU members in Manchester held a three-month overtime ban over job cuts, and BIFU RBS members ran a nine-week long overtime ban and work-to-contract on their pay offer (which included PRP). The bank responded by suspending 41 members in Glasgow for refusing to work contractual overtime. These suspensions were lifted after BIFU threatened legal action. However, the industrial action was called off after made it made no discernible impact on the bank's willingness to negotiate. In 1993, TSB BIFU members took their first ever national strike action (two one-day strikes) over compulsory redundancies after a 75%:25% vote. TSB claimed that 380 of its 1400 branches were shut while BIFU claimed 700 along with the cheque clearing centre. TSB admitted the strike's effectiveness surprised it (*Financial Times* 9 January 1993). BIFU computer members at Lloyds engaged in an overtime ban and work-to-rule for eight weeks on pay while Barclays BIFU clerical workers voted for their first ever national strike and BIFU NatWest members in Manchester engaged in overtime ban against compulsory redundancies. Meantime, in 1994, BIFU TSB members took action short off a strike over bonus pay after voting against strike action.

Putting together the different elements of balloting, ballot results and industrial action, a multi-faceted pattern of 'two steps forward, one step back' can be identified for the period 1990 to 1994. This then changed to become something akin to just 'two steps forward' from the mid- to late 1990s. In 1995, Clydesdale BIFU members struck for a day against the introduction of PRP and their sister members in the Yorkshire voted narrowly against for similar action on the same issue. The Clydesdale action was the first strike at the bank in sixty-six years. Meanwhile, joint-union action took place in LloydsTSB on Christmas Eve to maintain this as a half-day after a 65% vote for on a 37% turnout. NatWest union members voted similarly for a strike on same issue while agreements were reached with other banks so no disputes there came to a head. The situation at Barclays from 1995 onwards is recounted below in a separate section. The year, 1996, saw, in effect, a Scottish-wide bank strike by BIFU members at the RBS, BoS, Clydesdale and TSBScotland on 2 January to maintain this as a public (bank) holiday after a 69% vote for on a 52% turnout. NatWest Life joint-union members voted by 90%:10% in a preliminary ballot calling for a ballot on industrial action after the introduction of PRP while BIFU RBS London ended their action on London Weighting Allowance after a ballot with a low turn out effectively both rejected escalation and continuation. In 1996, an overtime ban by BIFU Yorkshire ended when members rejected escalation; members rejected their pay offer by 72%:28% on a 68% turnout with 60% supporting an overtime ban but only 47% supporting striking. The overtime ban run but the bank imposed the offer leading BIFU to ballot again for strike action, with only 38% in favour on a 49% turnout. Meantime, Clydesdale, also part of the NAG, imposed its offer. Finally in 1996, Midland BIFU members voted against strike action (64%:36%) on jobs losses and BIFU and NWSA agreed a pay deal in full with NatWest for time in twenty years after a pay freeze in 1995. Returning to the Yorkshire bank, it imposed its 1997 offer after 67% of BIFU members rejected it but on only a

33% turnout (and a ballot on PRP saw a 60%:40% vote on a 30% turnout result in no action). However, the imposition of the 1998 offer did lead to a one-day strike and a further one was called off after a marginally increased offer. The winter of 1997–1998 saw Clydesdale BIFU members strike against their pay offer as did Midland BIFU members to maintain their Christmas holiday arrangements after a 56%:44% on a 36% turnout. In Scotland, in both 1997 and 1998 BIFU members in the Clydesdale, RSB and TSB struck on 2 January in protest against this being a normal working day. BIFU BoS members did so on 2 January 1997 only. But according to the *Scotsman* (3 January 1998) the strikes' impact was negligible, and the battle was lost to keep this date as a public holiday. Some of this is explicable by the combination of attitudes of BIFU members to take this day as a holiday in any case and to strike to have the holiday. Consequently, picketlines lines even in the major cities like Edinburgh and Glasgow were almost non-existent while the banks remained open. Additionally, the numbers voting to strike were not particularly convincing. For the 1997 strike, RBS BIFU members voted by 50.02% to 49.98% for striking while their counter-parts in TSB voted 61% to 39% but on less than majority turnouts. The close of the decade witnessed the 5:1 rejection of LloydsTSB's 1998 pay offer which led to 2:1 vote to call a strike ballot and strike ballots in LloydsTSB and Barclays computer sections. In 1999, BIFU NatWest members voted against industrial action on pay despite the rejection of this offer in a prior consultative ballot by 90% on a 33% turnout. Throughout the decade, and involving BIFU members, there were also some small strikes in a number of the international/foreign banks like Bank of India (1991) and Sonali (1990, 1997), instances of industrial action short of a strike (e.g., Lloyds data processing, 1993, NatWest Manchester, 1992–1993, TSB insurance, 1994) and threats of industrial action short of a strike (e.g., Unisys Payment Services, 1997).

By contrast there were very few ballots for industrial action in insurance, with none at all in the building societies. Of the few ballots, action was rejected at the Guardian Royal Exchange in 1994 (see later). In 1990, MSF members at the Prudential engaged in a work-to-rule over changes to collective bargaining, whereupon some members were victimised and workers responded with a number of one-day strikes in response. In 1991, NUIW members at the Prudential instituted a 12-week work-to-rule against restructuring which ended following management threats of suspensions and sackings. The only strike on pay (by MSF members) took place at Pearl Assurance in 1993.

It is now appropriate to make an assessment of the industrial action. It recorded only a marginal impact on employers' business judged by closure of offices and the outcomes of the negotiations.[5] Some pay offers were slightly improved, the numbers of compulsory redundancies reduced and severance terms increased to

---

5   The strikes may have recorded a disproportionately greater and positive impact if they had lasted for longer or been more frequent. That said, one-day strikes became the hallmark of striking for nearly all workers in the 1990s, indicating its demonstratively tokenistic nature.

**INSET 4.2 Barclays – An Account of Growing Discontent**

Barclays experienced two major industrial disputes in the 1990s, with the first (1995) involving an estimated 20,000 striking union members and the second (1997) 28,000 striking union members (*Financial Times* 21 October 1997). Prior to the first one in 1995, it is worth noting that Barclays BIFU members voted for their first national strike in 1992 over the first below inflation level pay increase, in 1994 BGSU and BIFU members voted for striking against compulsory job losses but for BGSU members the majority did not exceed the constitutionally required 66% threshold, and in 1994 BIFU members in Birmingham struck for 2½ hours over gradings.

In 1995, workers were offered their fourth consecutive below inflation rise – of 2.75% when UNiFI had demanded 5%. A UNiFI ballot for strike action resulted in a 58% vote for on a 27% turnout. Although this amounted to only a 16% mandate (or 5,040 members), UNiFI decided to move forward given the support of the around 8,000 BIFU and many non-members not to cross its picketlines or carry out strike-bound work, and the belief on its part that the time to 'stand up and be counted' had come. Consequently, on 30 May 1995, UNiFI took its first ever intra-bank strike. Barclays claimed only 6,000 workers (10% of staff) took part with only 227 of the 2000 branches closed. UNiFI claimed some 400 were closed. Union strongholds were Liverpool, Wales, and south London. Barclays initially refused more talks then conceded them after threat of further action. These broke down and no new ones were arranged. The pay offer was imposed. A planned second strike was called off after BIFU decided not to join in and Barclays made a threat to sack staff and withdraw preferential loans if they continued to strike. Members showed less willing to sacrifice another day's pay (see *Times* 29 June 1995). Ultimately, UNiFI could not command sufficient membership support to carry on with active opposition but it ventured that '[s]taff were always feeling their way. It was always going to be a bit of an experiment' (*Times* 29 June 1995). Yet in the space of two years from disorderly retreat, UNiFI was able to regain lost ground and gained further new ground.

The issues of pay freezes through the use of PRP and reductions in pension entitlement for c.25,000 workers came to a head in 1997 (with 1996 seeing a 55% mandate for strike action not acted upon). Following breakdown in talks and two failures to agree, a number of joint UNiFI/BIFU actions were taken. A consultative ballot on the employer's proposals recorded 86% opposition on a 29% turnout, non-industrial action protests were staged and a ballot on industrial action short of strike, which recorded a 2:1 vote, led to a work-to-rule and overtime ban. What is noteworthy for what happened next was that at this initial stage, UNiFI members voted against striking by 53%:47% (compared to the 67%:33% vote for industrial action of a strike) while BIFU members voted for narrowly for both (53%:47%). However, these actions created no obvious leverage, and indeed, the overtime ban fizzled out after three weeks, so a strike ballot of 37,000 workers was issued. UNiFI recorded a 51%:49% for (36% turnout) of its 30,000 members while BIFU recorded a 55%:45% for (34% turnout) of its 7,000 members. In the first one-day strike UNiFI/

BIFU claimed 300 of the 1,985 branches were closed with 28,000 on strike – Barclays claimed 209 branches were shut with just 5,000 strikers. In the second strike, UNiFI/BIFU clamed the same numbers with Barclays reporting 176 branches were shut with 4,000 strikers. On the third strike, the employer claimed just 98 branches were shut with the unions refuting this. The strikes had their greatest impacts in London, Wales, and north-west England with more picketing and support recorded in many northern industrial towns. For example, the *Guardian* (9 November 1997) reported a 75% strike participation rate amongst the Liverpool call centre workforce, which the bank characterised as 'militant' and threatened to relocate the operations. Here, the management video recorded those on the picketlines (*Socialist Worker* 15 November 1997).

The 1997 strike was a watershed in a number of respects. The level of employer hostility was marked and reached levels associated with manufacturing and engineering industries. Thus, there were punitive retaliatory actions and threats, job losses predicted (*Financial Times* 7, 8 July 1997), some victimisation of activists, letters issued threatening suspension, and phonecalls to staff saying their jobs were at risk. Barclays also tried to buyoff IT staff with a much larger pay increase and opined that the voice of the silent majority (non-voting union members) was not being represented. The Barclays workers' action then became the first ever joint-union national strike which consisted of more than an actual (rather than intended or planned) one-day strike with three one day strikes being staged (*cf.* Gall 1997:223). The joint-union leadership again showed some boldness and mettle by acting in a qualified vanguardist manner because it detected a groundswell of opinion that would support its position. In the words of the UNiFI general secretary: 'Many staff have been holding back, thinking the bank would surely come to its senses and make some reasonable changes. Now it has become apparent that Barclays has no intention of treating staff fairly [and] the mood has changed dramatically' (*Financial Times* 7 July 1997).

This position was supported and exceeded by a minority within BIFU who called for a whole week's strike and by BIFU EUOs for the first time ever receiving phonecalls from members telling them not to call off the strike (*Socialist Worker* 3 January 1998) but these implorations were rejected as 'too damaging to the bank's business' (*Financial Times* 18 November 1997). Indeed, the fourth strike was called off as a result of the union leaderships' response to the bank re-opening negotiations. Similarly, it is worth noting that the unions 'want[ed] a short, sharp campaign that causes least disruption to customers but gets the message over to Barclay's management' (BIFU official quoted in *Financial Times* 25 July 1997). These responses were illuminating for the long-term impact of the strike, namely, the creation of a partnership agreement. In this regard, Unifi national secretary, Jim Lowe, stated: 'After the [dispute that led to the strike] was sorted out there was a consensus on both sides that things couldn't go on that way anymore and that maybe we should all start acting in a more rational manner' (Unifi *Fusion* magazine, February 2001). The result of the strike was not favourable. The performance and market related pay system was still introduced but in an extended phased in manner and with some improvements, and the principle of pay being fully determined by performance and market was established (BIFU *Report* February 1998, *Financial Times* 7 February 1998, IDS (1998c:25), UNiFI March 1998 No. 26 newsletter *Finance Industry Briefing*). With that, Barclays became the last major bank to have introduced PRP. Externally, the strike registered with many across the political spectrum. Tabloid newspapers like the *Daily Mail* were replete with opinions that 'normally mild mannered bank staff are ditching their genteel image in the face of management who have become aggressive and intransigent' while *Socialist Worker* (25 October 1997) ventured that 'the strike is also an indication of how groups of workers who previously have no tradition of industrial action have to turn to 'old style trade unionism' to get their voice heard'.

some extent but little success was recording in stopping the introduction of PRP, changes in holidays, the imposition of pay offers or huge swathes of voluntary redundancies (Gall 1997:224–225, 1999:130). Contrary to the expectations of Cressey and Scott, resistance to job losses was not common. In some instances, for example over the closure of final salary pensions schemes for new entrants and their replacement money purchase schemes, no action was taken. Despite having a greater extent of job security agreements than other sectors (Marginson 1999), stopping voluntary redundancies was particularly difficult for these agreements were about consultation not negotiation, and members acted here as individuals so collective leverage was not created. Nonetheless, psychologically the impact upon senior management was marked, precipitating what would be considered to be indications of traditional industrial relations employer responses as well as partnership agreements and favourable ramifications for collective consciousness and confidence (see below, Gall (1997:225, 231, 1999:130) and Lynch (1998:54)). Mass meetings of several hundreds became common for a while. For now, we can note that Snape (1994:56) reported that some membership increases had occurred after industrial action and the continuing salience of Hyman's (1976:129) observation that if grievances are sufficiently strong and strike action appears the only remedy, then conventional scruples about the legitimacy of striking cannot persist indefinitely. But at no point could BIFU's action be said to be 'militant' as Deery and Walsh (1999:263), Kelly (1996:92) and Wilkinson and Holden (2001:5) did. The activity of the 1990s was a clear departure for the staff unions, for earlier Morris (1986a:120) had stated that by the mid-1980s they still 'consistently deplored the use of sanctions or the rhetoric of a conflict of interests'. In summary, and compared to the mid- to late 1980s, greater number were involved, taking action and covering more than just BIFU members.

This detailed account has been necessary to give a contexualised feel to the bald data in Table 4.1. This government data clearly underestimated the number of workers and days not worked if the reporting of the strikes in the quality press is used, whereby it recorded 12,000 strikers and 12,000 days not worked for the three strikes of 1998 while in 1997 it recorded between 20,000 and 28,000 workers struck three times at Barclays quite apart from the seven other strikes of that year. And, of course, the data does not record industrial action short of a strike. It, nonetheless, shows that the period of the late 1980s to late 1990s, there was a growing, if uneven, move towards relatively greater collective combativity.

**Table 4.1     Strike Activity in the Finance Sector, 1982–2007**

| Year | No. of Strikes | Workers Involved | Days not Worked |
|------|----------------|------------------|-----------------|
| 2007 | 0 | 0 | 0 |
| 2006 | 0 | 0 | 0 |
| 2005 | 2 | 2,300 | 3,000 |
| 2004 | 1 | Negligible | Negligible |
| 2003 | 0 | 0 | 0 |
| 2002 | 0 | 0 | 0 |
| 2001 | 1 | 100 | 200 |
| 2000 | 0 | 0 | 0 |
| 1999 | 0 | 0 | 0 |
| 1998 | 3 | 2,900 | 2,500 |
| 1997 | 8 | 21,800 | 22,700 |
| 1996 | 2 | 20,000 | 10,000 |
| 1995 | 3 | 9,600 | 9,000 |
| 1994 | 3 | 4,000 | 7,000 |
| 1993 | 2 | 6,600 | 7,000 |
| 1992 | 1 | 800 | 1,000 |
| 1991 | 5 | 4,600 | 8,000 |
| 1990 | 2 | 1,000 | 1,000 |
| 1989 | 5 | 1,800 | 2,000 |
| 1988 | 2 | 600 | 1,000 |
| 1987 | 7 | 1,000 | 1,000 |
| 1986 | 6 | 1,200 | 5,000 |
| 1985 | 9 | 4,000 | 7,000 |
| 1984 | 7 | 11,100 | 20,000 |
| 1983 | 10 | 6,500 | 11,000 |
| 1982 | 5 | 5,000 | 4,000 |

*Source: Economic and Labour Market Review/ Labour Market Trends/Employment Gazette* (various) for the categories of financial intermediation, and financial and business services.

So whilst balloting for industrial action became common as was the taking of different forms of industrial action, often for the first time (Gall 1993, 1997), these developments were, nonetheless, underpinned by several limitations. First, industrial action continued to be rejected (even where the employers' offers were heavily rejected). Second, the existence of very high union density amongst the more unionate form of labour unionism did not guarantee industrial action. Third, where strike action was rejected, industrial action short of a strike was usually favoured. Fourth, majorities for action were often too slim to proceed on (as with Barclays data processing in 1996 where action was voted for by 51:49 on a 41% turnout), especially when they moved from being majorities to minorities when the non-voters were taken into account. In many cases, union leaderships successfully argued that these mandates should not be implemented because of management intransigence.  Although there was anger from certain sections of members to this, in only two cases (both concerning computer workers) did they proceed with the planned action against the wishes of their leaderships.[6] Fifth, the pattern of voting for action has been neither 'consistent' nor 'constant'. Thus, members in different employing organisations have voted inconsistently from one year to the next despite strongly held and widespread grievances. Sixth, BIFU members were still to the fore over staff union members. Seventh, the strikes were still mainly cautious and protestant in nature, and contrast with more robust action by fellow workers in other European countries (see concluding chapter). Eighth, the highpoint of 1997 may be argued to represent not much more than a return to previous levels of 1983–1984 (although the former should take on a qualified greater significance given that overall strike activity continued to decline (Gall 1997:223) but where MEB imposed a certain form of industrial restraint (see Chapter 3)). Ninth, the end of the decade saw the trajectory towards collective combativity thrown into quick and sharp reverse.

The unnerving of both employers and union leaders by the industrial conflict concomitant with the emergence of 'partnership' had an important part to play in explaining this reversal. The precursor of formal partnership was becoming clear in 1996, when NatWest faced and averted striking, with Dai Davies of NWSA stating: 'We are a ... union and our job is to fight job losses at all costs [but] by taking part in this consultative process we can ensure the best possible deal for those members who sadly have to lose their jobs' while Alan Ainsworth, BIFU assistant secretary, commented: 'This is a complete departure from previous arbitrary job culls. We welcome NatWest's attempt to minimise the impact on staff by involving staff and unions from the outset' (*Times* 1 May 1996). But so too was the influence of general political developments. The rising anti-Tory mood fed into, and was part of, the relative leftwards move by general populace, with this

---

6   Clearly then, there is no real sense in which the 'rank-and-file' can be talked about as a conscious and self-organised body of any significant size which has shown the capability and willingness to set the pace and resist the union leaderships where appropriate. For example, in Birmingham in the mid-1990s, the activist base amongst the 3,000 BIFU members was just forty (Gall 1997:232) and for much of the 1990s the Glasgow branch found it difficult to achieve a quorum at its meetings because, according to one activist: 'Members don't come to meetings because they see no point going because they are not getting a voice'. Neither can banks workers be said to become habituated in their strike activity. Therefore, caution must be taken not to over-exaggerate by categorising bank workers to be 'strike-prone'.

---

**INSET 4.3 Transmutation of the Halifax Building Society Staff Association**

Established in 1977, recognised by the employer in 1978 and gaining a certificate of independence in 1979, the HBSSA became the Independent Union of Halifax Staff in 1994 and Accord in 2002 to reflect the diversity of members it now encompassed (which included that of the Leeds Permanent Building Society Staff Association which joined it 1996). In 1996, the IUHS (*Accord* newsletter, February 1996) reported 'our successful approach is based on communication and negotiation not confrontation', with part of its objective being 'to foster mutual cooperation between members of the union and society' (IRS 1995a:8). This stood in some tension with a membership survey which indicated that members thought HBSSA was too closely identified with employer (*Accord* newsletter March 2000). This occasioned the change to the IUHS. Membership of 7,013 in 1979, rose to 11,064 (1985), 15,552 (1995) and 27,477 by 2006. After the Halifax took over Birmingham Midshires in 1999, the former staff association transferred to IUHS. So, along with the acquisition of the Leeds Permanent and Clerical Medical staff associations, far from all of Accord's membership was organic. In terms of internal democracy, activists in Unifi/Amicus/Unite were taken aback after the creation of HBoS whence they began working alongside Accord because of its domination by its leadership, its extremely close relationship with the employer and its lack of use of accountable, democratic method. On top of the absence of industrial action from its repertoire, indications of formal unionateness did not belie evidence of deeper, actual unionateness.

---

likely being true of bank workers and their industrial action. Come the election of 'new' Labour in 1997, the notion of self-activity amongst workers seemed to have less purchase as many looked to the new government, however mistakenly, to act on their behalf in pursuit of their interests.

*Organisational representations of unionateness*

The three most obvious forms of organisational representations of unionateness are mergers, changes in the nomenclature and affiliation to the TUC. The creation of Unifi, with c.180,000 members from BIFU, NWSA and UNiFI, on 18 May 1999 was argued by its proponents to create a viable 'industrial' union for the financial services sector, with the anticipation that it would become a pole of attraction for other finance sector staff unions[7] by virtue of its ability to cohere three quite different unions together in the first instance, its devolved, federalised structure and its ability to gain economies of size and scale. The basic argument deployed

---

7    BIFU (*BIFU Report* October 1998, May 1996) variously promoted the creation of Unifi as 'a start on the road towards our final aim – one specialist union for the finance industry', 'a single finance trade union covering all of the British economy' and 'a much wider finance union [that is] attractive to other staff bodies'.

in favour of merger was that collectively members would be more powerful *vis-à-vis* their employers and would be in a position to more easily recruit new members (see, for example, *Personnel Management* 18 June 2000). At the point of merger, BIFU had 135 staff, a headquarters and 7 regional offices and seconded representatives in 16 institutions, NWSA 25 staff, one office and 15 seconded reps while UNiFI had 104 staff, one office and three seconded reps. However, by 2004, Unifi was compelled by loss of members[8] and income to merge with Amicus, where it made a tie-up with the former MSF members employed in insurance (see next chapter), and competition between staff unionism and labour unionism within a number of major companies continued: for example, the LloydsTSB Group Union declined to be involved in the Unifi merger (see also Morris et al. (2001)). The Unifi merger was agreed by the following votes; BIFU – 95.7% on a 37% turnout, NWSA – 91.2% (43.5% turnout) and UNiFI – 93.3% (39% turnout) (Unifi 1999:6) and represented a significant move to end divided representation (in banking in particular), consequent upon the realisation that becoming a formidable bargaining partner required greater staff-side unity. Yet as early as 2001, Unifi began considering merging with the soon-to-be created Amicus (which was launched in January 2002), and other potential merger partners were the shop workers' union, USDAW, and CWU[9] (Unifi *Fusion* April/May 2001). This was influenced by the significant fall in membership to c.150,000 by 2003. But it was also influenced by Unifi's inability to become the quintessential pole of attraction for labour unionism in the sector as a result of further amalgamations (see next chapter). MSF did not merge in this period despite heavily falling overall membership, although it did court UNiFI (Morris et al. 2001:247). The overall growth of MSF's finance sector membership from c.60,000 in 1975 to c.75,000 by 1996 (Carter 1997:17) hides the rise and then fall of absolute membership within a period of growing sectoral employment. And while the LTU remained outside the fold of the major developments in the sector here, it did sign a bilateral cooperation agreement with MSF in 1997, indicating its preference to avoid dealing with BIFU.

In the rush to create Unifi, the battle-lines were drawn between the modernists/ progressives and internalists/conservatives and as a result of this polarisation of discourse, insufficient thought was given to how the union would meet the challenges facing it in providing effective interest representation. At a commonly superficial level, it was assumed that 'bigger' would be 'better', 'united' would better than 'divided' and so on. And while these were correct in the abstract, the premise applied to the actual context was unproven at the time. For instance, the notion that economies of scale would be achieved was open to doubt. Willman et al. (1993: 33, 183) showed it was not evidently clear that mergers with small unions bring economic benefit to the 'acquirer'. Indeed, they may lead to cross-subsidising by

---

8   It is, therefore, clear that Dolvik and Waddington (2002:366) were wrong to conclude that 'the formation of UNIFI [Unifi] … consolidated [union] organisation in banking'.

9   At this time, Unifi engaged in bi-lateral agreement with the CWU in regard of maintaining union membership when staff transferred between call centres.

the taking on of staff and organisation in an act of accommodation of the acquirer to the acquired. More importantly, the notion that greater numbers in one union make all those members and their union stronger *vis-à-vis* employers and government did not take account of the need for those members to be collectivised within a common identity[10] and then be mobilised in appropriate ways into a coherent and effective collective force (see also Gall (1997:234), (1999:133)). And the prospects for these mobilisations depended upon circumstances and consciousness, whereby it could not be assumed that the willingness to merge equated to the willingness to mobilise. Indeed, the vast majority of members in balloting for Unifi did not vote. Moreover, the federalised structure of the BIFU was reinforced and extended into Unifi so that the actuality of a single nation union was also open to some doubt (see Morris et al. (2001:249)). Heuristically setting aside that different groups of members were organised around different bargaining units which had different dynamics, the sense of all members being in the same union was considerably lessened by the degree of autonomy for company committees and thus also the former staff unions (UNiFI and NWSA) who operated as company committees.

The facilitating factors for merger were several over and above BIFU's fast continuing membership decline since 1990 and running a financial deficit since 1995 – representing a defensive merger as characterised by Undy et al. (1981) and a failure of NUBE/BIFU's diversification strategy. Both UNiFI and NWSA experienced declining membership over the decade before merger and their memberships were predicted to decline further (Morris et al. 2001:244, 246) although this did not have the same stark implications as it did for BIFU for both were not wholly dependent upon subscription income. For example, UNiFI gained c.50% of its income from the sale of financial services (Allen 1999:xi). To all three unions in Barclays and RBS/NatWest, the ability to work together more effectively and efficiently through merger seemed to be logical for under the pressure of hostile events, NWSA and BIFU had started working together in 1996 and BIFU and UNiFI together from 1995. This marked a change from the earlier period of the 1990s when BIFU's *Report* members' magazine regularly highlighted evidence of antagonism with BGSU (but not so much with the NWSA). Underpinning this realisation on the part of UNiFI and NWSA was that single institution-based unions were no longer viable in membership, bargaining and financial terms in the changed product and labour market environment of the 1990s. Moreover, both staff unions wanted to assert their independence from their employers and move towards the mainstream of labour unionism to do this (see also Morris et al. (2001)). Indeed, a NWSA membership survey came out in favour of merging as early as 1995/6 (but not with BIFU). But had BIFU not relinquished its historic mission to 'bury' these staff unions, these overtures would have fallen on deaf ears. BIFU's position against the three banking staff unions had weakened

---

10   One ramification of frequent union merging is that membership identity and affinity with the union is undermined by the change and the more generalised nature of the new union, particularly where little time exists in which to establish new identities.

in the 1980s and 1990s so it could act neither independently nor effectively. Rather then, BIFU saw the proposed merger not as a take-over but a three-way merger of equal partners (Morris et al. 2001:247). Thus, Ed Sweeney, BIFU general secretary, candidly expressed the view that:

> We [BIFU] have to merge – we can no longer be different. We have failed in our historical mission set in the sixties to organise all of the industry. Yes, we have taken in a number of small organisations along the way but we haven't resolved the major issue of divided staff representation. We don't seek to acquire or take-over but merge with other equal partners. We didn't oppose the affiliation of UNiFI to the TUC and have resolved our historic differences with MSF in 1996. There are some 29 staff organisations in finance; that's far too many and there will have to be mergers. If we don't, we won't survive. (British Universities Industrial Relations Association Conference 1997)

In personnel terms, the election of 'modernist' general secretaries in all three unions represented  a new set of internal but more outward looking politics and formed a key facilitator (see Morris et al. (2001:245), *cf.* Morris (1986a:130, 135)). Overall, the process by which the merger came about showed how far attitudes and environments had changed since the mid-1980s so the traditional stumbling blocks identified by Morris (1986a:136–7) with regard to the organisational representations of power, ideology and politics had been overcome by the movement of UNiFI and NWSA towards BIFU's position and *vice-versa*.[11] The point is worth dwelling upon. The merger represented the decline of internalism and the embracing of measures of greater unionateness, that is, not only the move away from mutual interests with one's own individual employer (and to some extent employers in general) but a shift to see the commonality of interests between finance workers in different companies. Without being overly-mechanical, the employers' actions compelled UNiFI and NWSA to move 'leftwards' in the environment of competition with BIFU. However the merger also represented BIFU moving onto the terrain of the staff unions and accommodation with them through the use of company committee autonomy when previously NUBE/BIFU would only countenance a centralised new union. It is also worth noting here that the employers did not seem fazed by Unifi's creation as a stronger, more unionate body for staff. For example, NatWest was reported not to be worried about NWSA becoming part of a 'more militant' union (*People Management* 18 June 2000). Indeed, NatWest and Barclays looked upon Unifi favourably because of streamlined bargaining arrangements and the cementing of an inward-company focus with the autonomy of the company committees.

---

11    Indeed, Morris's (1986a:139) pessimism about the prospects for merging became historically redundant. But internal records showed that pensioner vote was crucial to securing the merger outcome.

---

**INSET 4.4 A Financially Unviable Form of Labour Unionism?**

With 135 staff for a membership of c.113,000 in 1998, BIFU lived well beyond its means given that in 1982 it employed just over 100 staff with a membership of c.150,00. Of the staff in 1982, 37 were EUOs while in 1990 these numbered 45, and 50 by 1991. Unifi was not much better. Staff and officer ratios to members (but particularly the former) were significantly higher than for many industrial or general unions. This high ratio resulted from a) the absence of workplace unionism as it is conventionally understood so that EUOs filled the consequent 'gap', in tandem with b) low membership subscription rates and per capita income compared to other unions (Jenkins and Sherman 1979:67, Willman 1989:267, 268), largely consequent upon competition with subsidised staff unions and the counter-position of BIFU and its predecessors as a centralised, independent form of labour unionism, and c) the maintenance of the internal autonomy of company based-units of union organisation. The trajectory was added to by transfer of engagements leading to the staff of the transferring unions being kept on by NUBE/BIFU because of the compromise of transfer (see Melling 2004:86, Willman 2005:54). This involved the trade-off of staff associations joining an independent union but in doing so maintaining their autonomy and identity as distinct components.

---

There were also sixteen other mergers and transfers of engagement between 1990 and 1999.[12] In addition to those listed in Table 4.2, the following staff associations transferred Unifi/BIFU or MSF: AXA Sun Life, Britannia and CGNU while both the Town and Country and Gateway Building staff association transferred to WISA. However, this still left the financial services sector with 22 other staff associations/ unions in addition to Unifi and the soon to be Amicus (finance section). The rate of transfer/merger was comparable to that of the 1970s and 1980s but was likely to then decline whereby the remaining available partners were more resilient to merging, either through perspective and/or resources.

---

12  The Union of Royal and Sun Alliance staff joined NWSA in 1999 with an 88% vote for (33.7% turnout). The NUIW joined MSF following on a 97% vote for in 1999. The two unions had worked closely together in Confederation of Insurance Trade Unions, the AfF, and FSU (see below). Earlier in 1998, the United Friendly Field Managers' Association voted by 94% to join MSF.

**Table 4.2     Mergers and Transfers of Engagement, 1990–1999**

| | |
|---|---|
| 1999 | NUIW, Britannic Supervisory Union and United Friendly Agents Association to MSF, Union of Royal and Sun Alliance Staff Association (3,665 members) to NWSA |
| 1998 | Clerical Medical Staff Association (1,471 members) to IUHS |
| 1997 | National and Provincial Building Society Staff Association (2,500 members) to BIFU |
| 1994 | Newcastle Building Society Staff Association to BIFU |
| 1996 | Leeds Permanent Building Society (3,820 members) to IUHS |
| 1990 | Nationwide Group Staff Union formed following the amalgamation of the Anglia Building Society Staff Association and the Nationwide Building Society Staff Association, North East Building Society Staff Association to BIFU |

*Note*: The new owner of the National and Provincial, Abbey National, refused to recognise BIFU as it already recognised ANSA.

The moves towards merger and affiliation were in recognition of, and an attempt to redress, two main problems. The first was that of union dependence upon the employer and lack of independence from the employer. Using the example of the IUHS, its general secretary commented: 'Members told us that [IUHS] was too closely with identified the Halifax; that they suspected we were 'in cahoots' with management, that when 'push came to shove' we would always back down and that the Association 'was not a proper union'' (IUHS *Accord* March 2000). The second was that identified by Waddington (1995:186) who reported on 'the inability of a myriad of staff associations to present a united policy position, and the limited provision of bargaining services by staff associations'. But, another dynamic began to take deeper root – that of amalgamations directly arising in response to changing patterns of capital, whereby the staff unions/associations would join together because their employers had joined together. The logic here was plain: more tightly aligned common interests could be represented through unitary bodies which were numerically greater in numbers and could not be subject to 'divide and rule'. Nonetheless, the principle of internalism was still maintained so the degree of unionateness represented therein was limited. For example, following the merger of General Accident and the Commercial Union in 1998 to form Commercial General Union and then its subsequent merger with Norwich in 2000, the staff associations of General Accident and Commercial Union merged to form one for Commercial General Union and then a new one for Commercial General Norwich Union. But this did not immediately mean merging with MSF which had 3,000 members in Norwich Union and 4,000 in CGU (which did happen in 2002).

Also of note in the 1990s were the establishment of a number of pan-union bodies. The Alliance for Finance (AfF) was established in 1996 with 27 affiliates (unions and staff unions/associations from Abbey, Alliance and Leicester, Bank of Baroda, BIFU, Bradford and Bingley, Brittanic Field, Britannia, Clerical Medical, Commercial Union, CWU, Eagle Star, IUHS, Leeds Permanent, MSF, NUIW, NWSA, National Provident, National and Provincial, Nationwide, Scottish Equitable, Standard Life, Sun Life, TGWU, UNiFI, United Friendly, USDAW, Woolwich and Yorkshire), with this quickly rising to 36 affiliates. Its purpose was to be the lobby organisation for labour unionism in the sector by seeking to influence decision-makers in government, the Financial Services Authority (the sector's regulatory body) and the financial services industry in general to try to ensure that the interests of staff were properly taken into account when these organisations and agencies made decisions. These areas included training, mergers and acquisitions, and stakeholding where a collective industry approach was deemed desirable. Although not intended as a facilitator for union merger, AfF helped the Unifi merger (Morris et al. 2001:246). The Financial Services Staff Federation (FSSF) was established in 1994 and comprised 130,000 members from twelve affiliates (ANSA, ALGUS, BIFU, BBSA, BSA, IUHS, LTU, NGU, NPSA, NWSA, WISA and YISA). Its purpose was to act as a lobbying body on government and employers, facilitate the exchange of information between members, provide inter-union coordination on pay and conditions, and allow the exercise of membership collective consumer purchasing power. Also in 1994, the Finance Sector Unions (FSU) was established by MSF, comprising it, NUIW and the staff associations from the Clerical Medical, Eagle Star, Scottish Equitable and Sun Life. They were joined by NGSU and BIFU in 1997, UNiFI in 1998 and the IUHS in 1999. The FSU sought to provide similar roles to the FSSF for labour unionism in the insurance sector. Both the FSSF and FSU took back seats when the AfF was formed and became more informalised. Finally, the Financial Services Direct Staff Forum (FSDSF) was established in 1997 to facilitate the attainment of similar objectives in finance call centres.

Changes in nomenclature also continued to be evident. In addition to those in the Table 4.3, the following changed from being staff associations to staff unions (Alliance and Leicester, Britannia, Clerical-Medical and General, Derbyshire, Nationwide, and West Bromwich) while the Sun Alliance Staff Union became the Union of Royal and Sun Alliance Staff, Woolwich Independent Staff Association become WISA: the Union for Woolwich Staff, the Bradford and Bingley Building Society Staff Association became UBAC – the Union of Bradford and Bingley Staff and Staff in Associated Companies, and the Lloyds Group Staff Union became the Lloyds Group Trade Union (LTU).

In terms of TUC affiliation, IUHS and UNiFI did so in 1996, ALGUS, ANSA and UBAC did so in 1998 and in 1999 the BSU, NGSU, WISA and Unifi also did so. By 2001, and excluding Unifi and MSF, some 60,000 workers from these staff unions were now affiliated to the TUC. For these unions affiliating to the TUC, an ideological impulse to join the wider labour movement was not the primary motivation. Rather, a strong collective voice over employment issues and access to research facilities was.

**Table 4.3      Changes in Name, 1990–1999**

| | |
|---|---|
| 1999 | Abbey National Staff Association became ANSA- the independent union for Abbey National Staff |
| 1996 | Alliance and Leicester Building Society Staff Association (ALSA) became to Alliance and Leicester Group Union of Staff (ALTUS) |
| 1994 | Barclays Group Staff Union became UNiFI, Halifax Building Society Staff Association became Independent Union of Halifax Staff (IUHS) |
| 1990 | Lloyds Bank Group Staff Union to Lloyds Group Union |

*Membership attitudes*

Various observers identified the decline in trust that financial services sector workers traditionally placed in their employers and their employment conditions because of the erosion of the archetypical psychological contract (Gall 1997:230, 231, 1999:121, see also *BIFU Report* February 1998, *Herald* 10 February 1995, *New Statesman* 2 June 1995, *Personnel Today* 25 September 1994, *Times* 17 November 1997). Herein, attitudes towards employers were observed to be changing from those of respect, mutuality and commitment to hostility, derision and opposition (Gall 1999:121–122). These attitudinal shifts have been substantiated by research. For example, in their study of building societies, Snape et al. (1993:51) noted that staffs 'were expressing a demand for stronger collective representation as a protection against uncertainty' and Storey et al. (1999:16) observed that: 'Recent [industrial] relations ... have deteriorated as accumulated grievances have led ... to both threaten[ed] and undertake[n] disruptive action. ... Staff trust in management appears to be at a low ebb, producing the seeds for future conflicts'. For some BIFU union members, there was a growing, if wholly unquantifiable, sense in which collective action was now becoming more of an imperative:

> Attitudes have changed amongst many from 'aren't I lucky to have a job' to 'we have to do something about this'. (BIFU Midland member, 1995)

> I've never really been involved with the union before. I've just paid my subs. But for this I wanted to make a stand. You've got to show just how strong your feelings are. (BIFU Barclays member, 1997)

This, in turn, led to a furtherance of union consciousness amongst some BIFU members:

> For too long we have seen staff in the other banks and insurance companies as our rivals. When Barclays announce job losses, Lloyds staff duck their heads and heave a sigh of relief. It's time we stopped being so self-centred. We must

remember that we are all part of the same industry. A redundancy in the Midland is also an attack on jobs in the Clydesdale ... we must be prepared to act together ... and be prepared to act nationally. (BIFU TSB member, 1994)

People actually see the union as a bit more of a fighting organisation now. They've shown that they can stand up for themselves. This has given them a sense of their own strength and a sense of pride and purpose in their union. (BIFU Midland member, 1993)

Staff could not yet be described as 'militant', if you mean by that having completely oppositional ideas towards their employers and that they predominantly respond to strike ballots with big yes votes. But ... there is real derision at the way they're being treated ... and this is feeding through to them beginning to learn the traditions of what we associate with 'old-fashioned' trade unionism; more widespread 'them and us' attitudes; more confidence and organisation to mount a fight; higher votes for strikes; more taking part and more active strikes with picketlines. (BIFU Clydesdale member, 1998)

The 'good' members are those that seek out activists to find out what's been happening at this meeting and that, and what's the union doing about this or that issue. They're not active but they do want to be kept in the loop. The 'not-so-good' members are those that aren't really bothered what's going on until their employer hits them in the face. (Unifi HBoS member, 2003)

So the basis of the greater industrial combativity amongst bank workers was located in changes in their attitudes about themselves, their fellow workers and employers. Bank workers saw themselves increasingly as 'ordinary' finance sector workers and workers *per se*, having more in common than in difference with other these workers, rather than as a type of privileged elite or 'aristocracy of labour'. In this, the relationship between more unionate attitudes and propensity to take industrial action was a symbiotic one, whereby one fed the other and *vice-versa* as well as both running in train together. Some support for this assessment is provided by Deery and Walsh's (1999) survey of workers in NAG subsidiaries (Clydesdale, Yorkshire, Northern banks) and their co-workers in the mother company's operation in Australia in 1995. It highlighted that these bank workers in Britain were at least as collectively minded as their counterparts in Australia following the implementation of HRM, and that positive associations were found between collectivist work orientations, favourable union effectiveness perceptions and willingness to take industrial action. However, what is of contextual significance in Deery and Walsh's (1999) study is that the period covered witnessed an aggressive employer – not a partnership one (LRD 1997:8), a sharp rise in industrial conflict and the levels of union density in this employing organisation were very high (*cf.* Deery and Walsh 1999:262). The issue of the permanency of this attitudinal change will be addressed in the next chapter. But for the moment, is it worth noting that the suggestion by Deery and Walsh (1999:258, 262–263) that the 'worse' conditions get, the more that collectivism would develop has not been borne out for the workers they studied or for the sector, and this outcome is unlikely simply to be the result of less than conducive union strategy and paucity of opportunities to act.

In common with the tenor of what was argued in the preceding analysis of industrial action, most commentators (*Financial Times* 9 May 1995, *Herald* 17 December 1997) agreed with the assessment of the BIFU general secretary in 1997 which did not characterise the attitudinal changes in terms of militancy. Rather, '[m]embers are more assertive, rather than aggressive, in terms of what they want and what they expect the union *can get them* [emphasis added]'. Within this, staff unions were acknowledged to be less assertive than BIFU (*Financial Times* 9 January 1993, *New Statesman* 2 June 1995). But even these limited developments do not represent a simple 'one way' direction of travel for the picture is more complex and contradictory. Counter-developments existed for there was an uneven impact of processes upon different groups of workers and different workers within a single group. For example, Thornley et al. (1997:99–101) in their study of BIFU members at the highly unionised Cooperative Bank found membership attitudes of pessimism about, and antipathy towards, their union, and officials and activists well aware of the deleterious consequences of members' lack of participation. Centrepois and Jefferys (2004:115–116) found that union activists in Unifi comprised just 2% of the membership (or 3,000 individuals), this being lower than the 5% of members who were workplace reps (for workplace reps were not necessarily active). Moreover, they found that compared to their French CFDT counterparts, Unifi activists had lower levels of union consciousness and that these were predicated on instrumentalism rather than ideology (Centrepois and Jefferys 2003:8–9, 2004:118–120, Jeffreys and Centrepois 1999:7–8). Consequently, working with management was far more commonly advocated by Unifi activists than their French counterparts. In this regard, BIFU's pre-'partnership' stances were representative of a significant milieu of membership thought; it signed, along with the AEU, GMB, NCU, UCW and USDAW unions, the Industrial Partnership Association's 1993 document 'Towards Industrial Partnership: a new approach to relationships at work' (Undy et al. 1996:250) and on 23 November 1993, general secretary, Leif Mills, told the House of Commons Select Employment Committee Inquiry that BIFU was seeking partnership of interest with employers.

Centrepois and Jeffrey's findings are also broadly compatible with other research carried out by Hartley (1996) in her study of workers, rather than activists, in the cheque processing centres of a major retail bank in the mid-1990s. Thus, a preponderance of individual orientation toward BIFU as a form of purchased employment insurance was found, with little evidence of group identity or cohesion as union members and low levels of participation. Hartley's (1996) findings were consistent with Waddington and Whitson's (1997) findings across the union movement of instrumental rather than ideological reasons predominating in why workers join unions, where this instrumentalism was of primarily a passive and individual rather than an active and collective nature. Harrington (2001, 2005) also found a largely instrumental attitude towards joining BIFU amongst women. However, this took two forms – an individualist stance and a collective orientation, with the former being an atomised purchase and the latter being operationalised often in an active manner. Nonetheless, a collectivist political ideology was still marked by its relative absence. One caveat is in order here – Wills (1996) found a marked geographical dimension to the relative balance of instrumentalism and ideological conviction along a north-south axis in England as well as greater activism in the north than south.

---

**INSET 4.5 Barclays – A Long and Winding Path from Dependent to Independent Labour Unionism**

The evolution of the BBSA, established in 1919 as a defensive response by the bank to BIFU's forerunner, from a staff association to a *bona fide* union highlighted the slow and contradictory process of developing unionateness. Initially, membership was automatic-cum-compulsory, and it was not until 1940 that it became voluntary and by subscription. Formal institutional bargaining rights were not gained until 1968 and Martin's Bank Staff Association merged with BBSA in 1969 because of the merger of the two banks. In 1979, BBSA changed its name to the BGSU reflecting the first moves to reduce its dependence upon the employer. The BGSU executive was directly elected by members but it then appointed its EUOs. In 1969, the BBSA had 15,000 members compared to NUBE's 25,000 but by 1977, this position has reversed with the BGSU having 35,000 members and NUBE just 17,000 (Maksymiw et al. 1990:79–80). Even before the 1980s, the banks' bargaining stance was hardening as it refused from 1977 onwards to accede to an ACAS referral where there was a failure to agree as per the recognition agreement. In a series of industrial actions taken by BIFU members in Barclays, BGSU refused to support BIFU or become involved in the disputes even though the issues also affected its members. Institutionally, this competition was supported by existence of the CBU and the MEB machinery.

However, these attitudes of conservatism, mutuality and isolation began to change from the mid-1980s when relations with Barclays began to deteriorate. Thus, it imposed a pay deal for the first time (in 1987), instituted the first redundancies (in 1990), the first compulsory redundancies (in 1993), and ended final salary scheme for new entrants (in 1996). So BGSU proposed a merger with the NWSA which the latter rejected, and together with BIFU members, BGSU members voted for industrial action in 1985, on pay, and engaged in industrial action, in the form of an overtime ban for sixteen weeks against the imposed offer in 1987. In 1988, BGSU commissioned a study to consider affiliation to the TUC as a result of Barclays' hardening attitude. Affiliation was rejected, reflecting the continuing hegemony of the 'traditionalists' or inward looking 'old guard'. However in 1993, with new personnel at the head of the BGSU and the TUC and a more 'radical' BGSU executive along with continuing pressure on pay, conditions and industrial relations in the bank, a report on the future of the union was commissioned. As its conclusions were not universally welcomed by members, i.e., the 'traditionalists' rejected them, a membership opinion survey called 'Towards 2000' was commissioned which showed that a significant minority were in favour of progressive change. This process culminated in 1995 when the BGSU became UNiFI – Union in Finance - with the aim of embodying strong and independent unionism which sought to enlarge the scope of collective bargaining and representation to achieve the 'advancement of mutually productive relations' (in IRS 1996:14) with the company. In line with this, it reduced its dependence on seconded reps (Morris et al. 2001:245). UNiFi also sought to work more closely with the staff unions at NatWest and Lloyds, with the long-term goal of facilitating the unification of unions/associations in the sector. UNiFI's general secretary commented:

> The new name signals an awareness by UNiFI of the seismic change now shaking the finance industry and the need for a new brand of trade unionism to match the scale of that change. The new union pledges itself to continue to working for the elimination of the damaging divisions and influences which have weakened the employee interest over the years. (*New Statesman* 25 March 1995)

> The emergence of UNiFI represents a dramatic change of direction for UK finance industry unions. A new era has dawned: one in which banking and finance sector businesses, employers and their unions will work more closely than ever before to overcome the obstacles of an uncertain age. ... [UNiFI seeks to] build collective bargaining and representational arrangements for the advancement of mutually productive relations (IRS 1995b:3, see also Morris et al. (2001:248))

These quotes indicated that UNiFI saw that associating with other finance sectors unions and working in partnership were not incompatible (but in two *New Statesman* adverts (25 March, 2 June 1995) it choose not to put any emphasis on partnership). Indeed, given that BIFU, MSF and other staff unions also believed in this marriage of approaches, there was nothing particularly unusual about UNiFI's stance. Similarly, UNiFI, like other finance unions, had policy extolling high ethical standards in banking relations with customers/clients/consumers, and cooperation with consumer groups (IRS 1995b). With the support of BIFU, UNiFI affiliated to the TUC. Without BIFU's support, affiliation was unlikely to succeed. For this to happen, BIFU had had to move away from its mindset of enmity towards BGSU/UNiFI over competition and difference in the areas of recruitment, pay offers and strikes. Internally, UNiFI had its own factionalisation with the pro-affiliation faction centred around officials who had worked previously for TUC affiliate unions. At this point in time, UNiFI did not envisage merging with BIFU and, indeed, rejected this overture in 1995, although it did seek to develop closer relations with other finance sector unions and made calls for uniting all through merger to form a single industry union (IRS 1995b, Morris et al. 2001:246, *New Statesman* 3 May 1996). But by 1997, merger with BIFU became increasingly likely, either as a bilateral move or as part of a move towards multi-lateral merging. The more conservative faction favoured merger with MSF as their enmity towards BIFU ran deep. In the background was another factor, namely, that of financial viability. In 1989, the BGSU had a very low per capita income from subscriptions even though it was far from totally dependent on subscription income and it also ran a sizeable deficit (Willman et al. 1993:21, 25).

## Changing political complexions

Given that it is difficult to establish definite causal links between striking and political consciousness, not least because such developments may occur without, and separate from, striking, salient political developments towards unionateness are considered in this section. One might expect a broadly positive relationship between strike activity and voting for a party like the Labour Party with its links to the union movement and its heritage of social democracy. Although, no longitudinal data exists, Jefferys and Contrepois (2001:13, 17) found that 51% of BIFU activists interviewed at its 1998 conference saw their union activity as an extension of their (general) politics and 67% of these interview voted Labour in 1997. Meanwhile, the proportion of workplace reps who voted Labour in 1997 was lower at 36% and on a par with percentage of members who also voted Labour then (34%) (Centrepois and Jefferys 2003:5). Therefore, for the activists at least, there may have been some positive relationship. Alongside this, is it also worth noting that in 1997 BIFU established a political fund, joining MSF and the NUIW as the only labour unions in the sector then having one but leaving MSF as the only union in the sector affiliated to Labour. In terms of 'gender' politics, Harrington (2001, 2005), and Colgan and Creegan (2006) and Parker (2005) showed that both BIFU and Unifi had made limited progress towards attaining their formal diversity agendas despite much senior union formal support.[13] The context of this was that well over 50% of the banking workforce for the last thirty years had been women, with the lower rungs of organisational hierarchies of these employing organisations being heavily and disproportionately feminized. These phenomena found their parallels within the labour unionism of the sector – indeed, Harrington

---

13    To the extent that BIFU developed an 'equalities agenda' from the early 1990s, this was as much driven by recruitment imperatives as the ideology of gender politics, and was limited in comparison to a number of other unions (Harrington 2003). In 1991, it appointed an equalities officer for the first time and in 1990 elected its first woman vice-president and in 1991 its first women president. Yet activists still reported that negotiating EUOs were resistant to acting on union policy here.

(2005:125) argued that the situation Egan (1982) found with regard to BIFU had not much changed by the mid-1990s. So, the positive ramifications of industrial action and organisational representations of unionateness for wider social and political views of union members were not strong. This is not surprising given there is no mechanical link between them, and the many mediating factors that exist in between.

Examining political developments more widely, *inter alia*, BIFU officially supported the TUC and Unison national demonstration against low pay in Newcastle on 10 April 1999, supported the union movement's anti-racism work, the ambulance workers in their dispute in 1990 and the miners' union in 1992 over pit closures, and gave moral, public and some financial support to overseas finance workers (particularly when on strike). However, its support for, and donation to, the ambulance workers came in for criticism from some members as did its campaign against the poll tax – because the poll tax was a non-work issue, was too 'political' and too close to party politics. Others countered that as the poll tax affected its members, BIFU should take a position. By contrast, in the conference debates and journals of staff unions, it was difficult in this period and the next to find instances of debates, and policies formed thereafter, on 'political', 'outside' or 'non-work' issues. Over issues of company mergers with deleterious effects on members, it was noticeable that BIFU was keener to use parliamentary Private Members' Bills, referrals to the competition regulator and political lobbying to try to stop job losses by stopping the mergers themselves. This seemed 'moderate' behaviour unless industrial action was regarded as capable of preventing capital restructuring. Rather, the more appropriate criterion concerned whether BIFU used industrial action to prevent job losses once the mergers went ahead. It did not for reasons explained elsewhere.

The Broad Left worked towards and was successful in stopping employers attending annual conferences, gaining affiliations to solidarity campaigns and putting the agenda of electing EUOs and mandating delegates on conference agenda. With around 15 activists and 30 subs paying members, the Broad Left looked bigger than it was because it operated through sympathisers in sympathetic branches to bring motions to conference. Moreover, its activists commanded broader support as they were of a consistent perspective and consistently active – in a small and shrinking pool of activists – so that they gained positions of authority like the vice-presidency, chairs of company committees and membership of the national executive.[14] Alongside this development from BIFU into Unifi has been a counter-move with the arrival of UNiFI and NWSA activists. A Unifi activist from BIFU reported that 'we had to have the same battles again that we fought over ten or more years ago over issues of having women's committee, why we don't need a men's committee and why men shouldn't sit on the women's committee'.

---

14   There has not been an organisation of the right since the 1960s (see before). However, a minority of EUOs have been of the left and their activities have been tolerated as an interesting but not threatening sideshow.

Although no definite and positive relationship between union democracy and union bargaining effectiveness (*vis-à-vis* creating leverage) has been established, an essential part of union *modus operandi* is usually taken to be membership control secured through participation. Moreover, membership control is normally viewed as having virtues over and above those of bargaining effectiveness. Consequently, to the components of unionateness can legitimately be added that of a union being more unionate to the extent that it is more democratic – defined as rule by the many – in terms of word and deed. Here BIFU/Unifi was found to be severely wanting. Whilst there is a difficult contingent balance to be achieved between EUOs and lay officials leading and following members, the tendency was to both lead without robust mandate and close down options through not seeking to stimulate members. EUOs led and interpreted membership moods without much in the way of members setting the agenda. EUOs were wary of getting their fingers burnt by getting too far ahead of members but this often became a self-fulfilling prophecy whereby members were seldom challenged to act. Only a few EUOs bucked this trend, with most having the view of 'give me an army and [then] I'll go to war' according to one activist. In this sense, activists spoke of EUOs that saw their role as managing the union and managing membership problems. Occasionally, the confidence of EUOs to act more unionately was based on the confidence of members to act more unionately. Just as frequently, the EUOs acted robustly where the union's institutional rights were threatened. In terms of lay officials, few acted as delegates that sought mandates from members; rather most acted as individuals, speaking for themselves with their own agenda or rather passively accepting the lead of EUOs. Company committee (lay) officials were distanced from activists and members because they were neither union organisers nor grievance handlers, and subject to the confidentiality protocols of negotiations. Seconded reps handled formal and informal grievances – where the latter could not be dealt with by office reps – which meant they were neither organisers nor negotiators. An activist described them thus as 'social workers', and where the number of seconded reps was small relative to the size of the workforce, this was all these reps had time for. Only in a few cases, where the opposite was true, did the reps play a small and informal organising and recruitment role. A further aspect was that in Unifi, company committees had the autonomy to make agreements with their employers whereas in BIFU agreements proposed by company committees were subject to being in accordance with union policy via NEC approval. And because of the NEC was structurally more independent of the employers, it could be more assertive than the company committees. By contrast to much of this, in a few instances in MSF where there was workplace unionism, like at Scottish Widows, activists conducted their own bargaining without much recourse to EUOs, albeit within the scope of union policy.

**INSET 4.6 Advance – the UK Santander Group Union**

ANSA was created in 1977, gained its certificate of independence in 1978 and affiliated to the TUC in 1998. Along the way, it changed its name to the ANGU in 2001 and to Advance in 2007 in recognition of Abbey's integration into the Santander Group. Its membership grew from 4,895 (1979) to 6,575 (1985) to 8,210 (1991) before peaking at c.9,000 (1996) and then falling back to 7,216 by 2006. It has four secondees who are, in effect, the equivalent of EUOs and around 60 lay reps (one for every 150 members). It has commonly talked in terms of shared values and mutual objectives with the employer. Annual pay awards are not put out to membership ballots and there has been no failure to agree on issues between 1989 and 2004 (including on offshoring when ANGU believed that Abbey took part in open dialogue). De facto partnership has, therefore, been practiced - but only at the company not intra-company level for line management has been resistant to ANSA and workplace presence extremely underdevelopment (see also Bain et al. (2004)). Amicus was derecognised by Abbey when it took over Scottish Provident in 2002, and MSF derecognised in 1992 when Abbey took over Scottish Mutual. However, ANSA was derecognised by First National Bank after it was sold to General Electric. As with Accord, ANGU displayed only organisational moves toward, thus, limited unionateness.

### Explaining Moves Towards Adversarialism

This section examines the forces providing the trajectory towards adversarialism and oppositionalism, the sharpest manifestations of which were found in banking where labour unionism was able to respond in a relatively robust manner to more obdurate employers because of its greater strength than that found in insurance and building societies. Thus, the return to CLB in 1987 could not turn the clock back to the relative quiescence of c.1968 when MEB was introduced because developments towards unionateness could not be instantly undone. If the institutionalised employment relationship in banking can be characterised as a triangle with BIFU, the staff unions and the employers at its three corners, then despite the inter-union competition, the proximity of the relationship between the staff unions and employers was breaking down and the relative locus of proximity was shifting to between BIFU and the staff unions. This became a necessary but not sufficient condition, with the stimuli of collective grievances being the extra ingredient. The employers' actions, as a result of attempts to increase and or/ maintain levels of profitability under changing market conditions, produced such stimuli although not universally. An additional aspect of note was that CLB did not result in a move towards enterprise unionism such were the demands of employers and the growing unionateness. Thus, finance workers' collective interests were not fragmented by the ending of MEB. Moreover, because of decentralised bargaining in the situation, the conflict between unions and employer in each bank became sharper with the removal of the mediating forum of MEB, particularly with the return of inter-bank wage competition as a route to competitive advantage. Yet, the ending of MEB did not witness the focus of union activity onto the workplace but rather the centralised company level (as might have been expected given the historical tendency of independent labour unionism in the sector). But, unlike before, banking had no safety mechanism in the form of unilateral arbitration so that there was no institutional impediment to industrial action taking place, so again some rise in industrial action was likely to be experienced. Notwithstanding the multi-faceted influence of smaller units of capital in the sector outside of banking, labour unionism was in no position of organisation, let alone strength or unionateness, to contemplate the kind and extent of collective action taken by bank workers (see below).

**The Insurance and Building Society Sub-sectors**

Financial services workers in insurance were also subject to full-blown PRP (Danford et al. 2003:110, Poynter 2000:217, Swabe 1989) and a host of new management techniques, grouped around the concept of employee involvement. For example, General Accident introduced problem solving focus groups at the work group level in the early 1990s. Although still of a largely paternalistic and pluralist mindset but facing new market realities, General Accident choose to respond to the latter by introducing 'empowerment' in order to generate greater employee corporate commitment as a means to give it competitive advantage. In this, the union was consulted. In building societies, employee involvement and performance pay have also been evident (Wilkinson et al. 1998) but the use of individual PRP has been marked by its relative absence as a result of the enduring paternalistic and collectively orientated culture of these organisations. And, unlike in banking, a number of employers like Bristol and West, Standard Life and Zurich Insurance have used works councils as non- and anti-union forms of staff representation. Nonetheless, the general force of employer moves towards the intensification of the wage-effort bargain for their benefit can be detected in the two sub-sectors. Consequently, the issue becomes what explains the dissimilarity of response compared to bank workers. In insurance, union organisation had been in decline since the 1970s as a result of the impact of redundancies and restructuring, whereby the inability to push back management corroded the quality and quantity of union presence. The fate of the NUIW is instructive here (see Table 2.1) and those organisations joining ASTMS in the 1970s were not strengthened or made more unionate in the process. Indeed, there was little evidence of any organic growth where the structure of the labour unionism here militated against strategic organising of employers outside those already organised and little in the way of centralised intervention in each constituency to shore up membership levels. Moreover, Danford et al. (2003), Poynter (2000) and Upchurch and Danford

(2001) identified an atrophy of low densities, few activists, little activity and just a few hopeful sparks, where a self-reinforcing downward trajectory had been set in train. Notwithstanding its own weaknesses, the NUBE/BIFU centralised form of labour unionism provided a greater protection against the impulse towards enterprise-unionism within federalised labour unions like ASTMS and NUIW. In other words, for these reasons labour unionism in insurance did not have the capacity to respond robustly or effectively. In the case of building societies and despite demutualisation and mergers, the impact of staff associations being established relatively late in the day, their relatively small size and the doubly cooperative ethos of these organisations was to make unionate independent labour unionism slow to develop. Where unionateness has developed here, it has been of the organisational type. Again, labour unionism here did not have the capacity to respond robustly or effectively.

## Union Organising, Recruitment and Recognition

The nature of the labour market within which labour unionism in the sector sought to organise presented both challenge to and opportunity by which to reaffirm and advance itself at every turn. For example, the level of part-time workers rose from c.37,000 (12%) in 1986 to 72,300 (26%) in 1998 in retail banking (Morris et al. 2001:242) and by 1995 59% of the banking workforce were women, of which 25% worked part-time (Storey et al. 1999:139). Here, part-time workers have additional specific grievances but maybe less likely to be willing to join, and participate, in labour unionism while women's participation may also be low despite their specific grievances. Issues of casualisation, job insecurity and the like again similarly present challenge and opportunity. Whether the challenges became opportunities was influenced by the extant tradition of labour unionism. The tradition in the sector has been that of 'servicing' rather than 'organising', for 'servicing' has been characterised by relative membership passivity, where membership is regarded as a purchased service or commodity for the purposes of insurance (see also Colgan and Creegan (2006), Harrington (2005) and Wills (2004)). Alongside this has been relatively greater EUO activity in the setting of agendas and pursuit of these agendas. In particular, the labour unionism has comprised an absence of workplace unionism, with negotiation undertaken by seconded reps, individual casework carried out accredited reps and seconded reps, and union recruitment often carried out by travelling reps[15] and not seconded reps (see, for example, Jenkins and Sherman (1979:53), Luton (2001:239), Snape (1994:52), Willman et al. (1993:173), Wills (1996:366)). In other words, labour unionism was relatively centralised, office reps were still charged with the lowly tasks of being disseminators of union material and contact points, and

---

15   BIFU's travelling reps in 1989 recruited 4,776 members, 15% of all new recruits in 1991, with this rising to 21% in 1993 and 28% in 1994 (BIFU documents).

where membership existed and there were few or no activists, this created a self-perpetuating scenario of low density and/or passive members in the workplace (see, for example, Wills (1996:366–367)). Normally, there were between two to four seconded reps per medium to large sized company. Travelling reps were employed centrally to recruit members and were used since 1965 by NUBE/BIFU. However, they played no servicing or organising role. In concentrating on recruiting non-members, members who had no workplace reps and saw no other reps found this irritating (Wills 1996:367). Moreover, recruitment was carried out on a particularly individual basis because it was not part of workplace unionism given that recruitment and organisation were both geographically structured (see before). In terms of whether opportunities were taken advantage of as per above, the strength of the servicing-cum-insurance culture in the sector can be inferred in a number of aspects. From the *Labour Force Survey*, female union membership in the sector was higher than for males (1996: 56% to 41%, 2006: 28% to 21%), as it was for part-time workers than for full-time (1996: 55% to 48%, 2006: 30% to 23%). Yet, the rate of active union participation of women and part-time workers has been much lower than for men and full-time workers.

Come the era of 'union organising' from the mid- to late 1990s onwards, union recruitment predominated over union organising (including retention)[16] given the haemorrhaging of members (even though in the case of Unifi organising and bargaining were not separated as is common in many other unions). Thus, the key objective was to increase membership by 1% pa through the employment of 31 EUOs (IRS 1999b). In terms on infill-recruitment, there was a large terrain to work on for the free riding problem was large: 49% of the workforce in the sector was covered by collective bargaining but only 32% were union members (Kersley et al. 2006:180, 110). The structure of recruitment and organising remained regional whilst branches structures continued as a mix of geographical and institutional. Again this reinforced the centrality and power of the EUOs in the process, so that in common with many other unions, 'union organising' has had a tendency to come to mean continued reliance on EUOs with members being the subordinate 'spokes' in the union 'wheel'. Consequently, Colgan and Creegan (2006) found that to the extent that union organising existed in Unifi, it was dominated by EUOs – either the senior existing staff or the newly employed specialist organisers – in a managerialist manner (*cf.* Luton 2001:240). Lay activists were largely excluded, consciously or unconsciously, from the organising shift (Colgan and Creegan 2006:69) and the experience of involving new members as activists in 'winning the organised workplace' was poor (Colgan and Creegan 2006:78–79). This same broad picture also appears to be true for the 'union organising' activities

---

16   Given the significance of servicing, it was a weakness that little attention was given to retention because leaving was the main means by which members dissatisfied with servicing could express this. Another side to this coin was that because of the existence of servicing and the demands it generated on them, the activists were resistant to reducing the time they spent on this.

of MSF within the sector (see, for example, Danford et al. (2003:118), Tailby et al. (2007) and Upchurch et al. (2006)). Only latterly did Unifi provide for workplace committees although they were not explicitly referred to in its rulebook. Consequently, membership participation remained limited. This appeared to be a 'Catch-22' situation for a paucity of instrumental commitment to labour unionism amongst members provided a small pool of activists and members remained passive, wary of taking on tasks, as they preferred to be serviced (see, for example, Colgan and Creegan (2006:69,70, 75)). One further aspect is salient here, namely, existing EUOs and lay officials found it difficult to do organising work, such were the strictures of the extant servicing workload within existing time resources. Thus, one EUO told an activist, who supported union organising: 'So what bit of my job don't you want me to do?'

In addition to declining membership for BIFU, MSF and then Unifi, a particular challenge for labour unionism was that only 10% of the estimated 300,000–400,000 workers in the sector under the age of thirty were members (Unions21 n.d.), a task which the Unifi young members section called Unifi Active made specific attempts to address. Taken together, Tables 2.1, 4.4 and 4.5 indicate that the phrase 'running to stand still' is apt, if not a little generous, for Table 4.4 shows that IUHS/Accord and NGSU were the only unions of any significant size to record substantial growth (not all of which was organic), with the remainder either experiencing membership decline or insignificant growth in the wider scheme of things despite significant resources being deployed and significant numbers of new members recruited. For example, for IUHS/Accord to achieve 4% overall growth, it needed to recruit 20% more members. Looking at the situation more generally, and thus including banking, insurance building societies and other financial institutions and organisations, Table 4.6 makes it clear that the battle to maintain and augment presence was being lost.

Nonetheless, in historical terms, both the independent and dependent labour unionisms in banking and building societies had secured relatively high combined levels by the mid-1990s – levels which were significantly higher than the national average and growing while the latter shrank (see Table 4.6). As Tailby et al. (2007:213) noted: 'aggregate union density in the financial services [sector] rose in the 1980s'. The exception was insurance which recorded lower density levels compared to the other two sub-sectors and the national average (see above for explanation). Meantime, IRS (1995a:10) reported that in 1992 the staff associations of the largest building societies had densities ranging from 68% to 97% and Farnham and Giles (1995:18) showed that the largest and growing non-TUC affiliated staff unions between 1985 and 1991 were to be found in the financial services sector. Looking within banking, and starting with the big four banks (Barclays, Lloyds, Midland/HSBC, NatWest), the staff unions experienced growing levels of combined absolute and relative membership until the early 1990s when the impact of redundancy took its toll on absolute membership levels (Table 4.7, see also Gall (1997)). But what Tables 4.7 and 4.8 also reveal is that NUBE/BIFU was losing the battle on two fronts. First, its absolute growth rate

**Table 4.4  Labour Unionism Membership, 1992–2006**

| Year/Union (% women members) | Accord | ALGUS | AEGIS | ANGU | AXIS | BFSA | BGSU | BSU | CBBSA | CGUSA | DBSSA | DGSU |
|---|---|---|---|---|---|---|---|---|---|---|---|---|
| 1992 | 15,977 (75%) | 4,492 (n/a) | | | | | | 1,890 (n/a) | | | | |
| 1993 | | | | | | | | | | | | |
| 1994 | | | | | | | 48,500 (n/a) | | | | | |
| 1995 | 19,652 (65%) | 4,200 (n/a) | | | | | 47,606 (60%) | | | | | |
| 1996 | 25,124 (74%) | 4,000 (n/a) | | 9,000 (n/a) | | | 45,797 (60%) | 1,800 (n/a) | | 8,211 (n/a) | | |
| 1997 | 26,217 (73%) | 3,290 (n/a) | | 7,612 (80%) | 2,106 (n/a) | 1,663 (n/a) | 42,729 (60%) | 2,184 (n/a) | 347 (n/a) | 5,217 (n/a) | | 554 (n/a) |
| 1998 | 25,652 (73%) | 3,068 (80%) | | 7,468 (78%) | 2,763 (n/a) | 1,496 (n/a) | 41,924 (n/a) | 2,172 (74%) | 351 (n/a) | 5,243 (n/a) | | 549 (n/a) |
| 1999 | 25,263 (73%) | 2,820 (80%) | | 8,306 (78%) | | 1,512 (18%) | CE | 2,243 (76%) | | | | |
| 2000 | 23,995 (74%) | 2,717 (79%) | | 8,322 (77%) | | | | 2,353 (75%) | | | | |
| 2001 | 24,170 (72%) | 2,683 (79%) | | 8,514 (76%) | CE | | | 2,358 (75%) | | | | |
| 2002 | 23,772 (71%) | 2,838 (76%) | | 8,924 (75%) | | | | 2,352 (77%) | | 5,000 (n/a) | | 464 (n/a) |
| 2003 | 24,941 (70%) | 2,817 (75%) | | 8,874 (75%) | | | | 2,303 (n/a) | 449 (81%) | CE | 232 (80%) | 476 (77%) |
| 2004 | 25,759 (70%) | 2,454 (n/a) | 2,518 (60%) | 8,952 (74%) | | | | 2,337 (74%) | 411 (79%) | | 236 (77%) | 477 (79%) |
| 2005 | 25,936 (70%) | 2,519 (72%) | 2,693 (67%) | 8,063 (74%) | | | | 2,971 (74%) | 422 (82%) | | 250 (77%) | 498 (77%) |
| 2006 | 27,477 (68%) | CE | 2,484 (59%) | 7,216 (76%) | | | | 3,193 (73%) | 407 (84%) | | 286 (80%) | 504 (77%) |
| Company density 2004 or point of CE | | 44% | 59% | 35% | 66% | | | 76% | | | | |

*Sources*: Certification Office annual returns (various), Gall (1997), *New Statesman* annual TUC supplement (various), Maksymiw *et al.* (1990) and TUC Directories (various). Note: CE - ceased existence

# Table 4.4    (continued)

| Year/Union (% women members) | LBSSA | LTSBGU | NGSU | NPSA | NWSA | PGSA | SSA | SUWBS | UBAC | UFS | WISA | YISA |
|---|---|---|---|---|---|---|---|---|---|---|---|---|
| 1992 | | | 9,531 (n/a) | 2,467 (n/a) | | | | | 2,659 (n/a) | | 5,082 (n/a) | |
| 1993 | | | | | | | | | | | | |
| 1994 | | 29,424 (56%) | | | 41,187 (58%) | | | | | | | |
| 1995 | | | | | 37,339 (58%) | | 637 (n/a) | | 2,800 (n/a) | | | |
| 1996 | | | 9,300 (n/a) | 2,500 (n/a) | 35,806 (n/a) | | 748 (n/a) | | | | 5,200 (n/a) | 1,200 (n/a) |
| 1997 | | 28,340 (n/a) | 9,409 (n/a) | CE | 33,898 (n/a) | | | | 2,662 (64%) | 4,225 (n/a) | 5,000 (n/a) | 1,200 (n/a) |
| 1998 | | 30,472 (n/a) | 9,704 (n/a) | | 34,343 (n/a) | | | | 2,648 (65%) | 4,910 (n/a) | 5,832 (n/a) | 1,218 (n/a) |
| 1999 | | 36,039 (n/a) | 10,254 (76%) | | CE | | 1,276 (n/a) | | 2,584 (67%) | | 5,888 (74%) | 1,148 (n/a) |
| 2000 | | c.36,000 (n/a) | 11,018 (76%) | | | | 1,337 (66%) | | 2,803 (63%) | | 5,108 (73%) | 1,163 (n/a) |
| 2001 | | c.45,000 (n/a) | 11,291 (75%) | | | | 1,397 (n/a) | | 2,796 (65%) | | CE | 1,464 (75%) |
| 2002 | | c.45,000 (n/a) | 11,633 (75%) | | | | 1,366 (65%) | | 2,720 (63%) | | | 1,436 (74%) |
| 2003 | | 43,778 (64%) | 11,940 (75%) | | | 704 (63%) | 1,089 (67%) | 484 (60%) | 2,690 (62%) | 3,846 (n/a) | | 1,436 (74%) |
| 2004 | 122 (77%) | 43,848 (64%) | 12,078 (74%) | | | 741 (68%) | 1,337 (65%) | 493 (61%) | 1,813 (64%) | 4,343 (56%) | | 1,442 (72%) |
| 2005 | 126 (82%) | 44,411 (64%) | 12,402 (74%) | | | 1,090 (68%) | 1,310 (64%) | 547 (64%) | 1,568 (66%) | 4,040 (44%) | | 1,397 (71%) |
| 2006 | 119 (81%) | 41,998 (63%) | 12,832 (73%) | | | 1,425 (70%) | 1,434 (64%) | 615 (62%) | 1,593 (66%) | 3,739 (56%) | | 1,249 (69%) |
| Company density 2004 or point of CE | | 53% | 80% | | | | 67% | | | 74% | 85% | |

*Sources*: Certification Office annual returns (various), Gall (1997), *New Statesman* annual TUC supplement (various), Maksymiw *et al.* (1990) and TUC Directories (various), *Note*: CE - ceased existence

**Table 4.5    Levels of Membership Recruitment, Selected Years**

| Year/Union | BIFU/Unifi | MSF/Amicus | Unite | IUHS/Accord |
|---|---|---|---|---|
| 1990 | 21,429 (22,049) | – | – | – |
| 1991 | 19,378 (28,057) | – | – | – |
| 1993 | 9,141 | – | – | – |
| 1994 | 10,240 | – | – | – |
| 1996 | 10,154 | – | – | 4,745 (3,685) |
| 1998 | – | – | – | 4,675 (3,770) |
| 2000 | 12,000 (>12,000) | – | – | – |
| 2001 | 20,000 (25,000) | – | – | – |
| 2002 | 16,000 | 6,500 | – | – |
| 2003 | 16,000 | 10,000 | – | – |
| 2005 | – | 5,500 | 17,000 | – |
| 2006 | – | – | 25,173 | – |

*Sources*: Union documents, and secondary sources. Figures exclude any 'new' members as a result of mergers and amalgamations (with the exception of the Clerical Medical Staff Association joining IUHS in 1998 with its 1,471 members).

*Note*: Figures in brackets indicate members 'lost' per year. Danford et al. (2003:112) noted that MSF nationally achieved a high (but unspecified) level of new recruits.

was lower than the staff unions'. Second, the picture in relative terms showed that other than in the Midland where NUBE/BIFU faced no competition, it was being trounced by the staff unions. It is not hard to see why here BIFU was so keen on merger because while it was larger overall, in the key battles grounds, the staff unions were winning the war of attrition. Outside the big four banks, BIFU fared far better. For example, its density in the TSB moved from 83% in 1991 (comprising 95% in branches and 60% in administration) to 76% (1992) to 80% (1997) while in the Cooperative it was 90% in 1991. In the Clydesdale, density was 70%, and 80% in the Yorkshire in 1997.

The loss of the battle in the big four banks had at least two other dimensions for BIFU. First, bargaining and mobilising capacity were consequently limited unless united policy was promulgated and united action was taken with the staff unions.

**Table 4.6     Union Density in the Financial Services Sector, 1989–2007**

| Year/sector | Financial Intermediation | Banking and Building Societies | Insurance | UK-wide National Average for Whole Economy |
|---|---|---|---|---|
| 1989 | 39 | 49 | 36 | 39 |
| 1990 | 38 | 49 | 35 | 38 |
| 1991 | 37 | 49 | 39 | 37 |
| 1992 | 35 | 50 | 39 | 35 |
| 1993 | 35 | 52 | 39 | 35 |
| 1994 | 36 | 54 | 37 | 33 |
| 1995 | 37 | 51 | 34 | 32 |
| 1996 | 36 | 49 | 28 | 31 |
| 1997 | 33 | n/a | n/a | 30 |
| 1998 | 31 | n/a | n/a | 30 |
| 1999 | 30 | n/a | n/a | 30 |
| 2000 | 29 | n/a | n/a | 30 |
| 2001 | 27 | n/a | n/a | 29 |
| 2002 | 27 | n/a | n/a | 29 |
| 2003 | 26 | n/a | n/a | 29 |
| 2004 | 27 | n/a | n/a | 29 |
| 2005 | 24 | n/a | n/a | 29 |
| 2006 | 24 | n/a | n/a | 28 |
| 2007 | 22 | n/a | n/a | 28 |

*Source*: Labour Market Trends/Employment Gazette (various) using the Labour Force Survey.
*Note*: n/a – not available

**Table 4.7     NUBE/BIFU and Staff Association/Union Memberships, 1970–1995**

| Bank/ Year | Union | 1970 | 1980 | 1985 | 1990 | 1991 | 1995 |
|---|---|---|---|---|---|---|---|
| Barclays | BIFU | 24,977 | 14,506 | 15,346 | 13,358 | n/a | 7,582 |
|  | UNiFI | 18,925 | 37,004 | 47,047 | 49,421 | 50,533 | 47,606 |
| Lloyds | BIFU | 10,308 | 13,905 | 13,340 | 14,053 | n/a | 7,887 |
|  | LTU | 16,023 | 20,677 | 22,199 | 28,788 | 30,424 | 29,756 |
| Midland | BIFU | 10,192 | 18,810 | 22,239 | 27,521 | n/a | 25,619 |
|  | No SA | 10,488 | – | – | – | – | – |
| NatWest | BIFU | 19,567 | 14,943 | 17,391 | 22,128 | n/a | 13,692 |
|  | NWSA | 23,879 | 32,969 | 34,962 | 39,895 | 41,161 | 39,892 |

*Source*: BIFU Research Department, personal communication, 1996

**Table 4.8     NUBE/BIFU and Staff Association/Union Densities, 1970–1995**

| Bank/Year | 1970 | 1980 | 1985 | 1990 | 1995 |
|---|---|---|---|---|---|
| Barclays – overall | 80.0 | 75.2 | 79.0 | 74.1 | 90.2 |
| BIFU | 45.5 | 21.2 | 19.4 | 15.8 | 12.4 |
| UNiFI | 34.5 | 54.0 | 59.6 | 58.3 | 77.8 |
| Lloyds – overall | 80.0 | 80.8 | 75.3 | 73.1 | 87.8 |
| BIFU | 31.3 | 32.5 | 28.3 | 24.0 | 18.4 |
| LTU | 48.7 | 48.3 | 47.0 | 49.1 | 69.4 |
| Midland – overall | 45.4 | 36.0 | 44.3 | 58.4 | 59.0 |
| BIFU | 22.4 | 36.0 | 44.3 | 58.4 | 59.0 |
| No staff association | 23.0 | – | – | – | – |
| NatWest – overall | 74.9 | 72.7 | 71.1 | 72.2 | 87.9 |
| BIFU | 33.7 | 22.7 | 23.6 | 25.8 | 22.5 |
| NWSA | 41.2 | 50.0 | 47.5 | 46.4 | 65.4 |

*Source*: BIFU Research Department, personal communication, 1996.

**Table 4.9     BIFU Membership (in thousands) by Employer, 1990–1996**

| Year | Barclays | Lloyds | Midlands | NatWest | RBS | TSB | Total | Total Membership |
|---|---|---|---|---|---|---|---|---|
| 1996 | 8 | 8 | 28 | 15 | 16 | 19 | 94 | 76% |
| 1995 | 8 | 9 | 29 | 15 | 15 | 19 | 95 | 71% |
| 1994 | 8 | 9 | 28 | 16 | 16 | 18 | 95 | 71% |
| 1993 | 10 | 11 | 25 | 17 | 15 | 18 | 96 | 65% |
| 1992 | 10 | 11 | 24 | 19 | 15 | 18 | 97 | 63% |
| 1991 | 10 | 12 | 24 | 18 | 15 | 18 | 97 | 60% |
| 1990 | 11 | 11 | 22 | 18 | 14 | 19 | 95 | 56% |

*Source*: BIFU *Annual Reports* (1991–1997).

*Note*: The discrepancy in BIFU membership levels in Tables 4.7 and 4.9 is explicable by the former including all categories of membership and the latter only including working members.

Second, as Table 4.9 shows, BIFU had a sizeable and increasing dependence upon membership in a small number of large employers.[17] Yet, in the case of the big four, it was unable over the period to increase its membership there in order to strengthen its overall 'industry' position.

Within BIFU, and as alluded to earlier, certain regions were stronger in membership terms that others (and see Table 4.10). Taking into account the size of the potential memberships by region so that a relative measure is used, the stronger regions were the north west of England, Yorkshire, Wales and Scotland. By contrast, the south east and north east were markedly weaker. Coupled with mobilising traditions and union heritages (Gall 2005c, Wills 1996), the former regions were also stronger in terms of collective mobilisations (see before). In the only study which considered the geography of membership in banks in recent times, Wills (1996) found in 1993 a clear north-south divide whereby BIFU membership was higher in the north of England than the south-east, and BIFU membership was relatively more popular in the north when in competition with the staff unions with the position reversed in the south. Across Britain, Wills (1996:369) reported, the highest BIFU densities for 1989 were to be found in Scotland, north Wales and north-west England and in lowest East Anglia and the south-east of England. While overall density appears to have fallen (*cf.* Blackburn (1967:117) and Wills (1996:369)), the internal pattern of the early 1990s is different in as much from the early 1960s for, *inter alia*, Scotland has moved up while south Wales and the north-west of England have moved down the rankings.

**Table 4.10    BIFU Membership (in thousands) by Union Region, 1990–1996**

| Region | North East | North West | York- shire | Wales | Scot- land | London | Mid- lands | South East | South West |
|--------|------------|------------|-------------|-------|------------|--------|------------|------------|------------|
| 1996 | 4 | 15 | 9 | 6 | 16 | 19 | 13 | 8 | 9 |
| 1995 | 4 | 15 | 9 | 5 | 16 | 20 | 13 | 8 | 10 |
| 1994 | 4 | 14 | 9 | 5 | 15 | 21 | 13 | 8 | 11 |
| 1993 | 4 | 15 | 9 | 4 | 15 | 21 | 13 | 8 | 11 |
| 1992 | 4 | 14 | 8 | 4 | 14 | 22 | 13 | 8 | 11 |
| 1991 | 4 | 14 | 8 | 4 | 15 | 24 | 12 | 8 | 11 |
| 1990 | 3 | 14 | 8 | 4 | 14 | 25 | 12 | 8 | 11 |

*Source*: BIFU *Annual Reports* (1991–1997).

17    In 2001, 81% of Unifi members worked in HSBC, RBS, Barclays and LloydsTSB when previously this was 84% in 1999 (Unifi 2002:6) although other, earlier, figures contradict this.

**Table 4.11     New Recognition Agreements in the Financial Services Sector, 1990–1999**

| |
|---|
| BIFU Malayan Banking Berhad |
| BIFU Northern Rock Financial Planning and Financial Services |
| MSF Chartered Insurance Institute |
| MSF Municipal Mutual Insurance extension of recognition |
| MSF Legal and General Direct |
| BIFU TSB Telephone bank |
| BIFU First Direct |
| BIFU LloydsTSB for new areas and for senior managers BIFU |
| BIFU Manpower agency staff |
| BIFU Lloyds UDT |
| BIFU Membership Services Group |
| BIFU Unisys |
| BIFU Lloyds TSB offshore managers |
| BIFU Hill Samuel Jersey |
| BIFU Canara Bank |
| BIFU Adecco Alfred Marks |
| BIFU Membership General Services |
| BIFU First Direct (extension to Birmingham site) |
| BIFU B2B (Business to Business) |
| MSF Colonial |
| MSF Wesleyan Financial Services |
| MSF Zurich Financial Services |
| MSF London and Edinburgh call centre |
| MSF Scottish Provident (formerly Prolific before taken over) |
| MSF Petplan |
| MSF Pensions Investment Council |
| MSF Axa Insurance |
| BIFU Syndicate Bank |
| BIFU Barclays Stockbrokers |
| BIFU HSBC customer call centre |
| Unifi Barclays Sales Finance |

*Source*: Author's research (see Gall 2004, 2007).

*Note*: Listed in chronological order.

Now turning to the issue of union recognition, in common with most other labour unions, BIFU and MSF were affected by limited amounts of derecognition in the late 1980s to mid-1990s; for instance, North East Building Society[18], Royal Bank Insurance Services, Wesleyan Insurance, Prolific, Zurich Insurance, Barclays Private Bank (see also Gall and McKay (1994, 1999) for the period 1988–1998). In total, some 14 cases were recorded in the 1990s. However, and again in common with most other unions, the tide began to turn in the mid- to late 1990s where cases of gaining or regaining recognition far outstripped those cases of derecognition (which numbered just a few like Midland bank managers, RBS Trust Bank, United Bank, United Bank of Pakistan, Abbey National, Bank Hapaolim – see Gall (2004), (2007)). Table 4.11 represents a reasonably impressive list of 31 new recognition agreements. In this the late 1990s (and into the 2000s), MSF was organising for recognition in Newton Investments, Northern Star, London and Edinburgh, Zurich Financial Services, Virgin Direct, Churchill Insurance, American Express, Virgin One Account, Winterthur Life, Norwich Union Healthcare, Scottish Life and Canada Life. It encountered basic opposition like refusal to enter company premises and so progress was slow and faltering.

**The Decline of Collective Bargaining**

By the end of the 1990s, only a tiny minority of employers in the sector continued to bargain on collective 'across-the-board' rises. For example, in IDS's (2000a:12) review of pay settlements in 2000 in the sector, it reported only 20% of companies still paid across-the-board rises. The proportion that bargained over these was, therefore, smaller than the 20%. IRS (1997, 1999d) and Unite (2007) also confirmed this picture, and the 2004 *Workplace Employment Relations Survey* (Kersley et al. 2006:190) recorded the sector as that with the highest incidence of PRP. This change began in the late 1980s/early 1990s. For example, NatWest introduced PRP in 1988 and Lloyds in 1993. The same was true of PRP's emergence in insurance (Poynter 2000, Upchurch and Danford 2001). Initially, and in the 1980s, BIFU was against PRP *per se*. By the late 1980s, BIFU moderated its position so that it accepted PRP as long as it was not used to entirely determine members' pay rises – in other words, it accepted merit pay on top of across-the-board, cost-of-living rises. But the rise of merit pay became the proverbial 'thin edge of the wedge' as a precursor to full-blown PRP of a predominantly individual kind (as opposed to team, section or company-based performance pay) whereby employers introduced it on the basis that an ever more competitive marketplace required being able to motivate staff to respond in a desired manner to this through differentiation in reward. This move to PRP comprised a critical part of a wider downgrading of collective bargaining.

---

18   In 1990, the building society derecognised BIFU but recognition was regained in 1992.

What was left for BIFU and the staff unions to negotiate over was the size of the pot of money available for PRP, the criteria for its awarding and the grievances over subsequent individual awards (see also Heery (1997a)).[19] Playing these roles signified a multi-faceted problem for labour unionism. It wanted to play such a role for not being able to would mean being shut out from playing some part in the determination of members' conditions, and members wanted union representation on this form of pay determination. But in playing this role, they legitimised something they were not in favour of and legitimised their own marginalisation (*cf.* Heery 1997b). Moreover, PRP helped facilitate fragmentation of memberships as determination was based on sub-workforce groups (down to and including the individual) and outcomes put workers into different competitive bandings whereby workers received either no increase, just a cost-of-living increase or an above cost-of-living increase (albeit this does not lead to individualisation *per se* (see Gall (1999:124)). And furthermore, the territory the labour unionisms entered was to organise against the outcomes of the pay system not the pay system itself. Here, and although employee voice through labour unionism has been valued by affected individuals, contesting the outcomes is largely about individual case work not mass, collective action (save the Barclays 1997 strike), so the experience of the way labour unions operated here was not conducive to (re-)building collectivism. This is because each case is not readily generalisable and does not generate precedent setting for building union power, and, in turn, this can lead to unions being seen as (individual) service providers in the manner of an insurance service (*cf.* Danford et al. 2003:111, Samuel 2005:66–67, Heery 1997b). The context of this assessment is also important – for in the early to late 1990s, which witnessed five strikes against the introduction of PRP, the prospective of forming alliances of different sections of aggrieved workers seemed possible (see Gall (1999:124)). Similar, overall points to the above can be made about the introduction of new sickness/absence systems and assessment schemes like competence and market-based pay. In circumstances of relative weakness, these are aspects of the nature of the reluctant compromises that labour unionism is often forced to make.

## Conclusion

The development of oppositionalism was heavily confined the labour unionism in the banks, and BIFU in particular, although that did not mean that adversarialism was too. Employers engaged in an offensive throughout the sector but labour unionism was unable to respond outside banking in the way it did within banking. Furthermore, it was clear that the results of oppositionalism were far from successful.

---

19   The survey by Unite (2007) of bargaining amongst 16 banking and insurance companies between 2005 and 2007 indicated that the contraction of the scope of collective bargaining has continued. Thus, the criteria by which workers are judged and by ratings they are accorded are increasingly decided unilaterally.

**INSET 4.7 Not All One-way Traffic – Union Retrenchment and Stasis**
In contrast the relative advances made in banking, particularly with industrial action, two examples are a useful counter-balance:

*i) The Joint Credit Card Company*
In 1972, the JCCC with the Access card (subsequently Mastercard and Maestro) was established by NatWest, Lloyds, Midlands and RBS. BIFU secured recognition there, achieving density of 40%-60% between 1972 and 1989 with this falling to 15% in 1996 (Poynter 2000:99–100, 234). The company provided for one seconded rep (until 1993) and agreed to a system of accredited reps, whose number varied form 23 in 1988 to 13 in 1996 (Poynter 2000:100). As a result of the removal of the seconded rep and the refusal of the company to recognise a workplace organiser provided externally by BIFU, the accredited reps played the dual roles of organisers and representatives but they were increasingly supported by BIFU EUOs (Poynter 2000:101). This became ever more necessary as the company, particularly after its sale to an American owner, sought to marginalise the union's presence and activities in the 1990s. Recognition was confined to few small areas where there was little sense of leeway as the HRM agenda kicked in. Union density and activism fell and struggles were defensive ones, around the edges of managerial prerogative.

*ii) Guardian Royal Exchange*
The GRE Staff Union joined BIFU in 1979 after a ballot the previous year. BIFU was granted facility for four seconded reps, and had up to 80 reps in the early 1990s. However, around a third of the latter were regarded as merely 'post boxes' for the distribution of union materials (Poynter 2000:125–126). Membership density was c.60% of 6,000 workers in the early 1990s. This density declined through acquisition, selling off, rationalisation, new forms of employment, and establishing new business units like Guardian Direct. BIFU organisation suffered a severe blow when it unsuccessfully opposed the ending of CLB/move to intra-company level bargaining coupled with a pay freeze. BIFU balloted members on rejecting the proposals and on industrial action. In the first ballot, a majority voted against the proposals but the combination of those who did not vote or supported the proposals outweighed this and the second ballot showed insufficient support for one-days strikes (63:37 on a 67% turnout) (BIFU Report, November 1994). Thus, BIFU became a busted flush. Poynter (2000:139) reported that the members still thought of BIFU as a staff association rather than a union, reflecting their lack of unionateness. This weakness was compounded by labour shedding and work reorganisation leading the number of union activists to fall (Poynter 2000:140–144) as practices of HRM were implemented. The picture was one of a weakened union being overwhelmed by hostile changes despite a recruitment campaign in 1997 adding some 300 members and keeping density at around the 60% mark.

The salience of this was that while steps toward robust unionateness were taken, concomitant the organisational foundations of these were weak whereby, *inter alia*, BIFU's strategy of organic and inorganic growth and consolidation had run its unsuccessful course. The turning point of the creation of Unifi was an admission of weakness, not a sign of strength, and a hoped for basis for, but far from guaranteed, regeneration. It had, for example, not been able to turn the issue of redundancies into the basis of a campaign for job regulation in the light of the increased workload for those that staff that were left in post. Moreover, although labour unionism in banking had changed to reflect the changing material conditions a new model to deal effectively with these challenges had not emerged. Outside banking, changes in nomenclature and organisational association and affiliation were not the basis for robust and deep-seated moves toward unionateness, even if they were genuine expressions of such aspiration. This meant the situation across the sector was marked by heterogeneity not homogeneity.

# Chapter 5

# Blown Asunder: Dissolution, Disorganisation and Dislocation of Collective Organisation, 2000–2007

## Introduction

This chapter is concerned with the three 'D's of labour unionism – dissolution, dislocation and disorganisaton – in the sector. Dissolution concerns the contraction of labour unionism's presence, dislocation employment moving out of the realms of extant labour union organisation, and disorganisation atrophy of the influence of labour unionism. In journalese, these outcomes resulted from the 'shake out' of jobs and the 'shake up' of employment. It is worth stressing that the processes and outcomes of dissolution, dislocation and disorganisaton covered here stand on the basis labour unionism having made some significant, but nonetheless fragile, advances. Nevertheless, Poynter (2000:235) was correct to argue union organisation was 'ill prepared' for the cold winds of change blowing through the sector. The particularly pernicious aspect of the continuing employer offensive against wage labour was the use of partnership. Rather than outright confrontation, incorporation and demobilisation became the order of the day and existed almost as an antithesis to the dominant developments of the last chapter – and this proximate relationship requires explanation. Consequently, this period marks another turning point and in this chapter the study of partnership is undertaken after reviewing the moves towards unionateness, union organising and performance management. A necessary departure for this chapter is consideration of outsourcing and offshoring.

The juxtaposition of this three 'D's with the early period of the new millennium being one marked by record, huge and increasing profits for the main financial players was stark. LloydsTSB (2001–2: £1.6bn, 2002–3: £2.6bn, 2003–2004: £4.35bn), RBS (2001–2: £5.8bn, 2002–3: £6.45bn, 2003–4: £7.15bn), Barclays (Barclays 2003–4: £3.8bn 2004–5: £4.5bn), HSBC (2002–3: 6.9bn, 2003–4: £7.7bn, 2004–5: £9.6bn) and HBOS (2003–4: £3bn, 2004–5 £4.3bn) secured profits in the billions. Although these profits resulted in not insignificant bonuses being paid to many staff under profit-related pay schemes, these levels of profitability did not lead to any slackening up of the pressures for accumulation of profits amongst these units of capital. Indeed, the profits levels were testament to the increasing encroachment of the ideology of shareholder-value and return on investments. Looked at the other way around, one may venture that the three 'D's of labour unionism in the sector facilitated this level of accumulation *and* that its dissolution, dislocation and disorganisaton have been necessary to create this aforementioned level of accumulation. And while Unifi and Amicus propagandised against the company profits and the pay-offs and salaries of the company bosses, by contrasting these with the job losses, workers' pay and the profits generated per employee (see, for example, *BBC News Online* 30 March 2000), these were 'words' not backed up by 'deeds'.

## Employment Levels

The sector in Britain has for many decades been a highly visible and significant component of economic activity and employment within the wider economy. Unifi (2000a:2) estimated the sector's economic activity 'account[ed] for at least 7% of our national income' and this continued to be the case in the mid-2000s (FSSC 2006). Despite much intra-sectoral restructuring and re-composition, the workforce remained at between just under a million and just over a million in the period 1988– 2006 (IDS 1998a:13, 1999:13a, Table 5.1 below). Indeed, the total workforce has stabilised in recent years at just over 1m workers. This represents around 4% of employment in Britain. However, within this two processes were masked, namely, swathes of redundancies and the creation of new jobs. For example, between 2001 and 2006, around 26,600 jobs were shed each year, and meantime, a considerable number of new jobs were created – c.27,500 each year (calculated from Office of National Statistics' figures). Moreover, within the sector, banking recorded limited employment positive growth, insurance and pensions recorded negative growth and fund management registered considerable positive growth. Thus, between 2001 and 2006 and in a time of overall growing employment levels, c.45,000 jobs were destroyed in insurance (with no years of net growth), a net total of c.43,000 jobs were created in banking and a net total of c.63,000 jobs in fund management (FSSC 2006). And this trend was predicted to continue between 2006 and 2010 (FSSC 2006). This had serious implications for labour unionism because the decline in relative employment levels was taking place within the more unionised sub-sectors and much of the growth in employment was, by contrast, taking place in the non-unionised sub-sector. Here, then, there existed a stark case of double dislocation for labour unionism's position was weakened in its core areas and it had a mountain to climb to create a presence, much more an effective one, in the new, growing area of employment which was a far less hospitable terrain for it to operate on. In a separate calculation based entirely upon media reports, job losses in 2004 totalled at least jobs losses 22,590 amongst ten employers but only 1,500 jobs were created amongst three employers. This compared to c.25,000 jobs cuts in first eight months of 2001. Similar calculations based on media reports for the period 2000 to 2004 suggested that in the region of 50,000 jobs were shed while the number of new jobs created was around 10,000. The salience of this exercise is that despite what was happening overall (as per above), the impression that sector workers were likely to have developed from an awareness of these selfsame media reports was that jobs and employment security in the sector were continually under attack, and this, in turn, was likely – all other things being equal – to have had a dampening impact upon their willingness to mount collective resistance to their employers on a range of issues.

**Table 5.1    Aggregate Employment in the Financial Services Sector, 1992–2006**

| Year | Numbers employed |
|------|------------------|
| 1992 | 1.051m |
| 1993 | 1.017m |
| 1994 | 1.024m |
| 1995 | 1.044m |
| 1996 | 1.024m |
| 1997 | 1.039m |
| 1998 | 1.048m |
| 1999 | 1.075m |
| 2000 | 1.070m |
| 2001 | 1.089m |
| 2002 | 1.113m |
| 2003 | 1.104m |
| 2004 | 1.079m |
| 2005 | 1.083m |
| 2006 | 1.092m |

*Source*: Office of National Statistics (*Labour Market Trends / Economic and Labour Market Review*) for Standard Industrial Classifications 65–67.

**Organisational Representations of Unionateness**

The trend towards greater unionateness, evidenced by union mergers, nomenclature changes and TUC affiliations continued into the new millennium, albeit some caveats are in order. First, the rate slowed down. In part, this was to be expected given that the available pool from which this could arise became smaller and those that remained outside of Unifi/Amicus/Unite had a critical mass with which to survive. Second, several elements of unionateness have changed considerably. The notion of affiliating to Labour no longer had the same value as before given the ascendancy of neo-liberalism within it and as several of the more leftwing unions have either ceased or qualified their affiliations. In this situation, and where Labour was in office from 1997, affiliation to the TUC took on a different edge for the TUC provided a potential means of left-leaning opposition to both Labour and government. In practice, the TUC has tried to ride a middle way between the condemnation of, and partnership with, Labour governments because of the internal balance of politics and power within the TUC. Third, the goal of Unifi becoming the 'industry' union for the sector in the form of a viable, effective union as a result of organic (recruitment, organising and retention) and inorganic (amalgamation with former staff associations) did not transpire. Thus, LTU remained big enough in membership terms to continue on its own and was financially viable, while its domination of staff's preference over BIFU/Unifi/Amicus/Unite prevailed. These were buttressed by continuing reasonable relations between it and the employer and the domination of LTU by the internalist, 'old guard' mentality of the 1980s.

## Union merging

The major development here was the amalgamation of Unifi with Amicus in October 2004 and then the subsequent merger of Amicus in 2007 with the T&G general union (former TGWU) to form Unite (after the previous merger between MSF and the AEEU in 2002). The 2004 merger marked the end of the project to have a specific and singular finance 'industry' union, with the enlarged finance sector of Amicus comprising, according to the union, c.200,000 members. Unifi brought some 147,000 members and MSF quoted on different occasions in the run up to the merger that it had between 50,000–70,000 members (of which c.40,000 were working, subscription paying members (IRS 2004:23)).[1] Of this new, total membership, 52% were women. Ironically, Ed Sweeney, then Unifi joint-general secretary, proclaimed the merger as a major step along the road to the realisation of aim of a single union for the sector (*Financial Times* 15 April 2004) and the amalgamation was voted for by a 4:1 majority of the eighty delegates at Unifi's 2003 special conference. In a subsequent membership ballot, there was 91% support for on a 30% turnout. The arguments deployed in favour of amalgamation were that the Amicus finance section would have more resources in order to facilitate to growth, financial services sector workers would benefit by having greater strength by dint of being in a bigger union (particularly where employers were argued to be getting bigger and more powerful too) and that two thirds of union members in the sector would now be in same union, helping end divided representation. Alongside these, pledges of being able to retain aspects of existing autonomy and that the finance section would be an important internal union player because it would be the largest single section within the enlarged union were also made. Dressing up the case in arguments that are compelling in the general and abstract cannot, however, detract from the hard-headed recognition that Unifi was a sinking vessel in a turbulent sea it could not control. Given that merger talks with Amicus began late in 2002,

---

1   Some on the left questioned the sense of merging with Amicus when it had just c.50,000 finance sector members and was not a finance union whilst other sector unions existed with cumulatively more members. However, in the atmosphere generated by the leadership of 'merge or be doomed', these activists felt restricted in raising their concerns.

internal discussion preceded this by at least a year. Furthermore, when Unifi was created it inherited serious debts from is constituent parts. As a result, it began a discussion to identify possible merger partners in 2000. These included MSF as the most obvious one but other possible candidates included the AEEU, with its white-collar section (but problem of its 'manual' image and dominance by the former EEPTU and its form of democracy existed), USDAW, as retail finance increased (but USDAW organised only a few large employers where issues of its independence existed) and the CWU, if e-finance took off given the CWU's telecommunications side (but the union was deemed also to be quite strike-prone as a result of its Royal Mail members). These discussions gave some substance to the observation that Unifi was almost a stillborn organisation. However, publicly, in his first Unifi conference in May 2000, Ed Sweeney gave no sense of need to merge again as Unifi was presented as an independent body, working with its sister union, MSF, and he talked of growth and organising. He did, however, also state his belief that that Unifi would be the first step along the way to 'one industry, one union' albeit this would be a positive, free choice and feature not just MSF. And, under the welter of falling membership and consequent financial difficulties (which were not offset by asset or property sales), Unifi reduced its numbers of staff from 45 in its first three years. It only recorded a surplus in one year (2003 – its last year) of its short existence.

In the run up to amalgamation, MSF/Amicus-MSF and Unifi had begun the habit of working more closely together. Talks took place in 2000 and led, for example, to the signing of a cooperation deal with each other at Royal Sun Alliance in 2001, and MSF and Unifi engaged in single table bargaining at AXA following the Axis Staff Association of AXA Sun Life joining Unifi in 2000. In the light of this, one (underplayed) part of the 'industrial logic' of amalgamation with Amicus was that through the former-MSF, Unifi's brought its 14,000 members in insurance into the larger body of labour unionism there. But again here and with the amalgamation in general, larger numbers of workers associating with each other in a single union is not synonymous with their common and collective active mobilisation in defence and pursuit of their material interests. Indeed, it would be foolish to suggest that merger even necessarily facilitates such mobilisation for the number of members supporting merger was not a majority of all members and the sense in which those of the Amicus finance section (and, indeed, Unifi before it) were pulling or pushing in the same direction is open to doubt. This was particularly the case when a condition of merger was the continuation of a decentralised sectional structure which allowed the committees for each main company to act relatively autonomously. In this sense, the structure of the Amicus finance section replicated the earlier devolved-cum-autonomous structure of ASTMS (see earlier). Alongside, there was a question as to why the former MSF was the suitor given the roughly equal size of the LTU and the other extant staff unions. Asking this question suggests an answer of financial compulsion to find a quick and friendly partner (see below). MSF's merger with the AEEU in 2002 was also predicated on a defensive strategy to attempt to counter declining membership, influence and resources. For finance workers here, there was no particular sectoral logic, other than a promised stronger union resource base would be better for all union members wherever they worked. Of course, finance workers, as a 'distinct' minority, were subject to the general will of the majority of other members who felt compelled to merge as MSF appeared to be imploding.

Nonetheless, with the 2007 merger, the major component of labour unionism of the sector became part of the largest union in Britain and one which is a general industrial union rather than a service sector one. As with the MSF-AEEU merger, there was no sectoral logic for financial services sector workers (albeit the T&G had a tiny handful of finance workers) and the rationale for such a merger was a generic one. Moreover, and despite the creation of HBoS in 2001 with 72,000 staff in 2007, Accord and Unifi/Amicus/Unite still remain divided[2] as did LTU and BIFU/Unifi/Amicus/Unite despite the creation of LloydsTSB with c.67,000 staff in 1995 and c.72,000 in 2004. Indeed, LTU competition with BIFU/Unifi increased after Lloyds took over TSB. The reason for this continued separation was that both staff unions remained financially viable organisations with their current membership levels (and employer support) and on this basis were able to continue to resource their particular 'brand' of labour unionism. For these larger company-based unions as for the smaller staff unions, the issue of identity and union-membership connection are still salient when the alternative was becoming part of a union conglomerate.

In the same year, ALGUS (2,519 members) transferred to CWU, becoming the CWU-ALGUS national branch. This was occasioned by changes in ownership, and the Portman Group Staff Association transferred to the Nationwide Group Staff Union in 2008 following the takeover of the Portman Group by the Nationwide. In previous years, Cheltenham and Gloucester Staff Association transferred to Unifi following take over by LloydsTSB (3,800 members, becoming a company committee) in 2004, the Staffordshire Building Society Staff Association transferred to Portman Group Staff Association in 2003, while WISA (5,183 members) transferred to Unifi after Barclays took over the Woolwich, CGNU Staff Association (c.5,000 members) transferred to Amicus-MSF, and Girobank Senior Managers Association transferred to ALGUS in 2002. Finally, in 2001 AXIS AXA/Sun Life Staff Association transferred to Unifi (c.3,000 members) and in 2000 Hambro Staff Association transferred to Nationwide Group Staff Union and the Lloyds Register Staff Association to MSF. Of note was that ever more amalgamations were occasioned by the changing structure of capital, suggesting a slightly less robust version of unionateness than before. Nonetheless, it is worth taking stock here to observe that the number of staff unions/staff associations and independent labour unions declined from 40 in 1981 to 32 by 1997 to 16 by 2004. This number stayed the same by 2007.

---

2    The two began working closely together from 2001 but this took the form of Accord acting by following the lead from Unifi/Amicus/Unite if the latter took a lead.

*Other organisational and political developments*

Changes in nomenclature comprised the development of ANSA into ANGU and then Advance (see Inset 4.6), IUHS became Accord – the union for HBOS staff in 2002 and the Derbyshire Society Staff Association changed to the Derbyshire Group Staff Union in 2004. Also at the start of the period, the staff associations at the Yorkshire and Woolwich added 'independent' to their titles and WISA then became WISA- the Union for Woolwich staff. The number of TUC affiliations between 2000 and 2007 included Britannic Field Staff Association (which ceased to exist in 2002 following major redundancies) and YISA in 2000, the Derbyshire Building Society Staff Association in 2003 and the Skipton Staff Association in 2004.

In 2000, Unifi's members rejected – 57%:43% on a 25% turnout – creating a political fund (Unifi 2000c). This was a major blow to maintaining BIFU's campaigning tradition and was heavily influenced by the 'non-political' membership tendencies of former NWSA and UNiFI members. Activists reported that the major battle was to get annual conference to approve the decision and with that secured, the leadership expected the members 'to do as they were told' as one put it. The issue of affiliation to Labour was far from view given this was just a ballot on creating a political fund (and there was no sense that it was a pre-emptive move to achieve Labour affiliation). When Unifi amalgamated with Amicus, which had a political fund and was affiliated to Labour, ex-Unifi members wishing to contribute to one, either or both of these were required to opt in. Nonetheless, the Broad Left secured motions supporting Palestine in 2002 and opposing the Iraq invasion in 2003 as well as endorsing campaigns against low pay, poverty, and lesbian and gay rights. The federalised structure (*vis-à-vis* sectional autonomy) of Unifi was carried into Amicus and because the length of time between merger and Unite's creation was short and other demands were more pressing, it was not revised even though it was an anomaly for Amicus. However, with the creation of Unite and less organisational flux, the Broad Left signalled its intent to remedy this anomaly so that company committees become subject to the finance section executive and section policy. The Broad Left also set itself the task of securing the implementation of policy on electing EUOs. Finally, it is worth noting that the Alliance for Finance remained active until 2003 but was less far so from that time onwards.

## Union Organising

This section examines the moves toward attempting to organise the 750,000 plus finance sector non-union workers in terms of recruitment, recognition and retention.

*Union membership and density levels*

Amicus had just under 177,0000 members in the sector in 2006 and other unions and staff unions/ associations had, from Table 4.4, some 117,048 members in 2006 (including the IBOA's member in the north of Ireland, some ACTS (TGWU) and USDAW members in CIS, ALGUS members now in the CWU, and members of the staff associations/union in the Bank of Baroda and Leeds Building Society) giving a total of 293,926 members out of total employment compliment of 1.092m. This gave a 26.9% density for 2006 (although this also counted c.10,000 Amicus finance sector members in Eire). This means of calculation is some 3% higher than the Labour Force Survey (LFS) figure. Given that the LFS is scaled-up from a representative sample, there is no particular reason to think this study's calculation is any more or less inaccurate. Nonetheless, the higher figure is unlikely to bring much comfort or sustenance to the Amicus/Unite finance section even though it continued to engage in achieving similarly high levels of recruitment to those of its predecessors, MSF and Unifi, (see previous chapter, Colgan and Creegan (2006:66) and Danford et al. (2003:112)) because overall density continued to fall and sector density fell below national density for the first time (Table 5.2). With 161,269 finance section members in 2004, growing to 176,878 by 2006 (Amicus/Unite-Amicus section internal figures) through recruiting 25,173 in 2006 and some 17,000 in 2005 (*Amicus Finance Sector e-bulletin* 27 February 2007)[3], Amicus (2007:12) argued it was 'stemming the decline in membership ... [and] recruiting the highest number of new members'. Whilst this interpretation is some open to doubt in general terms and because membership fell to 167,674 (Unite internal figures) in 2008, membership retention has remained a huge challenge, whether as a result of job losses or turnover, so that just 'running to stand still' was still an ever present danger. In Unifi commissioned research (Waddington 2004), of those leaving, or stopping paying subs to, the union, 20% left the sector, 20% retired, 25% were made redundant, 21% changed job, 18% were dissatisfied with union and 16% gave another reason. If the first 65% of reasons are discounted and accepting that multiple choices were possible, c.39% either did not seek to renew their membership or deliberately left. This constituted a significant drain on recruitment, meaning that membership remained a fast turning set of revolving doors. Moreover, it questioned the appropriateness of both organising and servicing approaches in the light of membership demands. As with before (Colgan

---

3    To provide contextualisation, since Amicus was formed in 2004, it recruited 250,000 new members, of which 85,000 were recruited in 2005 and 74,000 in 2006 (Amicus 2007, *Amicus Financial services sector e-bulletin* 27 February 2007). Moreover, the T&G and Amicus in 2006 recruited 160,000 members but 'lost' 170,000 through redundancies and lapses (*T&G Record* May/June 2007). Both unions since 2004 recruited nearly 600,000 members but 'lost' just as many (Unite supplement in *Press Gazette* 14 September 2007). This suggests that the Amicus/Unite finance section performed better than its sister sections elsewhere.

**Table 5.2      Union Densities, 2000–2007**

| Year | Sector | National | Men (sector) | Women (sector) |
|------|--------|----------|--------------|----------------|
| 2007 | 22.3 | 28.0 | 17.8 | 27.2 |
| 2006 | 24.3 | 28.4 | 21.1 | 27.4 |
| 2005 | 24.4 | 29.0 | 19.8 | 28.5 |
| 2004 | 26.6 | 28.8 | 21.9 | 30.9 |
| 2003 | 25.9 | 29.3 | 21.9 | 29.7 |
| 2002 | 27.2 | 29.2 | 22.3 | 31.4 |
| 2001 | 27.0 | 29.3 | 23.0 | 30.5 |
| 2000 | 29.9 | 29.7 | 25.5 | 33.8 |

*Source*: *Labour Force Survey* annual union density reports.


and Creegan 2006, Danford et al. 2003), recruiting had been achieved primarily by EUO deployment (Amicus 2007:7), and this raised a number of issues, *inter alia*: was organising or recruitment taking priority, what role did members and activists play, were workplace unionisms (comprising these new members) self-sustainable to any significant degree, did servicing predominate rather than self-organising, and what EUOs resources were available to service these new members?

A number of staff unions (at 2004 or 2001 – see Table 4.4) had in excess of 50% density (AXIS, BSU, LTU, NGSU, SSA, UBAC and WISA) while others did not (ALGUS, ANGU). For example, the Britannia Staff Union had a density of 75% in 2003 and 76% in 2004. Heuristically, and ignoring for the moment their lower propensity towards unionateness, one could venture that the issue for these former staff unions was one of membership collective mobilisation for the pursuit of the effective representation of members' interests. Yet, no evidence existed of this (see later).

Part of the challenge of union recruitment and organising can be conveyed by comparing Tables 5.2 and 5.3 to see that free riding was not an insubstantial problem whilst non-union members often worked alongside union members. For Amicus-MSF, it had 40,000 members where an additional 50,000 (non-union) workers were covered in institutions where it only was recognised (in twenty instances).

The need for further self-reliance of, and self-organisation by, members or increased resources for servicing was accentuated by the significant increase in the number of bargaining units, either a result of the entrance of new players to sector or restructuring/de-merging of existing units. For example, Unifi (2002:6) reported that its members worked in 97 institutions in 1999 and 130 by 2001, while in 2001 it had recognition for 150 bargaining units which represented a one hundred per cent increase over the last two year (albeit this number was down to 120 by 2003). Of course, some compensation was availed to Unifi by the majority of its members being employed by a small number of very large

**Table 5.3      Union Presence and Collective Bargaining Coverage in Financial Intermediation, 2003–2007**

| Year | Workers whose terms and conditions covered by collective bargaining | Workers working in workplaces with a union presence |
|------|------|------|
| 2007 | 31.2% | 44.7% |
| 2006 | 31.4% | 46.3% |
| 2005 | 35.5% | 49.7% |
| 2004 | 36.1% | 49.3% |
| 2003 | 35.6% | 51.0% |

*Source*: *Labour Force Survey* annual union density reports.

employing organisations, whereby in 1999 75% of members worked for in Lloyds/ TSB, Barclays, NatWest and HSBC with this being 66% in 2001. Moreover, Unifi had members in 80 organisation without union recognition (IRS 2004:23). For Amicus, the problem was similar. Amicus-MSF had 80% of its 40,000 members in the insurance sector employed with 10 major insurers but it also had members in 400–plus other employers (IRS 2004:23).

*Union organising and recognition*

The practice of carrying out 'union organising' continued to be dominated by EUOs because of a 'Catch 22' situation. Recruitment (and retention) were recognised as being better where functioning office reps operated but these were hard to find and develop so that EUOs – still an expensive means of operating – stepped in to do so, compounding the problem. Unifi members in two surveys (Colgan and Creegan 2006:76–77, Unifi 2002:6–7) prioritised the rationale of help at work if they had a problem considerably more than other union members (see Waddington and Whitson (1996:56), (1997:521)) as they did over the rationale of improved pay and conditions. Given the dominant historical tradition of individualised orientation, this suggested in both cases that union members displayed an individualist instrumental approach to membership with the sense of 'what can the union do for me?' being to the fore, rather than the collective instrumentalism of 'what can we as the union do?'. This trajectory was, ironically, enhanced by Unifi not being believed to be well organised and judged to have too little influence in the workplace (see Colgan and Creegan 2006:73, 77) for there was an insufficient sense that members' action could produce a countervailing situation. In tandem, the visibility of existing reps to members was also poor and most members would seek advice on an issue from a EUO or seconded rep and not a workplace one or branch official (Unifi 2002:7, 18, 19). The difficulties in recruiting workplace reps remained acute. In the 2001 survey of Unifi members (Unifi 2002:8), when members were asked why they would not become reps, the top reasons were '[take up] too much time' and 'not interested'. Arguably, these were surface reasons for the actual underlying ones were that labour unionism was viewed as having no ideological appeal or instrumental efficacy for it there was ideological commitment and stronger unionism, many respondents may well have seen 'the point' of making the 'sacrifices' to be active in labour unionism. Whilst these phenomena were unlikely to be different from many other unions, the salience here was that the centralised form of labour unionism in sector accentuated these weaknesses.

Table 5.4 lists cases of new recognition agreements gained covering small foreign banks and specialist financial houses, extension of recognition to new or existing subsidiaries, agency, auxiliary and contracted out staff, and some re-recognition. Overall, the thirty-six cover c.40,000 workers. Notable here are Halifax Property Services with 4,000 staff (with IUHS and extended from the Halifax), AXA insurance's four new call centres (with MSF/BIFU-Unifi and extended from AXA), Capital Bank with 6,000 staff (with Unifi and extended from BoS), Barclaycall's three call centres (with 2,500) and the regaining of recognition for some 12,500 junior and middle managers at HSBC, Intelligent Finance's Edinburgh and Livingston centres with 1,000 staff (IUHS), London and Edinburgh's centre in Worthing, also with 1,000 staff (MSF), Prudential's takeover of Churchill Insurance facilitating recognition for these 1,200 workers through Amicus, and Unisys Insurance Services' Bournemouth centre with 850 staff (Unifi). Unifi's successfully used the *Employment Relations Act 1999* from 6 June 2000 to gain voluntary (Bank of Ceylon, Banco do Brasil) and statutory (Union Bank of Nigeria, Philippine National, Tejarat, Laiki) recognition agreements by applying for recognition through the Central Arbitration Committee (CAC). In the cases of Union Bank Nigeria, Banco do Brasil and Philippine National, there were indications of mild resistance such as employers commissioning their own polls and challenging the bargaining unit. And while these successes were helpful in normalising the presence of the union, their wider purchase must be tempered by acknowledgement that they are all small foreign banks, covering less than 400 workers in total. Moreover, this must be further situated and balanced by other developments where the Unifi lost in battles with determined anti-union employers. So Unifi lost at Turkiye Is Bankas in a statutory ballot where it recorded only 35% support despite having 83% membership after the employer organised workers to send to the CAC letters recording their opposition to union recognition, and Bank Hapoalim derecognised Unifi. But of more significance was Unifi's failure on two occasions to make a breakthrough at the Nottingham Building Society (with some 250 workers). Both applications passed the 10% membership threshold but not the majority support threshold. In the second attempt in 2003, the employer used a works council, anti-union literature and denied access to its workers to stymie the organising effort. The CAC ruled, after accepting the employer's argument for an expanded bargaining unit, that the Unifi had insufficient support to proceed. The results of bargaining under these new recognition agreements were on a par with more longstanding agreements (Gall 2005d). In similar terms, little success was

**Table 5.4      Cases of New Recognition Agreements in the Financial Services Sector, 2000–2007**

| |
|---|
| UNIFI HSBC – extended to auxiliary workers |
| Unifi Insurance Ombudsman Bureau |
| MSF London and Edinburgh |
| Unifi Capital Bank (BoS subsidiary) |
| Unifi HSBC for In-Store division which operates in Morrisons supermarkets |
| Unifi Barclaycall (Salford, Coventry, Sunderland) |
| IUHS Intelligent Finance call centres |
| Unifi Bank of Ceylon |
| Unifi Banca del Lavoro |
| Unifi Union Bank of Nigeria |
| Unifi Banco do Brasil |
| Unifi Banco do Roma |
| Unifi HSBC managers |
| Unifi IBM (staff transferred from BoS) |
| Unifi Unisys Insurance Services |
| LTU Scottish Widows |
| Unifi Barclays Stockbrokers |
| MSF Ethical Investment Research Services |
| Unifi Philippine National Bank |
| Unifi Tejarat Bank |
| Amicus–MSF CGNU |
| Unifi HSBC Asset Finance and Select insurance |
| Unifi Providian Card Services (Barclaycard) |
| Accord Equitable Life insurance |
| Amicus AMP UK financial services |
| Unifi Norton Finance |
| Unifi Direct Line (Croydon, Leeds) |
| Accord HBOS Card Services Credit |
| Accord Halifax Estate Agents |
| Accord Bank of Scotland Investment Services |
| Unifi Laiki Bank |
| Amicus Prudential (Churchill insurance) |
| Amicus Banca Intesa |
| Amicus Banca Popolare |
| Amicus Prudential (IT staff) |
| Amicus Alliance & Leicester |

*Source*: Author's own research (see Gall 2004, 2007).
*Note*: Listed in chronological order. Cases in Employer Resistance.

recorded in establishing a union presence, much less gaining union recognition, amongst new players like Sainsbury Bank, Tesco Bank, Standard Life Bank, Marks and Spencer Financial Services, and Virgin Financial Services as well as some longstanding players like Scottish Amicable (Prudential), Lloyds Abbey Life, Lloyds Insurance Direct, HFC, Norwich Union Healthcare, Colonnade, LloydsTSB Commercial Finance and Barclays Capital and some international operations of the older companies despite many years of on-off work.[4] The difficulties here arose as a result of employer hostility and insufficient worker enthusiasm. Finally, but of little obvious impact, the trajectory of labour unionism in the sector has not followed that of labour unionism generally, of fewer and smaller recognition gains after the initial surge of winning easy gains. Indeed, for the sector 1990–1999 saw 31 new agreements while 2000–2007 saw thirty-six (with just two cases of derecognition).

The two short studies of Egg and Standard Life (SL) indicate a number of salient features in the process and dynamics of employer resistance to granting union recognition. First was that such anti-union employers were prepared to spend considerable resources to promote compliant 'alternatives' to independent labour unionism (albeit this varied, with more or less resources given over at, say, SL, than at, say, Bristol and West or Barclaycall). This included facility time, salaries and training. Second was that they were prepared to show flexibility in revising the form of this strategy and by expending even higher levels of resources in pursuit of union avoidance. Third was that the goal of anti-unionism was not non-unionism *per se* but enhanced employer control of workers and, ultimately, enhanced productivity and commitment to the managerially determined organisational goals.

*Egg*

Egg is an internet bank. MSF had a very small number of members in the new Egg call centre in Derby that opened in 1999 (and which was owned by Prudential which recognised MSF in its other operations). MSF's campaign started at Easter 2000 with leafleting on four days in a two-week period, culminating in an 'Action Day' involving speakers and an innovative play about working in a call centre centred around stress levels. The speeches and play were run twice on the same day to take account of the shift system. During leafleting, EUOs remained outside the workplace for the rest of the day in the hope that workers would speak to them when they went out for lunch or left work after their shift. Meantime, in 2000, Egg set up its Egg People Forum (EPF) – an elected staff council with three seconded full-time members which was charged with representing the 'voice of all Egg People, to make working life great and help drive superior business results' by increasing employee involvement in business change and initiatives, building and maintaining effective relationships with all departments and independently

---

4   The 'Organise the City' campaign of 2002 was also not successful.

representing employees both collectively and individually (IPA website). There were 14 EPF representatives for the 2,000 staff across three sites including two for management grades. The EPF was jointly chaired by the employee side chair and Egg's CEO with members being elected for terms of three years. According to the IPA, information sharing and consultation take places on collective issues (company policies and strategy, benchmarking and salary structure, restructuring and reorganisation, people initiatives, health and safety, communications, terms and conditions and local departmental issues) while individual issues dealt with included bonuses, flexible working, performance management, general support and guidance, disciplinary issues, sickness reviews and redundancy hearings. Egg outlined the union avoidance and substitutionist rationale for the EPF when it stated:

> We have created an internal staff forum at Egg ... which ... has successfully provided us with the level of consultation and involvement our employees seek. ... we have not been approached by any staff requesting union representation within the workplace. (*Post Magazine* 12 April 2001)

MSF felt sufficient progress was made to warrant a similar exercise at Easter 2001 where it used a giant chicken to give out chocolate eggs and 'unions are good eggs' leaflets. Several months later, further leafleting was conducted around the issue of restricted toilet breaks with a protest outside the workplace using a giant toilet and stopwatch. In the intervening period, MSF campaigned on workplace stress arising from the use of targets and monitoring, stimulated by widespread publicity given to reports into call centre working. After Easter 2001, MSF's campaigned on pay and conditions inequality with other Prudential call centres which were covered by union recognition, citing, for example, that the Nottingham call centre workers were paid a basic of £10,500 with a pension while workers in Derby were paid a basic of £8,840 without a pension. In 2002, meetings took place between EPF officers and Amicus over access to recruit with a view to gaining union recognition but this led, with company support, to a reinvigoration of the EPF's ability to be involved in consultation exercises and the granting of higher visibility within the workplace. In turn, this acted as a renewed bulwark against Amicus. So denied access to the workforce by the EPF itself (*Times* 17 May 2005) and without reaching a critical mass, MSF/Amicus was forced to operate from the outside and here this was made more difficult by Egg preventing organisers from standing on company premises. The activity of the campaign became more sporadic but did not end, taking on more of a media war nature and punctuated by bursts of physical activity over redundancies and closures, and the inadequacy of consultation over these. In all, three requests for union recognition were made and all three were rebuffed by 2006.[5] Prudential then

---

5   Tuckman and Snook (2006, 2008) presented a quite different interpretation of the EPF, stressing its evolution into a quasi-effective and quasi-autonomous body. The counter-position was taken in Gall (2005a, 2005b).

sold Egg in 2007 to Citigroup as a part of a cost cutting exercise whereby Egg was a loss making business (of c.3,000 workers).

*Standard Life*

SL is a longstanding financial service provider of pensions, insurance, mortgages and investments. A staff consultation committee has existed within the company since 1970 and was relaunched as the LINK in 1998 as a result of the widespread perception of the former's ineffectiveness and lack of profile. LINK is the peak organisation for the five SL staff associations which correspond to its five divisions. These operate at three levels: local area representative (about 200 cover around 50 staff each, usually at the department level), some eighteen divisional or national representatives elected by the area representatives from each division; and four full-time representatives at central operations. Each full-time representative has a specific area of responsibility (training and development, compensation and benefits, communications, and chair). Representatives are elected for two years and recruited to national or central operations by their peers. The full-time representatives retain their current salary and benefits and are guaranteed re-entry into the business at the end of their term of office and at a level at least comparable with that at which they left for the secondment. The partnership, instituted in 2000, is based upon consultation and not negotiation and its principles comprise a joint commitment to the success of the enterprise as well as finding means of improving employment security, supporting openness and integrity and adding value. The remit of the partnership agreement concerns changes to pay, benefits, working practices and personnel policies, introduction of new technologies, and health, safety and welfare issues, with collective consultation over these. However, the IPA (website) commented: '... [surprisingly] given the level of investment in communication and consultation, there is, as yet little evidence of employee or representative involvement in business issues'.

SL had been a long time target of ASTMS/MSF. However, it was not until the late 1990s that it was able to make some limited progress in gaining a foothold of membership by virtue workers' concerns about job losses, contracting out, management bonuses, the prospects of takeover and demutualisation. The extent and depth of concern increased from 2005 over redundancies (which amounted to 4,500 prior to 2007), actual demutualisation, increased management and decreased staff bonuses. In this context, the issue of union recognition was first raised by Amicus. Events moved on apace in 2007, when Amicus recruited some 1,000 members out of 10,500 as a result of the company's proposals to reform the pension scheme from a final salary to average salary one in order to plug the deficit in the pension scheme. This added to its 200 existing members. At the same time, the company proposed another 1,000 job cuts. This increase in membership led to meetings with SL in a process whereby the company sought to delay and obfuscate in order to stymie the momentum Amicus was able to build up. Later, the company backtracked a little to both prevent a staff revolt and enhance the efficacy of LINK (staff member and union activist interviews). Thus, unwittingly aided by Amicus, LINK 'secured' its first victory over the company in the first crisis in employment relations at the organisation. In this situation, Amicus sought a voluntary union agreement with the threat of making a CAC application given that it had the requisite 10% membership density. However, the company stood firm, making clear that it would only deal with LINK and knowing that Amicus would also have to show that a majority of employees supported union recognition in a petition for the application to be accepted. SL rode out the crisis and subsequently the level of anger and membership dissipated.

### From Adversarialism to Partnership

As moves towards partnership became more entrenched and widespread, the tendency towards open conflict, adversarialism and unionateness was undercut, indicating their superficiality and transience, and that they were features of situational bargaining relationships rather than deep-seated changes in union and worldview consciousnesses of a sizeable number of members. 'Partnership' is marked by explicit ideological – rather than just pragmatic – and permanent co-operation and mutualism over compatible and common interests. Within such a commonly agreed framework, for labour unionism partnership involves moderated demands, compromise and accommodation, constituent demobilisation, emphasis on non-bargaining forums and consultation, and industrial quiescence. 'Partnership' is characterised as a phenomenon of intention (spirit), process (dialogue) and outcome in terms of substance (material rewards), codified means (procedures) and culture (attitudes, protocols like corporate social responsibility). It is less concerned with rule-making and enforcement compared to collective bargaining, and more concerned with achieving 'consensus'. Before looking at the evidence of active oppositionalism, it is worth restating that partnership had prior roots as previous chapters made clear – in this sense, partnership was not so innovative as it was necessarily of other sectors.

*Industrial action*

Although Storey et al. (1999:150) talked of 'the seeds of future conflict', Table 4.1 made clear that strike action was almost unheard of after 1998. Neither non-reporting nor underreporting (as per before, and which did occur) or even ballots for action and industrial action short of a strike substantially change this picture. There were two strikes in 2001; a one-day strike was by Unifi RBS members in London over their London allowance and a series of one- and two-day strikes over three months over pay by 100 workers at the Bank of India. In 2002, some 4,600 Unifi RBS in Scotland struck on 2 January over the day becoming a normal working day after a 64% vote for on a 31% turnout. However, as membership had fallen from 60% to 30% between 1997 and 2002, the strike did not make a large impact with few picketlines, and a third of branches remaining open. In 2005, USDAW members at Cooperative Insurance Services took two two-day strikes over contracts, workloads and pay, this being their first strike in 35 years. The major strike was at the HSBC in 2005 – where there was no partnership agreement with the employer – over pay. Amicus balloted it HSBC members on striking after a 3.5% rise in the available pot for PRP resulted in 10% of workers receiving no pay rise, and 40% receiving a below inflation rise. Concomitant, the bonus system was worsened. Members voted 2:1 (on 29% turnout) and the mobilisation saw the strike take place on the day of the company's AGM with a media campaign of mobile adverts, leafleting, press work and a customer poll. The strike was initially conceived of a 'series of one day strikes' (Amicus press release 29 March 2005). Amicus played the 'moderate workers spurned' card:

> This is unprecedented for a group of workers who are not naturally predisposed to strike action. (National Secretary, Rob O'Neill, *Guardian* 12 May 2005)

> People don't come any more 'middle England' and moderate than bank staff. Yet they have been pushed so far they see industrial action as the only way they can get their voice heard. (HSBC workers, *Amicus the Activist* journal June 2005)

> Bank staff are ... not the sort of people you might associate with union militancy or strike action. (*Amicus the Activist* journal June 2005)

On the left, the following observation was common: 'Although this was ... a 24-hour strike it has shown that finance sector workers are not the white-collar pushovers management think they are' (*Socialist* 2 June 2005). Very minor improvements were gained as a result of the strike threat, which were then imposed before the strike 'despite' being rejected by Amicus (*Financial Times* 6, 13 August 2005, *Guardian* 28 May 2005), with Amicus stating: 'even if the strike was total failure, the issue that caused the strike would not go away' (*Guardian* 28 May 2005). On the back of the strike, Amicus talked of organising a campaign against less than inflation rises. This did not transpire for in RBS, 22% of workers received a below inflation pay rise with no strike ballot organised. Similarly, the LTU threatened a strike ballot in 2005 after 33% of workers received no pay rise. Yet after a majority of members in a consultative ballot expressed a desire for an industrial action ballot on pay, no ballot was forthcoming. The closure of final salary pension schemes and introduction of money purchase schemes for new entrants did not elicit industrial action either. There were just a few cases of strikes being threatened in this regard (Prudential (2002), Scottish Widows (2002), Coop (2004)) with the employers making concessions because the cases either involved high union densities and/or IT workers.

In terms of other industrial action mobilisations, Unifi cheque clearing workers at IPSL won concessions on redundancy payments after balloting for strike action, Unifi EDS cheque clearing staff at NatWest/RBS raised their pay award from 2.2%

to 3.0% after voting for striking in 2002, and Unifi Directline IT workers voted to be balloted over strike action on the terms and existence of compulsory redundancies, by 96.8% on a 85% turnout in a consultative ballot, precipitating some concessions. Other than these, the threat to ballot or raising the spectre of striking were more routinely used (see also Unifi joint general secretary, Rory Murphy's comments in IRS (2004:22)). In 2001, the CWU did so over compulsory redundancies and more job cuts at the Alliance and Leicester Girobank. In 2003, Unifi successfully did so at HSBC over making ten agency staff at its Kirby processing centre permanent but did so unsuccessfully at First Direct over compulsory redundancies while Amicus at AXA threatened a ballot for striking over pensions cuts, increased employee contributions and raised retirement age and at the Bank of India used a strike ballot to win concessions on pay. In 2004, Securitas cash handling staff threatened a strike after the removal of London allowance following relocation, and this led to concessions. Finally, Amicus RBS call centre workers threatened a lunchtime walkout over removal of teabreaks. The sense of the unions attempting to 'manage' not 'fight' jobs was also palpable (*People Management* 2 March 2000, *Post Magazine* 22 February 2001, 24 October 2002).

In the building societies, again no industrial unrest was registered. In addition to points made in previous chapters regarding consciousness, culture and mobilisation, this state of affairs continued for, as in the case of the Bradford and Bingley closure of its call centre in 2000, there was 'full' consultation and information exchange so that staff felt that they had been 'kept informed' and they were given help to find other jobs. Thus, low expectations were satiated. In insurance, employers like Brittanic and Scottish Provident imposed pay and new terms and conditions without anything more than verbal protestation from Amicus, suggesting an inability of labour unionism to mobilise its members with moods of resignation predominant.

So the period was relatively barren in terms of widespread collective resistance (with industrial action against outsourcing included adding just one further case – see below), whereas the actions which predominated from Unifi/Amicus/Unite as well as LTU[6] were those of legal action (e.g., over pensions for part-time workers), trying to get the Department of Trade and Industry (DTI) to sanction investigations of proposed mergers and acquisitions, engaging in more extensive public relations work and campaigning (and see below on offshoring). There was no robust evidence of oppositionalism, this being attributable to the prevalence of partnership and the weakening of independent labour unionism (with just a couple of examples of obvious unrest in organisations with partnership agreements).

---

6    However, LTU supported the proposed takeover of Abbey by LloydsTSB in 2001 despite the likely job losses because it believed this would strengthen LloydsTSB (*Daily Telegraph* 14 April 2001).

## Partnership Agreements and Partnership Working

Partnership has affected the sector more so than any other in Britain judged by the number of employers and workers covered. This was the case in the late 1990s (Gall 2001) and was accentuated further by the mid-2000s, testifying to the longevity and development of the partnership deals (see Table 5.5 with 26 such agreements). To these could be added *de facto* partnership agreements or partnership working in a number of cases like that at Beneficial Bank (non-union), Birmingham Midshires, Bristol and West (from 2001, non-union), Nationwide Group, Portman Group, West Bromwich (Stuart et al. 2007, Tailby et al. 2007, Upchurch et al. 2006) and Woolwich building society. This brings the total to 33. Looked at another way, a third of these were signed in the space of three years after 1997 – the high point of open industrial conflict. Some obvious questions emerge, *inter alia*: why has the sector experienced so many partnership agreements?; what does this indicate about the sector?; and what does this say about the labour unionism in the sector? With regard to the first question, and drawing on studies of partnership agreements *per se* (see, for example, Kelly (2004, 2005)), it can be suggested that for the sector, the interplay of competition and accumulation strategies from employing organisations within a situation of general and significant specific market flux has led to overtures to establish these agreements.[7] In response, the moderate and weakened position of labour unionism has made it receptive to these overtures (see Inset 5.1). Although partnership was not 'the only game in town', as saying 'no' was a viable option, it was not an attractive option for it was not likely to be based on a worked out proposition of what an effective alternative would look like. The principle and practice of independent unionism had not so far produced an effective 'model' so that this could be fallen back upon. Alongside this, the servicing-orientated and centralised locus of power (national and company committee levels) of independent labour unionism made the overture attractive given that it was based on an exchange between employer and union at this level and in a centralised manner with attendant institutional support.

Nonetheless, and in light of the debate over the 'cycles' and 'waves' of participation (Marchington et al. 1992, Ramsay 1977), the rise of the partnership agreements should also be seen as an attempt to gain both greater worker commitment and lessen resistive capacity. Following from this, and in terms of the second question, it is hard not to come to the conclusion that the rise in partnership agreements is not closely linked to the process of workers developing disruptive capacity at a time of continuing market instability and change leading to organisational flux. What was crucial here was that the leadership of labour unionism blinked first (see below) whereby it believed that oppositionalism was too risky to continue with *vis-à-vis* employer retribution and too difficult to sustain

---

7 This would include the possibility that some employing organisations sought partnership agreements fearing that without they would not gain the benefits that others accrued, thus becoming competitively disadvantaged.

*vis-à-vis* members' preparedness and consciousness. In an ironic sense, the very issues which might have provided the foundation for robust responses buffeted labour unionism into stasis. Finally, and despite some fragile signs of a growing industrial prowess, the rush to partnership indicates a moderate form of labour unionism which did not conceive that it possessed alternative choices in material and ideological terms. Following from this, partnership looked like having some further longevity for agreements have been renewed on consecutive occasions where they have run for set periods of time and others have not been withdrawn from. The pressures for termination or erosion could come from the employers if membership densities fall so that the unions were no longer representative or

**Table 5.5     Partnership Agreements in the Financial Services Sector, 1993–2007**

| Employer | Date | Union(s) involved |
|---|---|---|
| London & Manchester Insurance | 1993 | MSF |
| National Westminster | 1996 | BIFU, NWSA |
| ANZ Banking | 1997 | MSF |
| Cooperative Bank | 1997, 2000 | BIFU/Unifi |
| LloydsTSB | 1997 | BIFU, LTU |
| Pearl Assurance | 1997, 2000 | MSF |
| Prudential Assurance | 1997 | NUIW |
| Legal and General | 1997 | MSF |
| Royal Liver | 1997 | BIFU |
| Abbey | 1998 | ANGU |
| AXA | 1998 | MSF |
| AXA Insurance | 1998 | BIFU, AXIS (AXA staff union) |
| Britannia Building Society | 1998 | Britannia Staff Union |
| Barclays | 1998, 2001, 2005 | BIFU, UNiFI then Unifi |
| Unisys | 1998 | BIFU |
| Das Legal | 1999 | MSF |
| Scottish Widows | 1999 | MSF |
| Capital Bank | 2000 | Unifi |
| Standard Life | 2000 | Link Staff Association |
| Zurich Financial Services | 2000 | UFS |
| Royal and Sun Alliance | 2001 | MSF, Unifi |
| Aviva | 2002 | MSF-Amicus/MSF |
| Unisys Insurance Service | 2002 | Unifi |
| Global Home Loans | 2003 | Unifi |
| Ulster Bank | 2003 | Amicus, IBOA |
| HBoS | 2007 | Unite-Amicus section, Accord |

*Source*: Various secondary sources.

worthwhile bargaining agents, or if crises of profitability 'compelled' erosion of terms and conditions of employment that made the conflict open. One Unifi EUO acknowledged the possibility of this latter scenario by stating: 'The unanswered question ... is what will happen when they want something very badly and we want very badly to stop it?' (Unifi 2001). From the labour union side, the sense

---

**INSET 5.1 Union Rationales for Partnership**

The desire for influence in a situation of little extant influence under the ideological offensive of 'Third Way' partnership proselytising (by the TUC, Industrial Participation Association, Industrial Society/Work Foundation, Unions21, and Labour Party/ Labour Government) led to rationales being constructed. Ed Sweeney (*Guardian* 14 September 1999) argued for '... a partnership of equals. You won't agree all the time, but if there's open and honest dialogue between the parties, differences can be worked through more easily than by going down the historical route of conflict. Partnerships have to be carefully negotiated – otherwise they could end up being sweetheart deals, where employers promise the earth tomorrow to get them through a difficult period today. Genuine partnership is based on mutual understanding of the business and an acceptance by employers that the workforce has a right to be included in decisions'. Meanwhile John Earls (2002), the then Unifi joint-head of research, tried to square the circle on partnership by marrying the case for strong, independent labour unionism with workers' desire for strong, independent and cooperative labour unionism by citing a survey of 2,000 Unifi members in 2001 (Unifi 2002) which showed the positive impact on a number of important members' working conditions of management being 'positive about the union in the workplace'. The problems for his argument were twofold. 'Being positive' about the union was not a self-evident simplism, for it was not clear what type or aspects of labour unionism management was positive about and what the union had done to receive this appellation (see Unifi (2002:12) where positivism concerns encouragement to membership and organisation).[1] Moreover, the evidence of the three 'D's did not sit well with the predominance of partnership throughout the sector. This could mean either that the partnership was past and present imperfect as a result of employer practice and the impact of product and labour markets, or that partnership was quintessentially antagonist to the interest of strong and independent labour unionism. Given the debate about partnership within Unifi, it is interesting that note that at its 2002 conference policy was revised so that deals were to be renewed every 5 years rather than the original, every 3 years.

---

1   Furthermore, it is interesting to note that the difference for positivism *vis-à-vis* job security in the eyes of union members was only 4%–44% in 'positive union workplaces' and 40% in 'negative union workplaces'.

of limited gain would have to be lessened and a sense of contamination increased whereby 'fairness' and equity become to be seen as incompatible with market outcomes. (These issues will be returned to below.)

Finally, it is important to acknowledge that partnership is subject to the underlying tensions in employment relations. Thus, within union recognition agreements, both parties sign up to an implicit tension, for these agreements state employers have the right to manage while unions have the right to represent members. Both rights imply effective rights, whose exercise is assumed to have favourable outcomes for each party. There is then ample room for the one to negate the other depending upon the balance of power. Partnership agreements seek to remove and/or manage this tension by concentrating on maximising perceived common interests but they cannot necessarily avoid the underlying expressions of interest conflict. Where a partnership agreement sits alongside an existing recognition agreement, the recognition agreement facilitates this and even at Barclays (*cf.* HBoS below), the agreement stated: 'Barclays [has the] right to take business decisions [and t]he unions [have the] right to challenge and influence those decisions'. With these initial comments, this section examines the stimuli to partnership, its nature, and process and outcomes, as well as presenting a case study of Barclays.

*Stimuli*

The original impetus derived in a number of companies from the belief by both employers and union leaders that a 'semi-permanent' state of conflict, as seemed to be the case in the 1990s, would be unsustainable for competitiveness and their bargaining relationship (see, for example, IRS 1999b). Having seen the 'precipice' both parties agreed to pull back for the conflict represented 'biting the hand that feeds you' for both sides. In Barclays, this was attested to by its chairman and employee relations director (TUC 1999a:12, IRS 1999b:6) and the unions (UNiFI/ BIFU/Barclays joint press release 1998). According to a Barclays BIFU member: 'The bank came up with the idea of partnership because it was worried about the spectre of industrial action' (see also *People Management* 25 February 1999). A similar dawning was also true for the Co-op Bank, Legal and General, NatWest, LloydsTSB, Royal and Sun Alliance, although their immediate points of departure were the unsettling influence on industrial relations and the bargaining relationship of widespread redundancies, rather than strike action. In these situations, employers were willing to 'to take on board' labour unionism with the ramifications for divulgence of information, and what might be done with this, in order to deploy them in their service. The employers' hope was that any potency of collective organisation would be neutralised through incorporation and participation and, specifically by, attitudinal restructuring and acclimatisation of EUOs and senior lay officials. This pertained to mobilising both the internal (workforce) and external (customers, public relations) environments (Gall 2001:366). In addition to the material in Inset 5.1 above, labour unionism was receptive to partnership because it offered regularised dialogue, institutional support and enhanced legitimacy at a time of financial pressure (e.g. BIFU/Unifi/Amicus finance section) and a low-cost way of responding to membership pressure to influence the employer as a result of redundancies and the like. It is worth stressing again the importance of the prior disposition to partnership *per se* (see, for example, *Financial Times* 12 May 1996, *Guardian* 13 May 1996, IRS (2000)). And in the case of MSF, its leadership pursued a more pragmatic than ideological approach towards the 'modernisation' of employment relations (Carter 1997, Martinez Lucio and Stuart 2005), and this was not blunted by MSF's merger with the AEEU to form Amicus.

Elsewhere in the sector, especially in insurance, the absence of overt conflict and rather the notion of 'best practice' building on existing features of industrial relations to promote competitiveness (such as those at Scottish Widows, Royal Liver, AXA, London and Manchester, Royal and Sun Alliance) was the driving force. Underneath this, the unions had reached an impasse in prosecuting their bargaining agenda through existing means. The major 'omissions' in the spread of partnership were the HSBC, NAG and RBS as well as a plethora of building societies. In the former, considerable degrees of open conflict were to the fore, for the employers deployed more aggressive and confrontational tactics with Unifi/Amicus. In the building societies, industrial relations continued as usual, therefore, not stimulating moves towards formal partnerships. The initial member and activist response to being asked to sign up to partnership was that only a minority current showed cynicism and scepticism (see IRS 1999c:15, Jacks et al. 2000). Most, despite the moves towards some oppositionalism and indicating the shallowness of these, were prepared to support the moves in either conditional or unconditional ways or positively or by default. Here the context was important: without independent means of significant collective influence, members and activists were subject to the hegemony of leadership, members expressed a desire for cooperation (without specifying explicitly their terms for this) and the continuing tranches of redundancies eroded confidence and capacity to collectively resist.

*Process and outcome*

In following a radical notion of power in employment relations, where power is a zero-sum phenomenon within a quintessentially antagonistic relationship between capital and labour[8], partnership agreements are viewed as intentions to both reinforce and extend managerial power and prerogative. Thus, regardless whether they are of a 'containment', 'nurturing, 'robust' or 'shallow' (Oxenbridge and Brown 2002, 2004, 2005) or 'adaptive', 'survival' or 'retrenchment' nature

---

8   That does not preclude recognition of the material basis for cooperation and compromise (see, for example, varying interpretations in Belanger and Edwards (2007), Edwards (1986), Edwards et al. (2006), and Gall (forthcoming) and Gall and Hebdon (2008)).

**INSET 5.2 Partnership at Barclays**

The Barclays agreement can be regarded as a 'model' one (*cf.* IDS 1996:1, IPA 1996, TUC 1999b) in terms of its principles *vis-à-vis* 'roles and responsibilities', 'behaviours', 'accountability', 'excellence', 'flexibility' and 'employability'. UNiFI (press release 4 June 1999) heralded the deal as: 'a rethink on pay and benefits [as] the result of both the bank and the unions recognising the need for a new approach to industrial relations. This means a move away from the adversarial/confrontational relationship of the past to a constructive and positive working relationship which is seen as an essential ingredient for the future success of the business'. The first agreement also included traditional components; three-year above inflation pay deal, private healthcare, improved sick pay and maternity provision, increases in minimum salaries and a removal of many maximum salary ceilings. Those components associated with partnership and which operationalised its principles were; the employer's right to take business decisions, the unions' right to challenge and influence those decisions, the employer's obligation to provide information and consult early on change initiatives, the unions' obligation to respect confidentiality, constructive communication to staff/union members and an undertaking that the employer will inform staff first about business decisions and plans without marginalising the unions. It thus combined the normal collective bargaining agreement as well as a 'memorandum of understanding' or 'declaration of intent' on working in partnership. Unifi (2000b) reported this led to a 'strengthening and deepening of the consultation and bargaining processes'. Criticism was aired of the deal producing insufficient progress after the strikes (*Morning Star* 17 March, 19 May 1999) and the unions being kept in the dark over job losses which were announced to the City first despite four months of consultation. This led the unions to stress their conditions for partnership were that they sought it from a position of strength with full union recognition and collective bargaining rights, and a recognition of underlying differences of interests between employer and union. In 2000, the partnership deal was renewed after an 87% vote for (Unifi 2000a) with one member venturing: 'I like the way we are moving forward towards partnership and away from the old industrial relations confrontation of the past' (*Channel 4 News* 14 September 1999). At this time, a flexible working hours agreement with improved maternity rights was gained and prior consultation and information on change management process, business strategy and redundancies took place. Unifi paraded all these as triumphs but was still sensitive to criticism. Unifi national secretary, Jim Lowe (Unifi *Fusion* magazine, February 2001) commented: 'I think the jury is still out. I accept the case for partnership still has to be proved. The top of the union and the top of the management are convinced but with the line managers and the union reps it could take another five years'. The agreement was renewed in 2005 alongside criticism of an agreement on annual hours and the extolling of an agreement on offshoring (see below).

Wills (2004:331) argued Unifi entered the partnership from a position of relative strength but this was contradicted – or at least not convincingly conceptualised and situated – by its desire to end its isolation, inability to sustain further adversarialism and lack of workplace presence (see Wills 2004:333–334,336). Moreover, Wills (2004:333, 336, 339, 340) made it evident that Barclays wanted to use partnership to attitudinally restructure Unifi through incorporation into their framework and that this resulted in curtailment of extant union democracy and union independence. Given the imbalance in power, the employer's interests and concerns predominated, with that not excluding Barclays having to throw the union some 'crumbs' to keep it on board. Nowhere did Wills (2004), like Samuel (2005, 2007), provide hard evidence that efficacy of union representation became better or greater. Giving the view of union representatives is not conclusive evidence for there was no triangulation, and 'on board' union representatives are likely to give a positive assessment because they have 'bought in' to partnership. Indeed, the prominence given to consultation suggests the union acquiesced in downgrading negotiation. So, for example, the creation of workplace representatives and the extension of recognition cannot be presumed to mean that Unifi avoided these representatives and recognition being captured by management for its purposes, and thus maintained its independence of agenda – assuming that it had an independent agenda (*cf.* Wills 2004:336–337, and see discussion of HBoS below). This is not to negate the potential benefit of having recognised, legitimate and resourced workplace representatives but to make it clear that a beneficial, unionate outcome should not be presupposed. Where there is evidence of membership growth (Wills 2004:338), further research is needed to determine whether this was retained and sustained, and whether membership led to participation given the auspices of partnership.

Turning to substantive outcomes, Barclays and Unifi signed an agreement for managing job security in the context of offshoring which involved early consultation, and with a view to avoiding compulsory redundancies, a register of all job vacancies for those whose jobs were being offshored, internal retraining, and a retraining allowance for those leaving the employ of Barclays. Lead Unifi negotiator, Keith Brookes, believed: 'The agreement represents what can be achieved through positive and progressive industrial relations in an atmosphere of partnership between unions and employers. Unifi has recognised Barclays need to reshape the business, and the bank has recognised the union's need to protect the employability and job security of its members' (*Telegraph* 6 January 2004). But it is pertinent to point out that consultation, particularly of the British-style under voluntary agreements, does not provide any leverage in and of itself. Some researchers, like Samuel (2005, 2007) and Wills (2004), have tended towards the simplism that 'knowledge is power' rather than mobilisation being the extra missing and essential ingredient. In terms of pay, the 1999 pay deal loosened the relation of pay rises with individual performance (*People Management* 21 February 1999, *Labour Research* September 1999). The pay pot deal of 2002–2004 paid an average rises of 2% to 3% while the 2004 three-year deal re-established the cost-of-living plus merit method. In 2007, Amicus secured an above inflation rise for 80% of staff (inflation plus merit award) with the remainder receiving an inflation only rise as part of a further three-year deal from 2008 (Amicus press release 15 October 2007). In response In response to Barclay's profits in 2008, Brookes commented: 'These results show ... Barclays' have done well to weather the storm in the financial markets. ... [S]taff ... must be congratulated for their hard work during these difficult economic conditions. Barclay's have recognised their contribution by delivering an inflation plus, three-year pay deal which sets a benchmark for the rest of the banking industry' (Unite press release 19 February 2008).

(Samuel 2007), these agreements seek to achieve certain constant macro-objectives within macro- and micro-contingent contexts. That is to say, whatever the specificities of the employing organisation and the labour and product markets in which it operates within, there are the constants of control and incorporation of labour and labour unionism at play. And here, the reason why partnership leads to the downgrading of bargaining and the enlargement of consultation is because of the existence of a mutual gains agenda where there is believed to be a high degree of overlap of interests. In these circumstances, there is no need of bargaining – it is almost superfluous – as any slight differences were to be sorted out through consultation. Many studies of partnership in the sector (see, for example, Samuel (2005, 2007) and Wills (2004)) have been unwilling to recognised this, primarily, because the 'wood' is missed for the' trees'. In other words, in a period of depleted labour union power and with commonly narrowed sights and vision, the crumbs of consultation of a British rather than European-type[9] arising from partnership, and attendant outcomes, are given far greater significance either in terms of historical significance or contemporary purchase than they warrant.[10] All this would not be so significant, it if was possible to show that partnership provided the basis for union revitalisation and renewal or growth in workers' collective and tangible influence at work. But there was no evidence of this because of the incorporating nature of partnership through institutional enclosure and attitudinal restructuring of unions, members and workers. The same is true of whether partnership could provide significant and demonstrable advances in terms and conditions of employment of workers or higher than market rates in the vein of substitutionist policies of paternalism. Indeed, in the case of Samuel's (2007) study of two insurance

---

9   Whilst negotiation has not been on the table, it is important to note that under the longstanding British version of consultation there has been no moral or legal obligation of employers to take on board or give full and proper consideration to any alternative actions that the workforce may suggest.

10   The same is true of the unions themselves – see, for example, Unifi press release (20 May 1999) and those by BIFU and NWSA quoted in Gall (2001:368).

companies, greater relative influence in one organisation was not shown to have produced a beneficial and discernible outcome for workers. By contrast, Kelly (1999, 2004, 2005) provided hard evidence that partnership was 'quite good for profits and not very good for jobs and unions' in the case of the sector. For example, Kelly (2005:201) reported that union membership fell by 11% and 7% respectively at Barclays and Cooperative banks between 1998 and 2001 while at NatWest, Abbey National and HSBC, the picture was mixed: +2%, +7% and –2% respectively over the period. And even where 'trust' existed in employing organisations, like Barclays and Legal and General, this should not necessarily be taken as a positive develop for the larger issue was trust around which and whose agenda (see also Kelly (2004:286)). In reviewing other available evidence of the experience of partnership below, these criteria will be used, and whilst recognising that there are other reasons for falls in membership and participation, it is still pertinent to place such an emphasis on these aspects given the importance of these for independent labour unionism. If partnership was unable to stop the decline or, indeed, helped the decline, this should at least facilitate the counter-factual question of: 'Would the union have been better off without partnership?'

The case of partnership at Legal and General from 1997 onwards is an indication that partnership agreements are signed from positions of weakness and impasse, no matter the intention to seek more strategic levers of influence (see *People Management* 4 December 1997). According to the IPA, the agreement sought to avoid conflict, share information, and allow for 'full and early participation in the decision-making process in areas of shared interest'. But Haynes and Allen's (2001) study indicated that the union was a busted flush, unable to move beyond achieving a ritualised annual wage claim set-to and unable to achieve membership mobilisation. The joint-employment policy forum was established to discuss business strategy, training and development, health and safety, reward and equal opportunities. Whilst the employer wanted cooperation and agreement from the union, its interests dominated and shaped the practice of partnership – contrary to the assertions from MSF/Amicus (*Guardian* 10 May 2003). Even if this was not the intention, Samuel (2005) showed under partnership, union density fell in the first two years after 1997 from 42% to 27% before recovering slightly to 34% in 2002 (Samuel 2005:67). Samuel also highlighted that there were some new activists but no more than before, and activists were more active but they were no aid to the increased membership participation and mobilisation (*cf.* Haynes and Allen 2001:172–173). No hard evidence was presented by Samuel (2005) of increased union efficacy but there was evidence of incorporation (Haynes and Allen 2001). The partnership was subject to workforce criticism (*People Management* 14 September 2000) by way of a joint-review in 2000 which exposed some disquiet on the union side about non-involvement and time-off work to carry out union duties. Nonetheless, a staff survey in 2001 revealed that 66% thought both union and employer benefited from the partnership and both parties celebrated its tenth anniversary (*People Management* 10 January 2008). This agreement became a sector pacesetter and was used as template by MSF/Amicus.

Similar outcomes were recorded by Danford and colleagues (Danford et al. 2003, Upchurch et al. 2006, 2008, Tailby et al. 2007) in their studies of seven companies in the sector. In one instance, that of Das Legal, an insurance company which recognised MSF from the 1970s, density was as high as 80% in the early 1990s but dropped significantly, fluctuating around 45% by the early 2000s (Tailby et al. 2007:215). After a threat to derecognise, the union signed a partnership agreement in the late 1990s and despite there being indications that the employer wanted an arrangement that would allow it a relationship with the majority of its employees and satisfy any future statutory consultation regulations, the mechanisms entailed in the partnership agreement did not increase union influence or presence (Tailby et al. 2007). Indeed, after the late 1990s, many members preferred individual, self-representation, an employment security agreement did not prevent redundancies, employee input took place within the straightjacket of a *fait accompli* system of consultation, and the downgrading of workplace representatives into just grievances and disciplinary handling representatives was apparent (Tailby et al. 2007).[11] Danford et al. (2003:105–106) showed that in this set up the union was a secondary afterthought for management. In another contrasting instance, of the Bristol and West, a former building society taken over by the Bank of Ireland, a partnership agreement was instituted with a non-union body to keep a *bona fide* union, Unifi, at bay (Tailby et al. 2007, Upchurch et al. 2006). Thus, in the period up to the early 2000s, the dependent staff association and existing works council[12] fell into disarray and dereliction whereupon Unifi attempted unsuccessfully to gain recognition, which in turn stimulated the employer to revamp and revitalise the works council with a full-time member of staff paid for by the company, and members *de facto* selected by managers. Thus, throughout the period since the late 1980s, the employer was prepared to deploy resources through a number of tactics to remain non-union. The revamped works council, called a 'partners' council', as all staff were deemed to be 'partners', was not entitled to negotiate on pay and is still a body beholden to, and dominated by, management's agenda (IPA website, Tailby et al. 2007, Upchurch et al. 2006). And whilst this mechanism was widely regarded by staff as ineffective, this did not mean that the 'union option' was a well-supported alternative, suggesting that management's strategy of union avoidance and employee control was being realised. All this appeared as democratic in as much that the company balloted staff in 2001 on the works council versus union/union recognition options – except that it was clear which option management preferred and promises were made about the effectiveness of the works council prior to its revamping (Tailby et al. 2007, Upchurch et al. 2006).

---

11    The observation of a longstanding Amicus NEC member suggested downgrading of workplace reps to this role was relatively common with Amicus/Unite-Amicus section (personal communication, 11 January 2008).

12    Bristol and West introduced a works council in 1992 as a means of pre-empting any unionisation, having expected employment relations changes under an anticipated Labour Government (Tailby et al. 2007).

Other research points in the same broad direction too. In Abbey, the primary union-employer interaction took place at company and business area levels, based on long-standing union recognition and a partnership agreement with ANGU (Hall 2003). The formal framework consisted of a group-level Joint Consultative Negotiating Committee (JCNC), which has four meetings a year, and several sub-committees to discuss issues such as health and safety, job security, and pay and conditions. In addition, there were a number of divisional or business area sub-committees. Participation in these bodies was only open to ANGU members. In some larger business areas, there were further lower level committees. The distinction in formal terms between consultation and negotiation was a little unclear for although Hall (2003) stated '[b]roadly speaking, negotiation takes place within the JCNC and its policy sub-committees, while the business area sub-committees are essentially used for consultation', Abbey also operated a range of direct communication and employee involvement initiatives and ANGU was firmly opposed to the participation of non-members in Abbey's consultative structures. The results of partnership over employment security have been mixed. Thus, a job security agreement at Abbey did not prevent the company from shedding jobs, closing offices and offshoring operations (Hall 2004) but it did allow some earlier redeployment and retraining of staff (IPA 2002). Moreover, support for independent labour unionism and conflict-based perceptions *vis-à-vis* management at Abbey did not find an outlet in ANGU despite an earlier revolt against an overly close and dependent relationship with the company and a frustration by some workplaces representatives at their restricted role (see Bain et al. 2004). Indeed, behind the rhetoric and partnership at the company-level, workplace reps believed the employer was antagonistic towards the idea and presence of labour unionism. In the early 2000s, overall union membership density stood at around 45%, with just 6.4% in a particular call centre (Bain et al. 2004:72)

HBoS signed a partnership agreement in mid-2007 with Accord and Unite whereby union membership and workplace organisation were to be encouraged (Unite press release 4 July 2007). Recognition of workplace representatives by the employer and the funding of their facility time were significant developments. However, it remained to be seen whether membership would actually increase and whether the newly created workplace reps would be independent of the company. Indeed, while the employer funded two seconded reps, with a workforce of some 72,000 staff at the time (most of whom worked in Britain) and the aim of having one workplace rep per site and/or one rep per fifty members, relatively little progress was made in 2008 in filling even 25% of this target. Some Unite finance sector activists in HBoS feared the partnership agreement would bring the union too close to the company so that potential members would not be attracted by a captured or compromised organisation which was not independent of management. Moreover, these activists also feared that the workplace reps would, under management pressure, to be dragooned into becoming solvers of individual grievances and disciplinaries, and on management terms, rather than union organisers and independent-minded workplace representatives. These fears were accentuated when it was discovered that the partnership agreement superseded (rather than sat alongside) the then existing recognition agreement so that the procedure of stages of disagreement was lost. This meant that there was no longer a procedure by which to progress disagreements.

Stuart and Martinez Lucio (2005) found evidence of extensive dialogue, consultation and involvement in two of their three partnership agreement case studies in insurance but from their account it was not clear whether negotiation, *de facto* or otherwise, took precedence or how consultation supported rather than contradicted or eroded negotiation. Similarly, the sub-text of partnership and union presence becoming part of the fabric of the employing organisation at the senior organisational level in terms of rule-making and process enforcement was interrogated insufficiently to ascertain whether the labour unionism there was able prosecute an independently derived agenda.

In the case of the AXA-MSF partnership, the employer decided to recognise MSF across the group in 1999 after it merged with Guardian Royal Exchange whence MSF designed the job evaluation scheme for the merged group as their EUOs had more awareness of different employees' job roles than the senior managers, a new staff handbook representing the harmonising terms and conditions was achieved and a one-off bonus was paid to staff for cooperation in the merger process. The TUC commented that 'unions and employees are now regularly *consulted* [emphasis added] on a range of issues' with the granting of greater than statutory minimum provision on family-friendly rights in 2003. Scottish Widows – now part of LloydsTSB – recognised MSF but until the partnership agreement in 1999, relations had been rather informal and sometimes problematic (and particularly so in 1998). The agreement expressed the desire to avoid conflict and to co-operate through information-sharing and consultation on an agreed range of agendas, and established a pay and partnership committee (with two staff from personnel and two representatives from the local union executive) as well as a works council. Committee communications were issued jointly where possible, and there was recourse to the grievance procedure if talks broke down. Royal and Sun Alliance recognised both MSF and BIFU when it was created from a merger. Following MSF taking the company to court because of a lack of prior consultation, the company revised its employee relations practices in the form of a partnership agreement after a range of other options including derecognition was considered. Consultation operated at three levels (local, business, corporate) and its parameters were set down, with it appearing more far-reaching at the two higher levels.

The partnership agreement at the Cooperative sought to provide a framework for 'the sensitive and effective use of change management' and employment security in exchange for employee commitment to change. Consequently, management agreed to engage and consult union representatives about business issues and change initiatives at an early stage (see also Marginson (1999)). According to the IPA, this enabled Unifi to help shape developments, and share concerns and ideas and, for the bank, led to union support to tackle problems jointly and speedier implementation once changes were agreed. Initial substantive outcomes concerned better family care facilities, greater job protection for temporary staff and more generous sick leave at Coop (*Financial Times* 3 April 1997). A second partnership agreement was signed in 2000, securing 4:1 backing from Unifi members in a secret ballot (of which around 70% of staff are union members). The other side to this was that 20% of members were receptive to the arguments of activists who argued that the union would be unable to maintain its independence and resist job losses under partnership. Following this, localised partnership forums were established to try to deepen the level of staff participation.

*Overview*

Standing back from the trees to see the wood, it is clear that none of agreements have been terminated or collapsed. This was not necessarily an indication of the absence of any problems. Rather, any problems and disputes were not sufficiently severe to engulf and overcome the agreements. Thus, agreements have been tested with significant issues and disputes (see section on outsourcing and offshoring, and *inter alia*, Barclays; closures, jobs, union recognition, LloydsTSB; closures, jobs, imposed pay, NatWest; jobs, pay, working time, consultation, AXA, Prudential and Scottish Widows; job cuts). But the other side to this is that the union leaderships felt they had little where else to go, other than sticking with partnerships. Indeed, on the issue of job losses, it seemed to them that it was better being 'inside the tent' than being outside in terms of influencing the numbers and severance terms because although, on the one hand, the unions opposed the job cuts, on the other hand, they believed themselves and their members unable to prevent such losses through widespread industrial action while many members volunteered for redundancy. Therefore, the unions appeared satisfied with prior notification, consultation and an assurance to avoid compulsory redundancies (through natural wastage and seeking volunteers) (IRS 2000, *People Management* 2 March 2000), allied to some success in limiting the extent of loses and securing agreements which enhanced severance packages and offered re-training, re-deployment and relocation. But partnership agreements' robustness was also attributable to employers' willingness to exchange information, which was previously solely their preserve, and to discuss many issues which had previously been solely management affairs (see Unifi 2001). In this sense, employers practiced the art of seduction on unions by talking to and involving them at an earlier stage than hitherto was the case. Both this point – and the following point – speak to impoverished union goals during a period of depleted power, where knowledge in and of itself was seen as augmenting bargaining expertise and prowess. Contrasting the outcomes of dialogue over job cuts in the early 1990s at the TSB (IRS 1991) with those from the partnership era indicates little difference, suggesting that union impotence in the face of employer aggression leads to a lowering of union expectations. Put another way, partnership on the issue of jobs security has not delivered more than was possible than before. Although partnership deals are voted on – like the one with Global Home Loans with 93% for on a 39% turnout, the deals have deleterious ramifications for the free play of internal union criticism and dissent because they closed down spaces for this as union leaderships sought to deliver their side to the partnership bargain of mutual gains. The key differentiating factor here, compared to before, has been the bringing of partnership to the fore, and in an explicit manner.

Standing back from the trees to see the wood also suggests that research has focussed on the minutia of differences without seeing the commonalities. The gains have been few and slight with regard to material outcomes, efficacy of worker voice and union renewal. McCracken and Sanderson (2004:282–284) found labour unionism was left to do little other than carry out individual case work because its negotiating role and ability had been eroded by employers. This then fed into workers' perceptions of what labour unions did. Different densities and sets of union organisation did not appear to have substantially altered this. But to some the gains might look good or reasonable given union weakness. If the defenders of partnership (conscious or unconscious, implicit or explicit) argue that these thresholds are too high or inappropriate, they need to demonstrate that workers and their unions would have been worse off without partnership.

Assuming that employers continue to benefit from partnership because their dominant position allows them to receive 'disproportionate' reward, the forces for the ending of the agreements will emanate from the union side. One scenario may be the belief by Unite's finance section leadership that partnership is failing to produce sufficient benefits for them as a bargaining partner in terms of organisational prowess as well as in maintaining their normal relationship with members. However this would be contingent upon the leadership being prepared to broach an alternative type of (robust) bargaining relationship. Another would be a 'membership revolt' based on activists mobilising themselves and members because 'organised cooperation' was seen to be failing to deliver and so a return towards 'conflict' was required because the unions had become too close to the employers, thus relinquishing independence of policy and action. This scenario could be envisaged for partnership was not membership led, there is no evidence of a deep-seated and permanent endorsement of partnership in attitude, and support for partnership in ballots did not suggest a positive vote for given the rhetoric, promises and absence of alternatives. But given the limited strength of the Broad Left, this option would most likely become a variant of the first scenario.

## European Works Councils

Because partnership agreements are predicated on consultation rather than negotiation, it is appropriate to make a slight detour here to discuss the purchase of European Works Councils (EWCs) for labour unionism in the sector. Indeed, the rise of EWCs predicated on consultation was another normalising pressure towards partnership. By 2000, EWCs existed in AXA, Barclays, Credit Lyonnais, General Accident, HSBC, NatWest, Norwich Union, LTSB, Guardian, Royal Insurance,

Sun Alliance and NAG. Many were set up rather begrudgingly (like NAG, Guardian, HSBC), and were confined to discussing matters of a pan-European nature. Whilst recognising that the capturing of such works councils by labour unions for the purposes of *de facto* negotiation was unlikely, a number of labour unionists and pro-labour union commentators have, nonetheless, been of the view that positive gains could be made from engagement with them. Nonetheless, in a subsequent situation of mostly inclusion and solicited involvement of unions by the employers, the gains appear to have been marginal, concerning obtaining information, relationship building with employers, and meeting brother and sister labour unionists rather than robust consultation (see, for example, Cressey (1998) and IRS (1999a, 2005)). Thus, the EWCs did not appear to have given any direct or indirect boost to labour union capacity building, and they also provided the employers with another opportunity to disseminate their cultural values of commitment, partnership stakeholding and corporate strategy.

## Performance Measurement

This section considers the continuing ramifications of performance measurement for the sector's workers. In a previous era, 'working to contract' was predominant, where the psychological contract embedded in the wage-effort bargain was that job security and decent wages and conditions, including pensions, would be given for meeting basic and undifferentiated obligations. The psychological contract has been remade through performance setting and measurement, primarily and most importantly at the individual level, making pay and progression contingent, where there is the sense of being required to 'work beyond contract'. The onus has been pushed back onto the individual worker to secure their own future employment, remunerated well-being and career advancement by extending their commitment to employer goals. So what may have been common for management has now become common for workers. In this regard, Snape et al. (1993:45) argued: '[t]he aim [has been] to retain the loyalty of the staff, but at the same time encourage them to go beyond mere compliance to administrative rules by showing greater personal initiative'. The most obvious and widely used mechanism in the sector to push this agenda has been PRP as a result of performance appraisals (see also Chapter 4). But other less common means include commission- and market-based pay as well as the operationalisation of 'employability' and 'flexicurity' where it becomes the worker's – rather than the employer's – responsibility to have the required skills and working patterns and attitudes in order to meet the employer's changing requirements. Introducing share option schemes and profit-related pay were further small signifiers of employers' attempts to sensitise workers to market priorities and company goals. *In toto*, there is now no one single 'contract' but a range of contracts the individual worker can choose to sign up to. Following the awarding of zero per cent and below inflation rises to considerable numbers of staff, and the feeling amongst the affected staff that good performers at tops of scales were not getting sufficient raises, Unifi started submitting across-the-board pay demands to HSBC, RBS and LloydsTSB in 2002–2003 in order to more robustly oppose PRP. But as highlighted above with regard to the impact of the HSBC strike, campaigning was not successful (with the exception of Barclays) and, despite the continuation of effective pay cuts, there was no evidence Amicus/Unite was able to create an active and effective alliance of aggrieved and altruistic to secure those who were paid a less than inflation pay rise a rise above inflation (although the issue was kept on the union agenda – see *Morning Star* 6 June 2008, Unite press release 5 June 2008). In the case of RBS, Unifi said it would not rule out industrial action but this was never acted upon. Instead, a postcard campaign was used. One further salient development, practiced by the likes of LloydsTSB, has been to use 'local market indicators' so that pay bands are aligned to local labour market conditions, with the effect that national pay scales are undermined and extant workforce commonality fragmented.

## Call Centres, Outsourcing and Offshoring

The internal and external reorganisation and relocation of functions and jobs amongst employing organisations within and across nation-state borders in financial services, through the deployment of call (or contact) centres utilising new information and communication technologies, have been categorised by different observers as a 'new industrial divide' on a par with previous epochal transitions. This is deemed to represent the transmutation from one historical paradigm to another. Whatever the merits and demerits of this analysis, the emergence and ascendancy of call centres inside and outside the primary employing organisations in the sector have posed major challenges to labour unionism there. And, it is one which has not yet been effectively responded to – albeit, this is not likely to be a problem confined to just the sector's labour unionism (see, for example, Bain and Taylor (2008) and Taylor and Bain (2007) on offshoring).

There is little doubt that employing organisations in the sector have utilised call centres to a relatively greater degree than other sectors of economic activity (see, for example, Rose (2002), Taylor and Bain (2003)). By 2003, some 150,000 workers were employed in call centres within the sector. Levels of union presence and recognition (involving collective bargaining) were generally higher than might have been expected as a result of the cooperative extension of facilitating provisions and agreements by the main employing organisations to their new operations here (IDS 1998b, 1999b, 2000, Taylor and Bain 2003). In other cases, some recognition was won after campaigning against resistant employers (like Barclaycard) but exclusion and avoidance have been evident (like Churchill insurance). Nonetheless, and although inter-union cooperation and exchange have been prominent (Bain and Taylor 2002), significant challenges to union organisation remained due to the configuration of the predominance of younger workers, staff turnover, low porosity for lay union work to be carried out as a result of call and target intensity, and the denial of physical access to the workforce particularly as a result of multi–occupancy of buildings and security entry. In this context, Bain et al. (2004), Bain and Taylor (2002, 2008) and Taylor and Bain (1999a, 1999b, 2001, 2007) highlighted that both density and the nature of workplace unionism in call centres in the sector varied from the relatively to strong through to the relatively weak, with there being no mechanical, positive connection between high levels of density and more robust workplace unionism. The factors influencing the differences related to issues of union (inter- and intra-) and management agency, and product and labour markets. In these cases, to varying degrees, some defensive resistance was affected as were incursions into the initial operating framework of these workplaces, with some limited contestation and amelioration, but no overturning, of the managerially determined work regime. In most ways, this should come as no great surprise given contemporary labour unionism in the sector is no more or less robust than much labour unionism found elsewhere. But while there may exist the attitudinal and ideological resources and characteristics amongst the workforce to create and sustain labour unionism with, these are necessary but far from sufficient to develop the actuality of collectivism, robust or otherwise, for these must be actively situated within an environment of 'structure' and 'agency' that lend themselves to their transformation into behavioural and institutional constructs (see also Bain et al. (2004:81)) and Kelly (1998) on opportunities to act). So, for example, the potential identified by Bain and Taylor (2002) and Taylor and Bain (1999a, 1999b) does not seem, in full or part, to have been realised a decade or so later on. In terms of creating robust labour unionism, Bain and Taylor's (2002:255, 256) survey showed a favourable degree of union commitment and support from members and non-members alike but not necessarily of the 'members as the union' type for the responses (chosen from a selection) were couched in terms of 'the union should do this or that' in the vein of a purchased service as per 'union servicing'. What is of note here is that although Taylorised targets and PRP have become increasingly common throughout the sector, they are more pervasive and persuasive in call centres because of the nature of the way work is organised. This cuts both ways, being both a potential stimulant and impediment to unionisation and oppositionalism so that, on balance, opportunities for resistance (see, for example, Callaghan and Thompson (2001)) are often not transformed into durable collective actions.[13] Added to this is that the Taylorisation of tasks means that most jobs in these call centres can also be opened up to agency, out-sourced and part-time workers whose propensity to unionise is generally lower than full-time, permanent staff. So again, the potential leverage

---

13   Some years on from research that identified the potential and possibilities, it behoves research and critical faculty to investigate whether the potential was realised, and if not, why not (*cf.* Bain and Taylor 2001, 2002, Taylor and Bain 1999a, 1999b, 2001 with Rose 2002).

that a call centre offers labour unionism as a strategic component in a workflow has been hard to realise.[14]

Turning to the specificities of offshoring, the *relative* ease (see, for example, Taylor and Bain (2004)) with which this has been achieved by employing organisations in the sector is testament to, *inter alia*, the logistical difficulties that afflict labour unionism in preventing divestment and relocation as well as the impact of workers' and members' resignation to such phenomena. By early 2008, the roll call of relocations of call centre and back office functions abroad included Abbey, American Express, Aviva, AXA, Barclays, Churchill, Friends Provident, HSBC, LloydsTSB, Norwich Union, Prudential, RBS, Royal and Sun Alliance, Scottish Provident and Scottish Widows involving some 45,000 jobs by 2006.[15] According to Amicus (2005), independent research predicted that from 2002 some 200,000 jobs would be offshored, located in finance and IT primarily, by 2008. The tone of labour unionism's response to offshoring was exemplified by Unifi general secretary, Ed Sweeney:

> to stand … implacable in the face of this force is … dishonest and doomed to failure. This does not mean that we simply roll over. We can and will seek to slow the process, limit its impact, cut the numbers involved and demand guarantees of no compulsory redundancies … . (Unifi *Fusion*, October 2003, see also *Fusion* February–March 2004)

Sometimes these objectives were gained (e.g., AXA, Barclays), sometimes they were not (e.g., Aviva, Scottish Widows). A key explanatory variable was that in the case of Aviva in 2004, Amicus' attitude was couched in terms of 'if our members want to strike, we will back them' leading to little leverage, rather than working proactively to build up a head of steam. The same can be said about Unifi issuing threats of industrial action *if* compulsory redundancies occurred (*Herald* 26 September 2003). Examining labour unionism's record opposing and ameliorating the effects of offshoring on jobs, Bain and Taylor (2008) and Taylor and Bain (2007) *de facto* concluded that in sector the response was no more or less effective than in others. Similarly, the salient differentiating factors were degrees and nature of membership mobilisation, membership attitudes and orientation and approach of national union leaderships. For example, they contrasted the activity of LTU in 2003 – which consisted of employer lobbying and public campaigning similar to that of the CWU over BT – and provided for little headway in preventing the job losses or securing enhanced severance arrangements to that of Amicus in Prudential in 2002

---

14   Thus, the impact of the first (one-day) strike in a call centre – by CWU members in BT in 1999 – was not one that permeated strongly through call centres (*cf.* Taylor and Bain's (2001:41) bombastically couched overestimation).

15   Call centre employment in the sector still then remains significant and on this bare-minimum level, at least remains, there exists the theoretical possibility of unionisation of non-union operations.

where Amicus was able to mobilise its local members with the genuine threat of industrial action to gain a job security package (whereby there was a parallel with the success of USDAW at Reality and PCS with Siemens Business Services). But when the agreement expired in 2006, Amicus was unable to repeat this advance, secure employment and prevent compulsory redundancies.[16] Of salience here is also the case of HSBC where the Unifi national leadership appeared to have misjudged the mood of a significant proportion of members and discounted their ability as workplace leaders to cohere wider numbers of members around a more robust response (see Bain and Taylor 2008).[17] Common to other labour unions, and notwithstanding resource-related difficulties, those in the sector seemed to have been incapable of implementing an effective strategy of simultaneously raising the costs of leaving one country and entering another in terms of the full array of potential levers (economic, political, industrial and social). To date, for example, UNI (Union Network International) has tried to facilitate the unionisation of call centres in India, Unifi gave £30,000 in 2004 to UNI to help in this task, and Unifi/Amicus/Unite has worked with and supported the UNITES union in India (Unifi *Fusion*, October 2003, *Morning Star* 4 June 2008). But this has been small beer. Consequently, in the sector the dominant approach by labour unionism has been characterised by press work, surveys of members/customers, urging customers to switch banks and make complaints to the Financial Services Authority, lobbying MPs/local councillors, arguing for government inquiry, holding consultative ballots, lunchtime protests, postcard campaigns, AGM protests, and promotion of non-offshoring employers. One particular aspect of the union media campaign has been to emphasise attrition rates in offshored operations leading to poorer customer quality, lower productivity and efficiency, and more mistakes given that companies were sensitive to 'bad' public relations as well as being open to corporate social responsibility issues over the social and economic costs of divestment. As with before (Chapter 4 and concluding chapter), there is nothing inherently moderate about this response unless it was implemented to the exclusion and subordination of industrial action – which it did seem to be.

Whilst offshoring has had the lion's share of attention, (domestic) outsourcing has been as much a threat to employment covered by the sector's labour unionism and the labour unionism itself. For example, Prudential outsourced 1,700 staff in 2007 to Capita. However, there has been less mobilisation against it because, in a period of sectoral industrial quiescence, the main method available to labour unionism has consisted of deploying and mobilising non-membership forces like the public, customers, opinion formers and so on to try to ameliorate offshoring. The crux of the difference was that mobilisation of these forces can be undertaken

---

16  However, the picture is slightly more complicated for LTU made a strike threat regarding the Newcastle call centre and balloted members there on conditions of transfer to Securicor which led to concessions.

17  Again, the picture is more ambiguous for at the initial reps meeting only 40% were present albeit this was a Saturday meeting.

because the employment was leaving the nation-state whereas as outsourcing was regarded as socially acceptable within the confines of the nation-state. In other words, there was a mobilising focus around offshoring as 'super' neo-liberalism while outsourcing is seen as 'normal' neo-liberalism. And as outlined above, seldom has there been industrial resistance to outsourcing – indeed, where there has been some such resistance, it has commonly focussed on IT workers because of their strategic position. The one case of industrial action was that of a successful one-day strike by Amicus IT members at Cooperative Insurance Services over pensions in 2004. Where industrial action, or threats thereof, was not used, Unifi/Amicus and MSF/Amicus were able to maintain pension entitlement and recognition with the new employers at Standard Chartered in 2001 and Barclays in 2002. In a further deal with Barclays for outsourcing in 2004, Unifi was able to gain a pledge of no compulsory redundancies for 6 years for the 1450 staff transferring to Accenture. However, success was far from dominant as with the outsourcing from Barclaycard to Xansa (Unifi *e-fusion* 22 April 2004).

**Conclusion**

For labour unionism, the early period of the new millennium was marked by stasis at the best, and the three 'D's' at the worst. The latter is a more robust conclusion as a result of the incorporation and control through partnership, the further encroachment of the managerial prerogative, the poor capacity to mobilise collective resistance, Unifi's inability to grow organically or inorganically despite the resources put into this and its federal structure and so on. Labour unionism was buffeted by pillar-to-post by successive reorganisations and initiatives taken by employers. The years as a whole thus mark another turning point, pointing to an uncertain future for independent labour unionism in the sector. The ratcheting up of the financial crisis in late 2008 and the prospect of a general recession, with job losses in the sector predicted at in excess of 100,000 as a consequence, only further served to emphasise the huge and overwhelming challenges facing the labour unionism of the finance workers. The merger of LloydsTSB and HBoS with thousands of ensuing redundancies was but only one of the most visible signs of capital restructuring and rationalisation that took place in late 2008.

# Chapter 6
# Putting Historical Processes into Perspective and Prospects for the Future

## Introduction

Although matters of labour relations are not conventionally conceived as being at centre of employer thinking because issues of labour exploitation are said to flow downstream from issues of market exploitation, they nonetheless remain a critical component in the pursuit of employer accumulation strategies. Part of this conventional conceptualisation arises from absence of persuasive and pervasive threats to the managerial prerogative from workers. If this was not the case, then it is reasonable to suggest that employers would be far more concerned that labour relations did not prevent the realisation of profit in the marketplace by disrupting the flow of good and services to it. In other words, this approach focuses attention on a number of substantive questions, namely, a) what is it that employers do to assure themselves of labour peace and the 'right' balance in the wage-effort bargain for them to be able to get their goods and services to market in order to realise the endpoint of their accumulation strategies?, b) what is that workers do to contest the employers' terms for the wage-effort bargain and the regime under which this is determined?, and c) what explains the relative success, or otherwise, of each party in prosecuting their strategies? Two further, counter-factual, questions can be asked here to try to get a measure of the issues: how much more freedom and control would management have had if there had been no labour unionism (*cf.* Holden 1999:226); and how much more infringement on the managerial prerogative could labour unionism have constituted? In the case of the financial services sector in Britain, it is clear that employers took considerable and distinct conscious steps to control independent labour unionism by deploying dependent labour unionism in their service. The effect of this was to limit independent unionism but not without dependent unionism becoming more unionate. Thus, employers expended considerable resource to counter a perceived threat and were not entirely successful in doing so (*cf.* Jenkins and Sherman 1979:52). The point of introducing the concluding chapter in this way is to argue that the study of labour unionism in the sector is not a study of processes and outcomes that were inconsequential or on the margins. To conclude otherwise is to not ask the salient questions about how and why employers maintained their hegemony as a result of their own actions and those of labour unionism.

So, this final chapter seeks to bring all the conclusions from the previous chapters together to form a coherent endpoint and in so doing provide more than just the customary summary and restatement. Thus, the thesis and its themes are considered; workplace unionism, turning points, forms and models of labour unionism, militancy and moderation, political complexions and so on. To aid the task of evaluation, a section considers the sister labour unionism in the Republic of Ireland (Eire). However, this chapter begins with a brief overview of the study so far.

## Summary Recapitulation

Notwithstanding its two variations, labour unionism in the financial services sector in Britain was historically able to gain a credible organisational presence under terms of relative employment relations stability, where latterly imposed radical and far-reaching changes in terms and conditions of employment provided a stimulus to collective industrial action on a hitherto unforeseen scale. However, the resistance was not sufficiently widespread or robust, and neither were results of this resistance sufficiently encouraging or powerful, to be a stimulus to further or more widespread action. The unions as organisations were unable to mobilise further or wider action given their historically informed weakness and the union leaderships moved towards a position of social partnership from previously advocating limited confrontation with the employers. Coupled with further and widespread deleterious changes to members' terms of employment, the existing collectivism became overwhelmed and weakened. Thus, membership levels have fallen in relative and absolute terms and union organisational cohesion has declined. The original project of ending much of the divided representation has achieved but it has been compelled through weakness.

## Workplace Unionism[1]

The central line of inquiry of this study has revolved around the combination of the absence and underdevelopment of workplace unionism within the original independent labour unionism and the subsequently reformed dependent labour unionism in the financial services sector. This can be summarised very succinctly by observing that there is no tangible sense in which employers in the sector have experienced a 'challenge from below' as other employers have experienced in the post-Second World War period. The locus where the contestation of the terms of the wage-effort bargain has taken place has been outside the workplace. Before reviewing the results of this inquiry, it is worth noting that since the early 1990s many other labour unions which previously were characterised by the marked presence of many robust workplace unionisms are now not – or certainly not to

---

1   To reiterate a point, the configuration of forces and attendant outcomes in insurance has been slightly different, and more so in building societies where unionateness has been less developed.

the extent they were before – as a result of atrophy. The salience of this is that without having developed its own workplace unionisms, labour unionism in the sector is now on a par with other labour unionisms as they have been pushed backwards. Moreover, the annual reports of BIFU and Unifi indicated that many of its smaller company sections and company committees were inactive and their newsletters gave a sense of membership disengagement from union. In this sense, the extra-workplace organisation of and relational links within BIFU/Unifi were also affected by the general retreat experienced here by labour unionism.

Although Blackburn's (1967) concept of 'unionateness' was used extensively in this study as a means by which to understand and measure developments in the *modus operandi* and values of labour unionism, this cannot be done without also using it critically. One highly salient dimension that requires adding to extend the purchase of unionateness concerns that of the 'form' of union practice, for form both reflects and influences the manifestations of, to use Blackburn's terms, completeness and character. Specifically here, the phenomenon of workplace unionism is central for it holds the potential to develop union members' bargaining awareness and capability as well as their collective mobilising capacity. The two together can represent a potent force. However, it is difficult to talk of the existence or development of workplace unionism in the sector in either substantial historical or contemporary terms as has been the case in, say, printing, manufacturing or engineering in Britain (see, for example, Terry (1983, 1995)). The reasons for this are primarily concerned with the contingent interplay of the high degree of employer hostility to labour unionism, the ramifications of the industry-wide nature and structure of many finance sector employers, and the adopted structure of labour unionism.[2] This analysis is quite different from the one-dimensional explanation put forward by Storey et al. (1999:149) concerning employer hostility. Before proceeding, and in full awareness of not setting the bar too high, *bona fide*, *de facto* workplace unionism would have the following main characteristic, namely, the deliberate and meaningful collective association between members within the workplace (in and across departments and sections), which is sufficiently independent of the employer to facilitate focusing upon workers' collective interests in the workplace. From this, one could expect the collective contestation of working conditions within the workplace and membership participation in the democratic processes of the union with regard to issues directly related to the workplace.[3] So the central focus would be on job control or regulation of immediate working conditions. The extremely widespread absence of this phenomenon has

---

2   One issue which has not been explored in this study is that of the implications of the trifurcation of the relationship in employment in the sector. Whilst employers have used the discourse of the customer, research is needed to explore the impact of worker-customer inter-action upon workplace unionism. The same is true of the use of employment agency workers here.

3   Salient issues thereafter would revolve around the ambitiousness of bargaining agendas and degrees and nature of resultant mobilisation and self-reliance.

to be viewed as the result of the interaction of the above factors in the context of a socially conservative group of workers who have been influenced *and* shaped by a socially conservative work and employment experience.[4] Each factor warrants some elucidation and explanation.

Firstly, employer hostility through substitution and suppression, rather than ambivalence and agnosticism, not only dampened the ability to develop independent unionism and favoured, supported and resourced the development of dependent unionism but it also conditioned the nature of independent unionism. This pertains to independent labour unionism within the workplace and the help and hindrance that it received from its own extra-workplace labour unionism. So employers imposed costs upon and gave rewards to those involved in the different types of unionism. Quite apart from their high degree of resources, employers were helped in this by the socially conservative and individually aspirational nature of those they recruited and did so using the cultural mechanisms of authoritarian paternalism rather than direct control.

Secondly, the ramifications of the 'industry'-wide nature and structure of a relatively small[5] number of finance sector employers refers to the historical influences of both the standardised and bureaucratised means of operation and terms and conditions of employment. On the one hand, the high degree of standardisation and uniformity of mass delivered products/services in each company (and to a large extent across companies) facilitated common operating and work practices, and common terms and conditions of employment[6], while on the other hand, the centralisation of command and control structures of financial services sector employers, constituted as large bureaucracies with a presence of national dimensions, reduced the room for job regulation. Consequently, no stimulus was given to develop the organs of collective representation at the workplace level. Both standardisation and centralisation were created by senior management, and in regard of the former, this was facilitated by the absence of highly skilled, specialist, professionalised or craft jobs and tasks. The overall effect here has been to create its own reflection in centralised operations of labour unions and staff associations which have prevented, by and large, the development of the ability and capacity to bargain in the workplace, leaving ordinary members as relatively passive onlookers in the determination of their terms and conditions of employment. Centralised collective bargaining of a sectoral or company nature has been another aspect of this phenomenon, where not even the contesting or ensuring the interpretation of national agreements has been available in the workplace to

---

4    It is conventionally understood that pay levels in the sector are not necessarily better than those for skilled manual workers but that the fringe benefits and status of such office work give the veneer of superiority which, for some, has been a disincentive to unionise.

5    This is the case when compared, for example, to the number of employers in printing, engineering and manufacturing.

6    The absence of piece work and payment-by-results systems and the presence of measured day work was another contributory factor here.

labour unionism. Although the staff associations have a different genesis, the same is true for them, albeit that the degree of employer interference and dependence represents a greater obstacle to the development of workplace unionism.

Thirdly, and to compound these matters, the form of organisation adopted by both labour unions and staff associations has been one centred on geographical rather than workplaces branches. Reflecting inhospitable environs, the absence of the implications for job regulation as a result of non-specialist work and the small size of many workplaces, where the perceived need was to draw together all the clutches of activists, regional rather than workplace branches were established. The creation of aggregate unionism in the form of ASTMS and NUBE in the 1970s cemented this trajectory by agreeing to terms of amalgamation which granted substantial autonomy to the former staff associations. For independent unionism in banking, the configuration of these factors is more complex. In attempting to provide a form of labour unionism which was independent of employers, it set itself up in juxtaposition to the staff associations. As they represented dependence in the form of single company internalist unionism, the BOG/NUBE constructed itself as industry-wide and geographically based to assert its independence and difference. Part of the rationale here was to avoid internal union pressures to end up as a federation of company unions under *de facto* pressure from its own members and external staff associations. This configured perspective of independence led to geographical expressions of organisation, with multi-employer branches.[7] Aside from any logistical difficulties for membership participation and the disinclination this can give rise to, this structure de-emphasised the workplace *per se* and specific workplaces and, in so doing, did not provide a stimulant to members participating in their union because their most immediate experience of the workplace was not given prominence (notwithstanding the impact of centralisation identified above). By the early 1990s, the majority of – but far from all – branches were institutional rather than geographical, multi-employer ones (and this was also true of Unifi upon its creation in 1999) but this did not make much positive difference as the focus remained outside the workplace and the branches were not well attended, in large part, due to the way they had operated before as multi-employer branches and because of the centralisation of union power in company committees. But in addition to these, there are two further factors that account for the 'underdevelopment' of workplace unionism in the sector, namely, the impact of national or industry-wide collective bargaining, and the consequences of employers granting of facility time.

The accession of MEB in 1968 in banking was also to consciously stymie the possibility of development of workplace unionism by NUBE, and in this regard, the banks were successful. In essence, this outcome had a number of dimensions. First, the form of MEB adopted did not give any impetus to workplace unionism for the content of these industry-wide negotiations was exclusive not complimentary.

---

7    Wills (1996:367) pointed out that in some cases members' branches were based on where they lived and not where they worked.

For example, some MEB was premised on the negotiations being the aggregation of the demands and strength of workplace unionism and, thereafter, there was the possibility of 'top-up' bargaining for those workplace unionisms that were capable of achieving this. This was not the case in banking. Second, MEB in the sector came into being before a workplace presence was developed in most instances so that it tended to freeze what was or was not already in existence by that point. Third, the form of union recognition accorded to NUBE (and the staff associations) was at the institutional level rather than also at any of its sub-levels like the workplace and so this acted as another bulwark against the development of workplace unionism and another support to the MEB structures. Again, this helped reinforce centralisation within NUBE at the national and company committee level.

The granting of recognition and facility time to lay officials had important consequences for workplace unionism. The seconded reps were full-time company level reps while the accredited reps were for sections of the company with some partial amount of facility time. The former engaged in dialogues with senior managers and the latter with lower and middle level managers. Employers granted this array of facility time as a result of the demonstration of sufficient membership support but this was seldom set at the threshold of majority support as employers sought orderly industrial relations. In other cases, union recognition was granted after which members were recruited. The salience of this was that union recognition and facility time were not gained through membership mobilisation and in situations of conflict where workers' consciousness was raised (as was the case in many other instances outside the sector). Consequently, the impact of the facility time was to substitute itself for what might have otherwise been the development of workplace activism. Moreover, the intention behind employers granting such facility time was to create responsible and orderly bargaining as well as representative agents that could deal with the problems the employers saw emerging and in a way they favoured. In this overall sense, the 'top' or leadership of the union in the workplace existed before the 'bottom' and members did. The dynamic that was then set up was one of regular form of atomised contact with members through newsletters and consultative ballot as referenda but without collective participation as part of a vibrant collective identity. Where some workplace unionism did develop, this has been the result of the dynamic and mutually reinforcing interplay of the positive ramifications of the creation of a very small number of centres of strategic operation per employing organisation, a reasonable size of workforce in such workplaces (like 100> workers), their location in conducive regional settings with regard to local labour union traditions, and the feeling of non-substitutability by dint of their skills and function amongst the concerned workers giving them air of (collective) confidence. On this basis, one can differentiate here, for example, between a call centre and a data processing centre. And, therefore, it did not take long for the employers to put IT/data processing workers into separate bargaining units so that their 'power' was ring-fenced. This task was eased by virtue of these workers not having the same occupational identity as finance workers and the ability and availability to work elsewhere.

There have been, *inter alia*, three important historical outcomes of this 'underdevelopment' of workplace unionism. One has been to reinforce the dominant historical sense of union membership as both bought service and business transaction, where an insurance-based protection scheme for a 'rainy day' is obtained. Consequently, this perspective of passivity does not envisage a role of self-activism and agency which are essential for workplace unionism, and here there was something of a 'Catch-22' situation. Part of the consequence of this configuration was also a separation of activists from members. The other was that come the time that the materialist basis for workplace unionism existed from the late 1980s onwards, in terms of the devolution of management responsibility and the introduction of aggressive and assertive managerial strategies in the form HRM practices like performance appraisals and PRP, the sector's labour unionism was not in much of a position to take up the cudgels and benefit from this. Its undue reliance on employer resource and goodwill during the epoch of paternalism and pluralism meant that it could not fall back on its own independent resource to do so. Labour unionism's weakness was further undermined by the constant state of market flux leading to organisational churn (see, for example, Taylor et al. (2005)), making the possibility of turning the 'potential' into 'actual' a low one. Therefore, the possibility of union renewal at this point and through this means was almost non-existent (*cf.* Fairbrother 1989, 2000). Another outcome has been that without an independent resource of workplace unionism, labour unionism in the sector has become dependent to a large extent upon employers for facility time and resources such that this has had the potential to limit its freedom of manoeuvre and choice with regard to *de facto* partnership, formal partnership and the tasks to which seconded and accredited reps are deployed.

## Junctures and Turning Points

Although always prone to the subjective gaze and never an exact science, there is a palpable sense that in the unfolding of social processes of the labour unionism of the sector, it has been both the victim and creator of specific junctures of history. These 'turning points' heuristically signify and embody in a stark, visible way the subterranean, almost invisible changes that take place. But there is also the sense in which these turning points create new social structures or psychological moods which compel or facilitate different directions to be embarked upon by the actors concerned. The chapters were based around the most important of these. The cumulative import of the turning points was to help be able to map out the direction of travel and to show that each staging post of development had a pre-history (sic) where legacies were important, but not in a *dirigiste* way, for subsequent processes and outcomes. A clear example concerns the *realpolitik* of why the BOG/NUBE desired MEB even though that was a difficult objective to gain: the BOG/NUBE did not want CLB as that would have reinforced internalism and the staff associations, make it difficult to differentiate itself from the staff associations and undermine its rationale to be a national union for bank workers. All this can be traced back to employers' actions in the immediate post-First World War juncture. Another example concerns the sense in which both independent and dependent unionism as overall agencies 'missed the boat' when they became more unionate because it was a case of 'too little, too late' to pose an effective challenge to the employers' interests, actions and policy initiatives (like partnership). Of course, within this there were subordinate currents urging more and sooner (see below). So, contrary to the hope of the then UNiFI general secretary (IRS 1996:12), UNiFI did not become the 'salvation' of labour unionism in the sector or of the union movement as a whole. Indeed, Unifi did not become the salvation of either because its creation signified the turning point that the 'old' cooperation and separation of labour unionism were no longer seen to be delivering upon their tasks at the time of the three 'D's.

## Struggles between Different Forms of Labour Unionism

Although the staff associations in banking were a response to the BOG and not *vice-versa*, the BOG/NUBE/BIFU and its policies and *modus vivendi* became essentially defined in opposition to them, such was the formers' potency and resilience. On the other hand, the BOG/NUBE/BIFU solidified the staff associations' existence and purpose for a long period of time. Indeed, as the staff associations demonstrated their adaptability, evolving into staff unions and jettisoning some of their internalist and mutual gains ideology, they remained defined, in large part, by not being the BOG/NUBE/BIFU. The dialectical sense of thesis and anti-thesis was, therefore, acute. Synthesis ultimately evolved as each represented the unstoppable force and the immovable object on a collision course with each other. Because neither side of labour unionism could inflict the 'killer blow' on the other, this was a long-drawn out war of attrition until the calculations of war were changed. If the victory has been that of independent unionism as the staff associations have become increasingly unionate, where independent unionism helped undermine the basis of internalism by pulling staff associations away from the employers and forcing the employers to facilitate greater staff association effectiveness, then it has been a rather pyrrhic one. In insurance, with a more diverse capital structuration, a similar but less powerful process of struggle and unification took place, where independent labour unionism far predated the creation of staff associations and there were more units of independent labourism. In building societies, staff associations were established much later, particularly as a result of combined pressure from the state and independent labour unionism, but again the same type of struggle and unification were evident.

In any and all of the sub-sectors, independent labour unionism faced the problematic of showing itself to be moderate but more effective than dependent labour unionism which necessitated creating independent leverage, especially where there was no unilateral arbitration available. But it commonly had too few members to put this strategy on a firm footing and being moderate and more effective were often not reconcilable ends. Indeed, employers took the fairly early step in banking of providing the staff associations with a means – unilateral arbitration – that underpinned them, made then more effective and obviated their need for the development of mobilising capacity. When this mechanism was withdrawn for both forms of labour unionism, in circumstances of work intensification, then both had to become more assertive and effective, undermining the basis of internalism and cooperation. When the staff associations moved 'leftwards', in part due to competition with independent unionisms, this allowed and forced independent unionisms 'leftwards' as well (albeit as below). It was this that pushed the centre of gravity unionate-wards. Outside of banking, without the detour of unilateral arbitration, the same pattern is again detectable in broad measure.

So there was a dialectical and symbiotic relationship between independent and dependent labour unionism. Each was founded on difference in approach albeit within the commonly agreed agenda of responsible, respectable, moderate and non-political worker representation and within the parameters of an environment heavily influenced by powerful employers. Each exerted a push and pull on the other to be different but not too different. Either faced degeneration if they were too far apart or too close together. However, over time the centre of gravity on which they did this shifted unionate-ward. This did not necessarily make the task of independent unionism any easier because there was still the same form of inter-union competition. That said, two caveats need to be entered into. The concessions to staff associations and internalism by independent unionism were greater in insurance (*vis-à-vis* federal structures) while amongst the building societies moves towards unionateness have been extremely limited, being organisational rather than collective action based. Stepping back from this, it is testament to the demand for independent, collective representation as well as it own underlying resilience and endurance that independent labour unionism was not snuffed out in its formative years. That said, the complexity of the processes involved meant that compromises were enforced upon independent labour unionism so that it did not operate as it wished. In this regard, the staff associations fulfilled a demand of what was possible and permitted as cheaper and adaptable 'second best'. But as Jenkins and Sherman (1979:52) argued: 'in the long run the staff association nearly always proves counter-productive to the employer who sponsored it in the first place'. So, overall, and to paraphrase the meaning of Marx again, workers here made their own history but not in ways and circumstances that they would have chosen or that favoured them.

**Unionateness: Militancy and Moderation**

One of the key aspects of the investigation of developing unionateness in response to changing environmental conditions has been the inquiry into the presence or absence of militancy amongst the financial services sector workers.

Three characteristics stand out amongst the salient studies. First, there have been conflicting analyses. For example, Upchurch et al. (2006:395) argued 'the independent unions [i.e., MSF/Amicus and BIFU/Unifi] [in] the sector ... have traditionally recorded low levels of militancy' while Deery and Walsh (1999:263) stated 'militancy has increased in the banking sector [in Britain in 1990s]'. Second, most studies have conflated militancy solely with the taking of strike activity (save Kelly (1996, 1998) for conceptualisation and Gall (1997, 2001) for empirical studies in the financial services sector). For example, Undy et al. (1981:79, 257–260) categorised both ASTMS and NUBE on many occasions as displaying militancy. Third, the sense of relativism has been pronounced whereby militancy has been judged in relation to only what happened immediately before. For example, one instance of a group of workers voting for strike action which had never before done so has been categorised as militant behaviour when it would be more appropriate to use the term if striking took place and then became part of a standard repertoire of industrial tactics. But this tendency does not just concern industrial action. Blackburn's (1967) study is replete with the uses of the term when describing BOG/NUBE's attitude and (non-industrial action based) behaviour to the staff associations. But not only are 'words'[8] easier than 'action' but using the staff associations as the point of reference is not particularly robust.

In line with these points and in previous works (Gall 1993, 1997, 1999, 2001), I did not argue that finance workers, and bank workers in particular, were becoming 'militant' or becoming 'more militant'. Indeed, in my first and widely cited analysis (Gall 1993), I did not use the terms 'militant' or 'militancy' because they were inappropriate for any group of finance or bank workers. Rather, I employed Blackburn's (1967) conceptualisation of unionateness and made nuanced and qualified points but did argue that what was happening was, nonetheless, clearly a departure for finance workers (*cf.* Edwards 1983, Hyman 1984:32) and for a rightwing, moderate union like BIFU. Despite this, a number of writers have wrongly interpreted what I argued as finance or bank workers doing just that (see Cressey and Scott (1993:72, 73), Edwards (1995:442), Danford et al. (2003:102–103), IRS (1993:6), Storey (1995:25), Storey et al. (1997:26–27), Upchurch and Danford (2001:105), Wills (1996:362))[9] despite my careful analysis and conscious choice of terms. Indeed, Storey et al. (1997:27) wrote that I 'suggested militancy among bank workers will become the norm'. I then went on in subsequent articles (Gall 1997, 1999, 2001) to point that this was an incorrect interpretation but to no avail. I, therefore, also believe that Deery and Walsh (1999:263) and Kelly (1996:92) were misguided to also categorise bank and finance workers as becoming

---

8   For example, Pugh (1998:34) reported that BIFU took a far more assertive position than IUHS on the implications for jobs as a result of a merger in the Halifax, this being relatively easy as BIFU had few members and could engage in competitive 'grandstanding'.

9   Indeed, Lawler and Serrano del Rosal (1999:159) were the only authors to have correctly characterised my argument.

'militant', certainly if one uses Kelly's (1996) own conceptualisation of militancy where the elements of mobilisation and goal-setting were not ambitious. This misdiagnosis arises because these writers have a one-dimensional view whereby they wrongly and simplistically conflate the mere taking of industrial action with militancy.

To restate the basic tenets of my argument then, strike action has still to affect the majority of workers in the sector (particularly the building societies and insurance companies) and there is no indication that taking industrial action has become a habitual or permanent state of affairs. Nevertheless, their strike activity was still salient as many workers not only took strike action for the first time in their histories but also struck twice in a period of less than five years, and in one case (Barclays) engaged in three one-day strikes in one dispute (*cf.* Gall 1997:223). This generally reflected that negotiations took longer, with more impositions of terms, more rejections of offers, more disputes and more industrial action ballots in the sector as a whole. Despite such caveats here and in the three previous chapters, strike action began to become a relatively more acceptable currency amongst union members and a relatively more 'normal' part of the industrial relations landscape within banking. Taken as a given that employers' actions are necessary to stimulate such responses and setting aside the particular nature of their actions and how these have varied over time, the forces pushing towards the greater use of strike action amongst bank workers were three-dimensional. Guided and directed by the EUOs as well-regarded leaders of the national unions, and supported by the majority of activists, the membership became willing to endorse these infrequently used methods of bargaining on a more regular basis. Critical to understanding this process was the wish of the EUOs to prevent the erosion of the unions' bargaining strength with increasingly unilateralist employers and to maintain their credibility with their members as effective bargaining agents at a time of greater member receptiveness to these non-traditional methods of operation. This process was itself associated with, and ran alongside, a considerable and credible membership density in this period. Specifically, taking such a path towards oppositionalism was possible given this membership base. But since the late 1990s, these developments have been thrown into reverse by the combined effect of the decline in industrial action and the rise of partnership agreements. These developments were influenced and affected by parallel developments with regard to the overall decline in industrial action and the rise of partnership agreements across the economy. This emphasises the contingent and transitory nature of the advances towards unionateness.

In assessing and explaining what has been shown to be the generally moderate approach of independent labour unionism in the pursuit of finance workers' interest representation, a considerable amount of nuance and sophistication are needed for it is an erroneous oversimplification to, for example, make the positive correlation between the absence of significant or widespread strike action and moderation because issues of power and effectiveness need to be integrated into any calculation. Thus, strike action can be called by a group of workers, suggesting militancy, but if it is called without the credible chance of success then it is ill-conceived and damaging for, all other things being equal, it will disincline workers to strike in the future. Alternatively, not striking or calling off a strike might be a rational and credible course of action where there is no majority support for such a strike. Moreover, the taking of lower forms of industrial action may subsequently help facilitate the taking of higher forms of industrial action if collective confidence and consciousness are developed as a result. Here, the other issue concerned what kinds of non-industrial action were compatible and/or supportive of industrial action. So in regard of the relationship of taking strike action (without attention to the ambitiousness or otherwise of demands) and militancy, there is a complex set of potential relationships. This is multiplied (Gall 2003) when one considers the other dimensions of militancy outlined by Kelly (1996, 1998) such as mobilisation, institutional deployment, methods and ideology. Taken as a (decontextualised) collection of means and tactics, the following survey of activities relating to pay, jobs and conditions could attest to clear evidence of moderation. After the survey, examination will be made of whether this is, in fact, the case and whether it represents evidence of ideological or instrumentally contingent moderation.

Legal means of redress over, *inter alia*, repetitive strain injury (RSI), pension entitlement, fixed term contracts and equal pay, have been deployed in terms of fighting individual personal compensation claims and test cases (which are pursued with a view to establishing precedence in order to exert legal and extra-legal leverage over the situation of others) through Industrial/Employment Tribunals, and civil and high court cases. Other legal means have utilised the application of existing legislation like Equal Pay Audits. Direct approaches to employers have been based on meetings in which the company has been cross-examined on their business cases for their intended or taken actions as a way of trying to, and in the hope of showing, the companies the errors of their ways in terms of customer relations and brand recognition damage. Sometimes research has been commissioned to help do this.

Independent labour unionism has also deployed political lobbying to a large degree. Beginning with press and media work through releases and responses, and often deploying petitions and surveys of members and customers, this activity has been used to try to exert influence on opinion formers and policy makers (like the Scottish Financial Services Strategy Group), regulators (like the Financial Services Authority) and legislators (central and devolved governments as well as individual MPs, MSPs, AMs and local councillors) either through publicity or behind-the-scenes lobbying by EUOs. Here the targeted outcomes have been parliamentary investigations, government inquiries, and positive statements to indirectly influence employers or facilitate direct policy changes by employers. The premise of the attempt to influence the employers through the media has been that employers do not like 'bad' or 'negative' publicity. Sometimes, newspaper adverts have been paid for to do this. And since the new millennium, attempts have been used to run with, and benefit from, the corporate social responsibility (CSR) agenda. Seldom have there been instances of using these initial means (petitions, surveys, publicity) as ways to create extensive membership or popular mobilisation in order to try to exert leverage on these aforementioned political bodies.

Where membership mobilisation has occurred, it has primarily taken the form of the use of consultative ballots, petitioning, lunchtime protests, public leafleting, postcards campaigns, protests at employer AGMs and so on. Other than the consultative ballots and petitioning, very small groups of members, that is, essentially just activists and workplace reps were involved in organising and taking part in the protests, leafleting and petitioning (and these activists and reps do not in themselves constitute large numbers). Those means that are more extensive in terms of involving a wider array of members (ballots, petitions, postcards) had been based on a small level of involvement and activity. More importantly here, seldom were the ballots intended to be used or used as tools to mobilise for further and greater membership activity (such as industrial action ballots) which potentially disrupt the operations of the employer. Rather, they have been used to send symbolic messages to employers to try to strengthen the union negotiating hand at the bargaining table. Customer mobilisation has also been attempted through encouraging customers to switch accounts and make complaints to the financial services companies. So, notwithstanding the historic developments outlined elsewhere in this study, on the occasions when industrial action has been utilised since the 1980s, it has been on a tokenistic, protestant and demonstrative rather than hard-hitting nature. More often that not, the aim has been to bring employers back to the bargaining table rather than gain significant concessions at the bargaining table. Looked at another way, the action has been to say to employers, 'Look at what we can do – don't make us do more!' rather than 'Now that we've shut down your operations, you must give in!'

Turning to the nature of membership attitudes and values, the dominant characteristic has been instrumental, rather than ideological, collectivism[10] and within which the EUOs in the unions have remained hegemonic. Most members have attitudes which coalesce around a distant relationship with their national union, an extremely low level of involvement in workplace and branch union affairs, and politically conservative or moderate views (where 'new' Labour has ceased to be a social democratic party). Such members currently wish to be 'serviced'. Only a minority have engaged in higher levels of union involvement where instrumentalism is more evenly balanced by ideological commitment to collectivism. These are predominantly found in the large employers. Following from this, the relationship between members and EUOs in finance unions is best described as a mixture of 'professional' and 'managerial', rather than 'participative', unionism (see below). Even in BIFU/Unifi, few initiatives have come from the membership and membership is encouraged throughout the unions by a servicing

---

10   Hartley (1996) argued that the individually-orientated instrumental attitudes toward union membership in the financial services sector may not be very different from that found in other labour unions.

culture of professional representation. This has not been significantly altered by the rise of the 'organising culture' since the late 1990s.

One aspect of the deprioritisation of more robust, collective responses (and collective bargaining as the *modus operandi*) by both independent and dependent forms of labour unionism, under the strain on general union retreat, was the re-emphasis of the advocacy and practice of an individual-based servicing relationship with members. The instances of this comprise Uniservice, a wholly owned subsidiary of Unifi whose remit was to provide financial services and benefits to its members and those of other unions, the job agency for redundant members called Unifi4jobs.com which was established in 2003 and Rory Murphy[11], former MSF official and NWSA general secretary and then joint-general secretary of Unifi, advocating a new type of highly individualised union membership called 'pay as you go' (*Independent* 14 September 1999, *Unions Today* January 2000), whereby clients would phone a call centre in the first instance for support and advice and lay structures would become superfluous. Of course, this type of activity is not historically entirely new in the labour unionism of the sector and it is not just that the main organ of independent labour unionism practiced it. For example, the LTU commented 'LTU membership is, in many ways, like a form of insurance' (LTU *Newsletter* 26 July 2000) where it argued that its role was to give information and advice, and interpret and act on members' concerns without any hint of the desirability of self-activity or 'organising'. Meantime, the NWSA in its members' magazine, *Counterpoints* (May 1999) stated: 'Joining a trade union is like paying your car or house insurance. You pay your subscriptions – just in case – not after the disaster has happened. Your union is funded by members' subscriptions, so to expect immediate help without paying your dues is basically sponging off your colleagues'.

Before moving to an overall assessment of this *prima facie* moderation, the specific case of employment retrenchment is considered. Thus, in the early 1990s, BIFU had what would have been regarded in the 1980s as fairly standard labour union policy on job cuts/redundancies, job security and job creation, but which now from the vantage point of the new millennium looked more radical: casuals laid off before staff, a four-day, 28–hour week and so on. When one turns to examine operationalisation, the means involved raising concerns, disseminating the policy and winning support for it amongst members (given the policy emanated from conference decisions which are more a reflection of activists than members) and other allies and agencies. In addition to the small number of specific instances

---

11    Interestingly, he became HR director at outsourcing consultancy, Morgan Chambers, as its human resource director because he believed he could make a bigger and better difference for employees from the other side of the fence (*Personnel Today* 7 June 2005). However, within a year he left to join FirstAssist, part of the Legal and General insurance group. His trajectory can be taken as indicative of the continuing prevalence of the perspective of moderation in Unifi and its successors amongst members and activists, if not also EUOs.

of industrial action covered elsewhere, BIFU/Unifi/Amicus used awareness raising campaigns amongst staff and its own members through petitions, lobbied local politicians (seeking them to ask questions in Parliament) and consumer and business groups. The arguments BIFU/Unifi/Amicus deployed concerned pushing for a socially sensitive approach to redundancies and closures in terms of their effect on customers and communities, making criticisms that job cuts were being made in haste and for short-term, profit-driven ends which would damage the business, brand and reputation of the employers, and attempting to influence the Department of Trade and Industry to refer potential mergers to Competition Commission in order to consider the ramifications for employment numbers. More latterly, labour unionism has attempted to use the arguments of 'employability', that is, the duty of employers to provide transferable skills to allow redundant workers to gain employment elsewhere (inside or outside the company or sector) because job security agreements of the past are no longer adequate to deal with the extent and pace of employment restructuring, and because that restructuring is unstoppable. Turning to the staff associations, the LTU is largely typical of these staff bodies (ANGU/Advance, BSU, IUHS/Accord, NGSU, UBAC). With the exception of its activities over offshoring (see before), the LTU has been critical in words but not in deeds for it has undertaken no mobilisation consequent upon its criticisms. For example, in its communications with members (such as its fortnightly newsletters), it has kept members informed but not involved, where it has clearly stated its opposition or disagreement with employer policy, action and inaction. In face-to-face dialogue (information, consultation and negotiation meetings) and correspondence with the employer, the LTU has not sought to augment its arguments by outside membership strength. To a limited degree, it has practiced the common repertoire of wider political, behind the scene lobbying.

Now turning back to the overall assessment of moderation, it is worth noting that some commentators (for example, *Herald* 8 October 2004) have praised the modernity, innovation and effectiveness of these campaigning methods where no industrial action has been involved. The key means by which to interrogate the *prima facie* case of moderation concern the criteria of efficacy, proportionality and appropriateness. This means not assuming in an a *priori* manner that moderation is ineffective or prizing the (preferred) method (of militancy) over attested outcome. Thus, political lobbying *per se* is neither inherently militant nor moderate for it should not necessarily be negatively counter-posed with industrial action.

The means deployed have not been successful (either as individual tactics or used in conjunction with each other) if the criteria of efficacy is concerned with more than just making successful propaganda, namely, organising agitation and mobilisation with a view to changing employer behaviour which benefits finance workers. Neither has there been clear or abundant evidence that the means deployed helped build a greater collective confidence and consciousness amongst finance workers in transformational and transitional manners (like non-strike action facilitating striking). Of course, it is not possible to demonstrate in a counter-factual manner how much worse the situation would have been without the array of aforementioned actions being taken. This possibility cannot be discounted but equally well neither can the possibility that such actions may have helped prevent the emergence of other, more potentially efficacious means. The notion of proportionality specifically concerns whether the means deployed were up to the size and scale of the objective in question. In the case of redundancies and offshoring, the aim was not to stop these but ameliorate their extent and improve the terms for these. With that recognised, campaigns to mobilise customer and public opinion, for example, do not appear in general, or as practiced, to have been capable of exerting specific leverage on individual employers because the aggregation of atomised individuals into a collective force is not manifest or sustainable. Appropriateness concerns what is possible in regard of creating effective worker agency, and is thus a much more indeterminate and open ended issue to judge. As part of the developing unionateness, BIFU/Unifi/Amicus did not reject more militant *modus operandi* on specifically ideological grounds – that is to say by arguing that such means were inappropriate for finance workers *per se* because they were politically and socially (too) conservative. The leadership of this independent labour unionism did, however, routinely judge that the majorities of the salient groups of finance workers on an affected case-by-case basis were unlikely to support more robust actions and industrial actions because they were unaccustomed to it, did not believe that their fellow workers would support it or that the action would be effective even if widely supported. Thus, certain means were promoted and others rejected, whereby EUOs believed that the members concerned would not support more robust action so less robust action was proposed. In this process, more robust action was de-legitimised. This was, therefore, an assessment concerned with instrumentalism. Whether it was an accurate one is another matter though. There is certainly the possibility that these were poorly worked out and researched estimations and assessments and that each time such estimations and assessment were made this compounded the state of inertia and conservatism. Although involving risks, and thus potential membership rejection and compounding weakness in front of employers, seldom were leaderships prepared to be bold and carry out the work necessary to minimise the associated risks. The potential or window of opportunity to build up a culture of more robust action was not utilised on the few occasions it arose (like 1997). One caveat is necessary here. In the balancing the tension between leading and following (see Gall 2003), this process of leadership accommodation to members' perceived lower levels of consciousness is not uncommon to other unions. It may appear to be more pervasive with financial services sector workers because they did not participate in the rise of robust collectivism during the 1960s and 1970s that other groups of workers did.

So, overall then, there is substantial evidence of moderation but for a number of contingent and highly contextualised reasons. What looked like *prima facie* evidence of moderate behaviour was, indeed, overwhelming evidence of moderate and moderated behaviour.

**Political Complexions of Labour Unionism**

Within the labour unionism of the sector, and by contrast with much of the rest of the labour movement, there has been a historical and dominant strain of centre-right or right-wing union politics. Often was this posited as moderation (see, for example, *Guardian* 31 May 1995, *Independent* 25 May 1995), with militancy being the inverse cipher for leftwing-ness. This dominant strain pertains not just to the slow development of unionateness by both labour unionisms, partnership working and the absence of militancy (*vis-à-vis* ambitious bargaining agendas, attendant collective mobilisation and radical worldviews), but also the absence of an internal influential left, the *de facto* promotion of membership passivity and the absence of practical association with the rest of the labour movement (in terms of its causes and the participation of members and activists in these causes). And, as outlined already, this historical trajectory began to change in some limited but marked ways. However, because of the limited breadth and depth of these overall changes, it is useful to examine the political trajectory of NUBE/BIFU/Unifi as the strongest manifestation of these. This can be done through the lens of its general secretaries because they reflected in a more identifiable way the changes and because they were also key movers in the changes themselves.[12]

So, the changes in BIFU were as much exemplified by the change in personage at its apex in 1995 as any other indicator. Leif Mills was appointed general secretary in 1972 by the NUBE executive and was of 'the old school' in terms of his upper class background, his 'posh' schooling – reputedly held to be at both Eton and Oxbridge – and his love of classical music and appreciation of Greek (see, for example, *Financial Times* 12 September 1995). This gave him the air of a refined gentleman which was, so the argument ran, suitable for dealing with the conservative and staid world of bank directors in the halcyon days of respect and reverence for banks by the rest of society. Mills was not just know as a moderate (*Independent* 2 May 1992) but also an ultra-moderate and right-winger within the wider labour union movement.[13] Ed Sweeney was elected upon Mill's retirement in 1995. Coming from Liverpool and educated at a combination of urban universities (Warwick in politics and law and the London School of Economics in industrial relations and labour law) but having worked for NUBE since 1977, Sweeney was a breathe of fresh air in terms of his non-conservative, non-staid personae. Indeed, Sweeney was the first directly elected general secretary, and on a three (17,387 votes) to one (6,213 votes) margin over another longstanding BIFU employed official (John Brawley) on an 18% turnout. By contrast, Mills

---

12    Although there were many differences and the period was different, the personage of Clive Jenkins as general secretary of ASTMS can also be used heuristically in the same way for he can be read as representing certain aspirations of sections of his then (finance sector) members (see Jenkins 1990, Melling 2004).

13    A predecessor of Mills from 1959–1962, Hornby, was an active Conservative (Blackburn 1967:83).

was appointed prior to the Conservative's creation of legislation regulating unions' internal affairs in the 1980s and when required to stand for election in 1989 by this legislation, was returned unopposed. Unlike Mills, Sweeney was willing to criticise then Labour and opposition leader, Tony Blair, for his deliberate non-intervention over likely jobs losses following the creation of LloydsTSB. This, the *Independent* (20 November 1995) observed, was 'a decisive break with the intently loyalist approach of his predecessor – and the present acquiescence of other union leaders'. Sweeney also 'declared his intention to oppose the 'short-termism' of the City using Parliamentary lobbying and industrial action if necessary. … [And u]nlike the present general secretary, Leif Mills, Mr Sweeney seems to feel free to speak out about the shortcomings of the Labour leadership and senior management' (*Independent* 20 November 1995). For the membership of BIFU, Sweeney's election was an indication that as the sector had changed so too had the union. So, as the financial services sector was transformed into a more shareholder-driven business, where profits, operating costs and market shares became the hegemonic criteria, BIFU was seen to need to shed its old aloofness from traditional labour unionism and become more of an assertive, independent-minded, almost 'industrial', union, operating without fear or favour in regard of the employers, political parties and government. Of course, the degree of change was limited for a number of reasons (see Chapter 4) even though Sweeney was an expression of collective mood – a mood of having actions taken for it rather than carrying out the actions itself.

A Broad Left has operated in BIFU for many years that carried itself into Unifi/Amicus/Unite. Although it met regularly, generated counter-policy and argued for this, its overall, direct impact was marginal in terms of union policy and actions. Yet, two caveats need to be entered into. First, the impact of the Broad Left was greater on non-domestic issues like international policy that were of lesser consequence and cost compared to domestic issues of challenging partnership, performance related pay and the like. Second, and of a less tangible and manifest nature, has been the Broad Left's impact on unionateness. It constantly pushed for this direction of travel and although it never fully gained what it sought, it helped hastened and sharpened this trajectory by familiarising members with what greater unionateness, in effect, was. At annual conferences and recognising the disjunction between (formal) policy and (actual) practice, the Broad Left's influence was out of all proportion to its actual numerical strength on the ground amongst members or within the bureaucracy of the union's organisation. Here it was sometimes able to force the pace of debate, introduce new issues for debate and highlight different causes as well as win some occasional votes. Because Broad Left activists were consistent in their activity and positions, their conference presence – in terms of physical presence and participation in debates – made them look bigger and better organised than they actually were. Many of their leading activists were well-respected because of the way they were able to concretely and credibly relate issues to left policies. And with the absence of other lefts or a divided left as in some other unions, they became a singular pole of attraction for those who believed the response of the union leadership was insufficiently robust and critical. Consequently, members of the Broad Left slate were elected to the NEC of NUBE/ BIFU/Unifi and then for the allocated National Executive positions for the finance section of Amicus. In 2004, the left through the Broad Left won the presidency of Unifi by 58% to 42% for the rightwing candidate on an 11% turnout. Subsequent to this, the Broad Left of Unifi was given some extra sustenance when it joined with that of Amicus and its finance section in 2004 but was also compelled to divert its attention to wider internal-Amicus and the Unite left-right battles.

## Sources of Labour Union Power

According to Batstone (1988), workers' labour union power is derived from three basic sources: ability to disrupt the production, distribution and exchange of goods and services, scarcity of labour and political influence. Looking at the case of the BOG/NUBE/BIFU, its political leverage was low as it operated as a non-political organisation so that lobbying directly and through the TUC and international trade group affiliations was the sum of its activities as it eschewed affiliation to Labour. This necessarily increased the importance of what leverage it could create through the two other arenas. And even with strong internal labour markets in banking, BOG/NUBE/BIFU encountered the consequences of organising a group of workers which were not craft workers and which were not subject to jointly-controlled apprenticeships – banking exams not being an equivalent. Thus, it could do little to influence entry into the labour market for the workers it organised (and pre- or post-entry closed shops were not on the agenda for reasons, *inter alia*, of the presence of the preferred staff associations). This turned even greater attention to its ability to exercise disruptive power. While Allen and William's (1960) criticisms of the BOG may have been rather premature, it is hard to get away from the view that BOG/NUBE/BIFU showed insufficient willingness to *try* to develop the kind of capacity, especially workplace unionism, that was either capable of mobilising or being mobilised for more assertive actions. Turning to the GIO/NUIW/ASTMS/ MSF labour unionism for insurance, affiliation to Labour did not appear to deliver any significant benefits. Whether this was due to the nature of the demands and the lobbying to support them, the restricted nature of Labour as a social democratic party or Labour being out of office is immaterial in as much as the logic of the situation suggested that attention should then be focussed on the two other arenas. Therein, the same points made about independent labour unionism in banking can be made about GIO/NUIW/ASTMS/MSF. In relation to these judgements, there is no hard or clear evidence that mergers have strengthened the hand of labour unionism in the sector or even staved off its further decline. This is because mergers *per se* do not deliver increased bargaining power – that is down to issues of consciousness and mobilisation. The most one could venture is that mergers have stopped employers playing further divide and rule (although members being in different sister unions is not an insuperable barrier to joint industrial action as the 1990s showed).

In making these judgements, it would be wrong and erroneous to consider independent and dependent labour unionism in the financial services sector in complete isolation from other labour unionisms in Britain. As a point of reference, the labour unionism in the sector has been, explicitly and implicitly, compared and contrasted with labour unionism in the printing, vehicle building, port, engineering and manufacturing industries in order to elucidate the issues of developing both unionateness and workplace unionism. However, an equally valid point of reference would have also been weaker and less unionate forms of labour unionism such as the predominant forms of NALGO in the gas industry and local government, or USDAW in retailing. This would have highlighted that the nature, dynamics and outcomes of independent labour unionism in the financial services sector are not wholly peculiar or specific to itself.

### Forms and Models of Labour Unionism

In the explaining the absence of workplace unionism, two aspects of the labour union form are particularly salient. One is the economistic nature of the bargaining undertaken by independent unionism in the sector. Under this approach, concentration was put on the remunerative aspects of the wage-effort bargain, these being financial remuneration like wages and non-financial remuneration like holidays, and not the conditions under which the wage-effort bargain was conducted on like line management control, productivity measurement, staffing levels and work organisation. The focus of union organisation was not then the workplace but the locus of company power, the organisational apex, in the form of the negotiators and personnel department acting on behalf of the board of directors of each company. This extra-workplace focus was strengthened by the demand for, and then realisation of, MEB in banking. Following from this is the second aspect. Unlike many others labour unionisms, when the BOG was formed it was created straight away as a putative national, single 'industry', all grade union making demands on companies *per se* and the 'industry' as well. In a sense it was, therefore, formed outside the workplace, whence forth it sought to gain members in workplaces for its aims and objectives of centralised bargaining. The same is true for the GIO although the format of this was different given the company-based unionism and its federations. Ironically for the long battles independent unionism previously fought, it has become noticeably dependent upon employer subsidy for operating through facility time and ICT equipment. This again is another aspect of the salience of union form, particularly where this subsidy is received and spent in a centralised, bureaucratic and institutionalised manner. Of course, dependent unionism was, and is, even more dependent upon employer subsidy. But, in an era of greater employer aggressiveness and declining mutualism, this is an ever more contingent resource of self-interest and goodwill.

Heery and Kelly (1994) proposed a threefold schema of types of labour unionism in Britain. Professional unionism, they argued, characterised labour unionism in the period of the 1940s to 1960s where a servicing relationship predominated. Managerial unionism, dominant since the 1980s onwards, is still servicing based but predicated on more individualised relationships between union and members, and where market research on members' needs and wants is used to determine services. Participative unionism predominated, Heery and Kelly argued, in the 1960s and 1970s. To use Heery and Kelly's (1994) schema of types of labour unionism, as was not intended by them, NUBE/BIFU/Unifi and ASTMS/MSF/Amicus-MSF have over time embodied 'professional' and 'managerial' unionisms with a small and internally subordinate move towards 'participative' unionism en route in the 1980s and 1990s. The professional phase ran later than specified as did the participative strand whilst the managerial phase could be detected earlier than the 1980s.[14] In other words, these trajectories are similar to the patterns of transformative development experienced by a number of other white-collar unions but of a later period and of a weaker form. Both professional and managerial unionisms suggest an orientation on 'servicing' rather 'organising'. Indeed, NUBE/BIFU/Unifi, and to a slightly lesser extent ASTMS/MSF/Amicus-MSF, developed a relatively unaccountable and undemocratic *modus operandi*, whereby EUOs and full-facility time company committees chairs exerted a predominant influence on the union-side determination of bargaining outcomes over terms and conditions of employment. These milieus negotiated the annual pay claims without recourse to any significant degree of active involvement of, much less direction from, members over claims and offers. Consultative ballots on offers were used as validatory referenda. This *modus operandi* developed in response to the need to exert leadership in the face of relative membership disinterest and passivity and an inability to find means by which to stimulate and engage with membership interest. But over time, this *modus operandi* became institutionalised such that it compounded the problems of membership disinterest and passivity whereby few attempts were made to stimulate interest and involvement. The belief on the part of officials and EUOs of the need to act on behalf of the members in the absence of membership interest has become self-perpetuating. This represented another Catch-22 situation. Historically, the roots of this *modus operandi* lie in the lack of workplace unionism (see above). This tendency was less pronounced in ASTMS/MSF/Amicus-MSF because of the crossover influence of different union traditions within a union that organised other white-collar workers outside the financial services sector and its different trade group structure. Notwithstanding moves towards unionateness, a further salient historical aspect is that it is open to doubt whether the model of independent labour unionism in the sector as outlined above (in terms of Heery and Kelly's (1994) schema) was still suitable or viable for a period in which the principal foundation on which that model operated

---

14   It has been noted earlier why EUO domination historically occurred in the BOG/NUBE/BIFU and why this set in train the financial weakness of this form of unionism.

had been withdrawn, i.e., structured employer paternalism and institutionalised support. The difficulty facing labour unionism was that any emergence of a new, more appropriate model would come out of the old and, thus, maintain some degree of historical continuity with its forebearer. In other words, the new would be developed within, and simultaneously limited, by the old.

Despite differences of inter-union structures, the development and form of independent labour unionism in banking and insurance could be taken as confirmation of Clegg's (1976) thesis that the nature of collective bargaining, primarily its structures, determines labour union behaviour where a union has as its main function the protection and advancement of its members' interests through collective bargaining. However, it may be a case of a perverse confirmation in as much as, and until the late 1960s, there was little collective bargaining (as per Clegg) with independent unionism to speak of, the very restricted collective bargaining that did exist was *de facto* rather than *de jure* and took place with dependent unionism on CLB basis against which independent unionism reacted, and in doing so confirmed its earlier historical mission. The variations, represented by the turning points of the late 1960s and late 1980s did not change the perverse confirmation. But if the perversion is too much, then it is surely a case that the behaviour of labour unionism is heavily influenced by employers acting firstly as 'primary organisations' (Offe and Wisenthal 1980, *cf.* Muller-Jentsch 1985) and then secondly as employers seeking surplus value through the selection of one of a number of available meso-means. Labour unionism's historic mission is a consequence of the existence and purpose of employers in a capitalist society, and thereafter, in the case of the financial services sector at any rate, a specific response to the employer strategy of non-unionism turning into what Bain (1970:131) called 'peaceful competition' (rather than 'forcible opposition'). Indeed, the aspect of a reaction against, not a validation of, structures of bargaining is apposite in the case of independent labour unionism. The preferred company-level focussed organisations and relationships found their antithesis in attempts at extra- and multi-company level organisations and relationships. And while Clegg (1976:118) maintained that the 'external structure of trade unions is not directly shaped by the dimensions of collective bargaining', in the case of this study, those structures – and the values supporting them – heavily influenced the internal structures too and well after collective bargaining began. In turn, this raises the question of what influences collective bargaining structures (see above) which Clegg did not adequately address or answer.

**Potential, Possibility and Probability for Labour Unionism**

It is a correct convention for left academics to point to the potential and possibilities for the growth of the presence and power of labour unionism after their analyses of extant practice and outcomes. This is true of studies of labour unionism in the financial services sector (see, for example, Danford et al. (2003), and Gall (1999)).

The common currency here has been to emphasise the quantitative existence of activists without considering their qualitative aspects (see, for example, Danford et al. (2003:100)) or to emphasise the existence of grievances as a foundation for labour unionism through its actions to collectivising these and in so doing form collective identity, oppositional consciousness and collective mobilisation, whereupon redress of grievances solidifies these facets. In the banks, the battle against PRP indicated that there was some validity to this perspective for in the 1990s there were five strikes against PRP and its consequences (Lloyds, RBS, Barclays, Yorkshire, Clydesdale). But these strikes were unsuccessful in rolling back PRP and there have been few other instances to validate this left perspective. At one level, there has been no shortage of issues around which labour unionism can attempt to relate to and mobilise members and workers – bullying, long working hours, targets, low pay, RSI, stress, job security, imposed pay, job security, sickness/absence policies, inadequate information and consultation (see, for example, *FSU Finance Update* February 1999, *People Management* 14 October 1999). Consequently, and as alluded to in the last chapter, it is therefore incumbent upon left academics to perform three tasks. First, translate potential and possibilities into probabilities by using more exacting criteria to map out the likely array of future trajectories. This might involve, for example, analysing the impact on workers' labour market power as a result of the reduction in task specialisation (see Storey et al. (1997:33)) or the impact of partnership deals. Second, to revisit their 'predictions' and use counter-factual and counter-intuitive methods to ask why the potential and possibilities were not been realised. This has been attempted on a number of occasions in this study – for example, in chapter four, on PRP. This would not only deepen our understanding but be of more use to labour unionism. And third, to make such calculations on the basis of an acknowledgement of the specificity of the form of labour unionism in the sector, whereby there is sometimes little in the way of grassroots oppositional consciousness, let alone grassroots oppositional organisation.

**Capital Restructuring**

The consequence of capital restructuring for labour unionism in the sector has been several-fold. It has occasioned – as a result of deliberate employer will – new organisational structures and new micro-accumulation strategies. These have become increasingly entrepreneurially orientated in terms of exacting performance targets and revenue generating internal cultures. Whilst this presents both opportunity and challenge for labour unionism in terms of the representation of workers' collective interests (see, for example, Fairbrother (1989, 2000) on 'union renewal'), the balance has been more towards challenge than opportunity. In line with the tenor of the argument made elsewhere in this study, and on balance, labour unionism in the sector has been historically and contemporaneously ill-suited to matching such powerful and capricious employers. Quite apart from the content and nature of the capital restructuring, the dislocation of intra-company labour union structures, processes and relationships has also been occasioned, which again is of a double-edged opportunity-and-challenge paradigm. Again, this has taken the form of more challenge than opportunity in terms of capacity building and 'union renewal'. Some of this flows from labour unions being 'secondary organisations' (Offe and Wisenthal 1985, *cf.* Muller-Jentsch 1985) and thus necessarily reactive and under-resourced compared to employers. Yet some of this is also due to the specificity of the geographical rather than workplaces structures of labour unionism. Moreover, the ending of particular often longstanding relationships between managers and union officer holders has created a transaction cost for labour unions of having to establish new relationships, where new managers under the new, more competitive regime of accumulation are often less receptive and more antagonist towards labour unionism (see, for example, Danford et al. (2003: chapter 5)). Indeed, sometimes with the scaling down of the human resource function and the devolution of such tasks to line managers, the loss of a regularised, profession-based approach by the former has been noticeable (see, for example, Danford et al. (2003:106)). Intertwined with these issues has been the rise in the intensiveness and extensiveness of work and the closer monitoring of performance through targets and PRP. This means, on the one hand, union activity is looked upon rather less favourably than it once may have been (within the limitations as they then existed), and, on the other hand, there is now less porosity at work in terms of time and spaces which can be utilised for union activity (see, for example, Danford et al. (2003:107–108)). Given that there has been little *de jure* facility time in most employing organisations at the workplace level, this has been a significant and deleterious change.

In terms of the implications of (capitalist) capital restructuring for employment, and from general observation across the private and public sectors in Britain, the financial services sectors unions have not been particularly any more or less successful than most other unions in opposing redundancies through restructuring, offshoring and outsourcing (notwithstanding the employment security agreements). In common, with most other unions they have demanded no compulsory redundancies, the use of voluntary redundancies, early retirements and the like and the application of TUPE (Transfer of Undertakings – Protection of Employment) principles. It is difficult to ascertain whether the finance unions have been any more or less successful than other unions in attaining more beneficial severance packages for voluntary leavers, retraining and redeployment because this information is not generally available in the public domain. Similarly, it is difficult to ascertain[15] overall whether the financial service sector unions and unions in general were able to gain such outcomes like the absence of compulsory

---

15   This is all the more so the case because one would have to be able to identify the 'behind the scenes' characteristics and dynamics of the intentions at the outset of both parties as well as the subsequent processes and outcomes of the collective interchange to clearly work out what give and take, and from whom, eventually emerged.

redundancies because of leverage they created and used over the employing organisations or, alternatively, because the employing organisations were already prepared to offer such terms in a process of negotiation whereby they would allow it to be seen that they had been negotiated into such a position through attitudinal restructuring in order to clinch the deal and in doing so sell the unions something they not actually won.

## Class Issues

This study has not sought to generalise out from a study of labour unionism to construct an analysis of class position and consciousness for the sector (*cf.* Crompton 1976, Hyman 1983) because the objective of the study was labour unionism *per se* and because the research methods and questions deployed were not appropriate for performing such a task. Nonetheless, some reflection on these wider issues is still warranted and possible. Compared to the situation in a number of other economic sectors, the full historical development of an objective working class in the financial services sector took some time due to the length of time by which the process of managerial functions were distilled and reified into the social structure of the sector. By contrast, the development of a subjective working class in the sector took much longer for reasons of the early social base of financial service workers, their aspirations and employer strategy. It is something of a paradox that when both dependent and independent forms of labour unionism begin to move towards greater forms of unionateness from the late 1980s, the wider union movement could be said to have begun moving in the opposite direction (and one which labour unionism in the sector was then subject to). It was almost as if finance workers were a quarter of a century too late for the springtide of labour unionism and, when they had their own springtide, theirs was pulled back by the wider ebb tide.

## Bank and Finance Worker Union Organisation Elsewhere

An obvious point of comparison for finance workers' collective organisation in Britain is with sister organisations in other western countries. Although a number of comparative studies have been undertaken (see, for example, Anderson (1997), Centrepois and Jefferys (2004), Deery and Walsh (1999), Haipeter and Pernod-Lemattre (2005), Holden (1999), Lawler and Serrano del Rosal (1999), Thornley et al. (1997), *cf.* the single countries of Regini et al. (1999)), this is not necessarily a particularly worthwhile exercise within a brief overview for the structures of organised labour as well as the bargaining structures, for example, in a number of other western European economies (like Belgium, France, Germany, Greece, Italy and Norway) are sufficiently different as to render close and meaningful comparison impractical. In these aforementioned countries, structures of different intra-labour movement affiliations based on political and religious beliefs, collective bargaining of an industry-wide nature (which is highly inclusive of financial services sector employers), longstanding statutory voice workplace mechanisms such as works councils and works committees, and – for different historical reasons – significant state and public policy support for the maintenance of these types of bargaining arrangements all exist (or have existed) in these countries (see, for example, Haipeter (2002), Lawler and Serrano del Rosal (1999), Luton (2001), Mueller (1997)). Indeed, union density and mobilisation capacity vary so greatly (see Dolvik and Waddington (2005:282–283)) that it is difficult not to be overwhelmed by the disparities. Furthermore, there has not been the struggle for union recognition as in Britain, and the company unionism as per the staff associations has not existed on the same scale and in the same way.

So while finance workers in these other western European countries have experienced a similarity of impacts of capitalist accumulation upon their working conditions – leading to, *inter alia*, job intensification, redrawing the 'frontier of control' through introducing new technologies, company mergers, restructurings and job retrenchment and the like – albeit from different baselines *vis-à-vis* the relative 'health' of companies and national sectors  (European Foundation for the Improvement of Living and Working Conditions 2001, European Monitoring Centre on Change 2003, 2004) and displayed some common responses to these challenges (for example, union mergers in Australia, Germany and Norway), the nature and extent of the more assertive and combative reaction[16] through striking is believed to be heavily contingent upon the bargaining structures and the relatively conducive and supportive conditions for unions which arise from these in terms of collective mobilisation. The thrust of this point of greater difference than commonality is sharpened by the situation where the research resources available (without extensive funding and fieldwork) comprised secondary data examining the institutional aspects of employment relations and labour unionism of the financial services sectors in a number of western European economies through sources like the European Employment Relations Observatory (Eironline), IRS's *European Industrial Relations Review*, IDS's *Employment Europe* and coverage by quality broadsheets in each country accessible through Lexis-Nexis. In this situation, and for these two reasons of context and resource, meaningful comparative analysis with the study of financial services sector workers in Britain could not be accomplished.

Consequently, a more useful comparison is to look at sister unionism in the Republic of Ireland (Eire). And while the situation in Eire is different from that in Britain by virtue of the absence of staff associations, the national level social

---

16    Large strikes have taken place in the financial services sector in the following recent years: Belgium (1999, 2003), France (1999, 2002, 2003), Germany (1999, 2002), Greece (1998, 2000, 2002, 2005), Italy (1999, 2002, 2004) and Norway (2006). This list excludes any other industrial action which has taken place within the financial services sector in these countries as a result of wider actions such as general strikes.

partnership (and wage rise) agreements of recent decades and the relatively greater recourse to collective legal redress, the commonalities are sufficiently strong to make this a more worthwhile exercise. These commonalities include CLB, a single peak union organisation (and its attendant effects), similar internal union representative structures, the operation of a British based-union (through MSF/Amicus/Unite with some 10,000 members in the early 2000s), similar dominant company characteristics of the sector (including the presence of some British banks) and similar levels of union density. Overall union density in Eire fell from 60% in 1980 to 46% in 1994 to 35% in 2004 despite a rise in absolute membership (*Industrial Relations News* 14 September 2005). Somewhat similarly, in the financial and other business services, density has fallen from 34% (33,000 members) to 23% (46,000 members) over the 1994–2004 period with density for the private sector being 21% in 1994 and that for men and women being equal (*Industrial Relations News* 14 September 2005). Consequently, a thumbnail account of the Irish Bank Officials' Association (IBOA)[17], which organises in the north (Northern Ireland) and south of Ireland (Eire), follows.

The challenges facing the initial group of activists who formed the IBOA in September 1917 were difficult ones – the banks vehemently opposed any collective dealing with staff (only countenancing individual relations and using a policy of fear), and bank staff were badly paid with no pension provision. Notwithstanding these difficulties, the then IBOA recruited over 80% of bank officials and this was the catalyst that changed the banks' minds, whereby the IBOA balloted its members on striking to force the banks to engage with it. The banks responded by threatening to lockout strikers and replace them with scab labour from Britain. However, IBOA stood firm and members voted by a majority for striking, leading to union recognition in late 1919 and an agreement that salaries and terms and conditions be referred to arbitration. Subsequent arbitration awards (through the Industrial Court) produced minimum starting salaries, incremental scales, pensions, holiday entitlement and allowances by the early 1930s. Only a few years after this initial advance, the banks sought to introduce a recruitment grade (without automatic progression) and tax bank official's salaries. The latter eventually led to the calling of a national strike in 1946, forcing a compromise resolution which the IBOA accepted but which members subsequently wanted to gain redress on.

Between 1946 and 1950, IBOA secured lunch breaks, overtime payments, and Sunday and Bank Holiday attendance to be voluntary but this was not sufficient to satiate members' desire for further improvements, and between 1950 and 1951 the union conducted a seven-week strike which delivered increased salaries, rank allowances, and overtime rates. As IBOA put it: 'This strike set the scene for future relations ... clearly put[ting] the balance of power in the hands of the [IBOA]' (IBOA website). Further improvements were gained thereafter: withdrawal of the need for Bank permission for marriage, introduction of uniforms, Saturday

---

17    This sketch is derived from materials from EIROnline, IBOA, the authoritative and indigenous fortnightly *IRN* periodical and the *Lexis-Nexis* database of newspapers.

half-days, improved overtime arrangements and the introduction of the five-day week. A major strike in 1966 introduced a modernised salary scale structure while the 1970 strike over pay rises during a period of rising inflation saw a six-month lockout but resulted in the gaining of pay increases similar to other groups of workers. The period of the 1970s saw progress made for bank workers on equal pay, introduction of a seven-hour working day and pension parity although it took a long strike in 1976 to gain an acceptable wage settlement. In the early 1980s, IBOA successfully gained from a new technology agreement by dint of securing increased salaries, early retirement and increased annual leave.

Geary and Trif (2008:9–10) described the overall union-employer relationship of the 1970s and 1980s as at best an 'arms'-length' one and at worst 'adversarial in orientation'. And the later 1980s witnessed a more aggressive and re-assertive management which seemed intent upon breaking the IBOA's power in a 'reforming conflict' (see Gall 2003). For example, in 1987 bitter disputes took place in the Bank of Ireland and Allied Irish Bank over the ramifications of the introduction of new technology, leading to industrial action being taken before a final agreement was arrived at. As part of reasserting managerial prerogative, individual contracts for managers with PRP and benefits were introduced within the ascendancy of HRM techniques. This culminated in 1992 when banks awarded their managers pay increases in excess of the National Wage Agreement but limited pay increases to non-managerial staff to national norms. When IBOA began limited industrial action in response, the banks retaliated by using a combination of reduction in staff salaries or as in the case of AIB, immediate suspensions of staff. According to IBOA (IBOA website): '[w]hat followed was one of the bitterest disputes in the history of this union ... [and after three months] the banks' attempt to break this union had failed'. As a result of the strike, IBOA expelled 4,000 members for strike-breaking. Other assessments of IBOA's performance were less generous (see, for example, *Irish Independent* 17 February 2007), and the strike resulted, under the prevailing conditions, in a consequent decade without of strikes (and without their threat and mobilisation for through balloting and serving of strike notifications).

As part of its rebuilding after the 1992 strike, IBOA joined the Irish Congress of Trades Unions in 1993 and began using legal means of redress more frequently as well as offering more services to members. In the early 2000s, IBOA rebranded itself as 'IBOA – the finance union' given that it represented members outside the main three banks, including other financial houses and where IT contracts have been outsourced to non-financial services sector organisations. By 2006, membership had increased back to just over 20,000 workers (of which 72% were women), with a 10% aggregate growth between 2003 and 2006 (computed from figures on Certification Office website) as a result of organising and recruitment drives. Consequently, Irish banking is highly unionised and IBOA is widely regarded as being a very strong and influential union, representing c.60% of sub-sector's workforce (with c.80% in retail banking) (Geary and Trif 2008:2). In the last decade, IBOA has prosecuted a reasonably resolute position of defending its members' interests on the downward revision of pensions, the introduction of PRP, outsourcing of jobs and functions, and job cuts through redundancy programmes. Thus, although sectoral bargaining ended after 1992, IBOA found it was able to use inter-bank labour market competition to its own benefit to some extent.

As alluded to above, the IBOA's mobilisations for strikes – in the various forms of the process leading up to a strike – and more latterly strikes themselves have been deployed quite frequently. However, this has been less the case after 1992 when striking in the sector has remained at a very low comparative level (although relatively high compared to Britain on a proportionate basis). For example, in 2004 there were two strikes involving 220 workers and 2,280 days not worked (LRC2005a:2). Moreover, banking has been affected by partnership agreements. This was preceded by some moves towards partnership working approaches since the mid-1990s on the part of the IBOA, following its strike defeat in 1992. Consequently, there are partnership agreements in the Allied Irish Bank (from 2001), Ulster Bank (from 2003, part of NatWest then RBS) and National Irish Bank (owned by the Danish Danske Bank). In the case of the Bank of Ireland, there is no partnership agreement following a period of attempts of union marginalisation but latterly some moves towards rapprochement (LRC 2005b).

So what salient themes and issues emerge from this brief sketch? Although both BOG/NUBE/BIFU and the IBOA faced fierce employer opposition to first gaining recognition and then attained their bargaining agendas, the strategy adopted by the employers in Ireland was more akin to one of 'forcible opposition' (Bain 1970:131) than 'internalism' and substitutionism/'peaceful competition' (Bain 1970:133) adopted by the employers in Britain. The use of the 'iron fist' (rather than 'velvet glove') with its greater tendency to leave workers with an unambiguous sense of what employers' interests are, how these conflicted with their own and how employers would enforce them is likely to have helped develop bank workers' union consciousness further than the situation faced in Britain where employers created a more dominant perception of paternalism and compatibility of interests. Under these conditions in Ireland, it would appear that independent, collective representation prosecuted through robust collective mobilisation was understood to be necessary to respond to employers. This picture was not muddied by the existence of employer-sponsored forms of worker representation (like staff councils or staff associations). By contrast in Britain, not only were there two avenues of representation open to workers but the staff association avenue was clearly the favoured one and was allowed to succeed by employers within its own terms. So the situation is not as simple as saying that the 'history of struggle' shaped the union in Ireland for its specificity and contingency has to be understood to fully appreciate why a particular type of response from employers heavily influenced the union's development there as well as why the union chose to respond in a certain manner. Therefore, what can be said is that the overtly hostile and well resourced response from employers was a key (but not the only) influence in facilitating a robust and quasi-militant response from IBOA. Moreover, granting of recognition – which BOG/NUBE/BIFU was prepared to take industrial action to gain – in Ireland did not lead to a calming of the situation through the formalisation and regularisation (if not incorporation) of the conflict capacity of the union *vis-à-vis* its agenda and methods. Rather, and compared to the situation in Britain, the employers continued to contest the union's role and function in an overtly forceful and confrontational way, again inclining the IBOA to respond in an equally robust manner.

Some of the difference in bargaining capacity between IBOA and its British sister unions can be attributed to a relatively greater collective mobilisation capacity, which itself appears to the product of a (relatively) greater role given over to lay representatives and the dominant internal culture of IBOA. In terms of the former, the IBOA's workplace representatives played a role more akin to that of a shop steward and the lay district secretaries played an organising role. In regard of the latter, the internal union culture is more of a democratic, participative and unionate consciousness one where, for example, the union reminds members that it is a 'union run by bank staff for bank staff', '[their representatives are] IBOA members elected to their posts by their peers working in the industry', and 'IBOA is only as strong as its members and if members stick together significant improvements can be made' (IBOA website). Indeed, in a celebration of the union's ninetieth anniversary in 2007, IBOA mounted an exhibition of its history which emphasised the continual nature of the battle with employers to defend and improve members' conditions, and the use of collective mobilisation to do so. The exhibition concluded that: '[members] should be proud of [the union's] history [and] ... members have a responsibility to maintain that history by participating in and supporting their Union which seeks to protect their jobs and terms and conditions [of employment]' (IBOA website). Arguably, IBOA learnt a profound lesson much earlier than the BOG in as much as it was prepared to strike to gain *de facto* recognition, although Blackburn (1967:248–249) pointed out IBOA did not face staff associations and did have majority membership unlike BOG. However, the case of the GIO (and to a lesser extent the SBA) may go some way to undermining the force of Blackburn's case because it faced a much more similar situation to the BOG but did deploy strike action successfully for this end.

The salience of IBOA is twofold. First, it was able to create a more robust form of independent labour unionism under certain conditions but where the importance of its own choice should not be discounted. Second, after a defeat, it has been prone to accepting partnership working where offered. Thus, for independent labour unionism in the sector in Britain, this reaffirms the evaluation of a relationship of circumstance and choice, where the balance has not always been fixed.

## Final Remarks

There will be some readers of this study from a variety of left persuasions who will interpret its thrust as one which is erroneously pessimistic and downbeat. They will point to this or that instance of resistance and struggle, and this or that survey, and say this shows what is possible and what the potential is for labour unionism. But two swallows can never make a summer and this type of faith and hope over reason and evidence approach is seriously misplaced. Potential and possibility are not probabilities and certainly not actualities – the former couple can only be put forward for so long without the rescue of real events to support them. Otherwise, they look increasingly hollow and forlorn. This faith-based approach is not up to the task of fully comprehending and understanding the nature of financial services sector labour unionism in both historical and contemporary, and general and specific, terms. Neither is it capable of understanding where this labour unionism is actually situated in terms of levers of power and sources of resource in order to concretely appreciate how to construct robust collectivism. Of course, for those that ignore the study of organised labour in the sector, as is the want of the uncritical ideology of HRM, an equally serious error is made. The underlying dynamic of conflict of interest in the employment relationship and the inherently collective nature of work (as per Marx's 'collective worker') will find expression in some form or other and poke its head above the parapet of cooperation (instrumental or ideological) and quiescence from time to time because there can be no conclusive resolution to the fundamental antagonism arising from labour exploitation under the regime of capitalism.

So this study has demonstrated that independent labour unionism triumphed over dependent unionism and won the battle *vis-à-vis* employers on this front. This is not something Blackburn (1967:256–267, 262) could have contemplated, particularly in terms of the fusion of respectability and effectiveness. Either dependent unionism was subsumed by independent labour unionism, or it became increasingly unionate. But the spoils of victory for independent labour unionism have been poor because the backers of the vanquished staff associations remain powerful and intransigent opponents and the wider war has been fought on other fronts. Indeed, employers have shown tactical deftness by replacing the form and practice of dependent unionism – the staff associations – with its spirit infused into independent unionism via partnership. An irony was that independent labour unionism in the sector 'came of age' at the time when a general malaise was affecting labour unionism, and independent labour unionism in the sector is, thus, now as 'weak' or 'strong' as most other labour unionisms. Another was that when management responsibility was decentralised to some degree (albeit in a tight manner), the stimulus for workplace unionism was present but labour unionism was unable to take advantage of this opportunity. And for the future, having most of the labour unionism in the sector constituted within a single, independent union (Unite – finance sector) where it is the single largest intra-union component of the biggest union in Britain is not the boon that it might otherwise have been expected to be. It is a sign of weakness not strength and the anticipated increased unionateness of workers from dependent unionism coming across to independent unionism is far from assured. For this study, reaching the bar of being able to construct robust and effective collectivism in sector is exacting but an objective progressive labour unionists in the sector must still strive to attain. In the absence of being displaced by non-union or alternative channels of representation, labour unionism still has an opportunity to do so. But it will be a difficult task for weak and weakened labour unionism is not a particularly attractive prospect – it seems expensive and irrelevant to prospective members or activists. And yet there is no way of avoiding the necessity of squaring the circle that more members and more active members are needed as the means by which to make the unionism stronger and more attractive. Hopefully, this study will have been some use to these activists in showing them that patience and determination are needed here if they are in for the necessary 'long haul'.

# References

Allen, M. (1999) 'Shaping up for the millennium' *New Statesman Trade Union Guide 1999*, ppx-xi.

Allen, V. (1966) *Militant Trade Unionism: a re-analysis of industrial action in an inflationary situation*, Merlin, London.

Allen, V. (1971) *The Sociology of Industrial Relations*, Longman, London.

Allen, V. and Williams, S. (1960) 'The growth of trade unionism in banking 1914–1927' *Manchester School of Economics and Social Studies*, 28/3:299–318

Amicus (n.d.) *History of MSF*, Amicus website.

Amicus (2005) *Offshoring: the exporting of UK jobs to offshore locations is one of the most significant issues now facing trade unions*, Amicus, London

Amicus (2007) *Industrial Report 2006 – financial services sector*, Amicus, London

Andersen, T. (1997) 'Do institutions matter? Convergence and national diversity in the restructuring of employment in British and Danish banking' *European Journal of Industrial Relations*, 3/1:107–124.

Bain, G. (1970) *The Growth of White Collar Unionism*, Clarendon Press, Oxford.

Bain, G. and Price, R. (1983) 'Union growth: dimensions, determinants and destiny' in Bain, G. (ed.) *Industrial Relations in Britain*, Blackwell, Oxford, pp3–34.

Bain, P., and Taylor, P. (2001) 'Seizing the time? Union recruitment potential in Scottish call centres' *Scottish Affairs*, 37:104–128.

Bain, P. and Taylor, P. (2002) 'Ringing the changes? Union recognition and organisation in call centres in the UK finance sector' *Industrial Relations Journal*, 33/2:246–261.

Bain, P. and Taylor, P. (2008) 'No passage to India? Initial responses of UK trade unions to call centre offshoring' *Industrial Relations Journal*, 39/1:5–23.

Bain, P., Taylor, P., Gilbert, K., and Gall, G. (2004) 'Failing to organize or organizing to fail? Challenge, opportunity and the limitations of union policy in four call centres' in Healy, G., Heery, E., Taylor, P. and Brown, W. (eds) *The Future of Worker Representation,* Palgrave Macmillan, Basingstoke, pp62–81.

Batstone, E., Gourlay, S., Levie, H. and Moore, R, (1987) *New Technology and the Process of Labour* Regulation, Clarendon Press, Oxford.

Batstone, E. (1988) 'The frontier of control' in Gallie, D. (ed.) *Employment in Britain*, Blackwell, Oxford, pp218–247.

Belanger, J. and Edwards, P. (2007) 'The conditions promoting compromise in the workplace' *British Journal of Industrial Relations*, 45/4:713–734.

BIFU (1982) *Microtechnology: a programme for action*, Banking, Insurance and Finance Union, London.

BIFU (various years) *Annual Report*, Banking, Insurance and Finance Union, London.

BIFU (1992) *History of the Union*, Banking, Insurance and Finance Union, London.

Blackburn, R. (1967) *Union Character and Social Class: a study of white-collar unionism*, Batsford, London.

Buchanan, R. (1981) 'Mergers in British trade unions, 1949–1979' *Industrial Relations Journal*, 12/3:40–49.

Callaghan, G. and Thompson, P. (2001) 'Edwards revisited: technical control and call centres' *Economic and Industrial Democracy*, 22/1:13–37.

Cameron, A. (1995) *Bank of Scotland, 1995–1995: a very singular institution*, Mainstream, Edinburgh.

Carter, B. (1997) 'Adversity and opportunity: union renewal in MSF' *Capital and Class*, 61:8–18.

Checkland, S. (1975) *Scottish Banking: a history, 1695–1973*, Collins, Glasgow.

Clegg, H. (1976) *Trade Unionism under Collective Bargaining: a theory based on comparisons of six countries*, Blackwell, Oxford.

Coates, K. and Topham, T. (1988) *Trade Unions in Britain*, third edition, Fontana London.

Colgan, F. and Creegan, C. (2006) 'Organising and diversity in banking and insurance: reflections on the approach of Unifi' in Gall, G. (ed.) *Union Recognition: Organising and Bargaining Outcomes*, Routledge, Abingdon, pp64–82.

Contrepois, S. and Jeffreys, S. (2003) 'The future of activism: continuities and renewal among trade union bank sector workplace activities in France and Britain' International Industrial Relations Association conference, Berlin.

Contrepois, S. and Jeffreys, S. (2004) 'Founding values or instrumentalism: comparing trade union activists in Britain and France' *Industrielle Beziehungen*, 11/1+2:112–28.

Cowling, A. and Newman, K. (1995) 'Banking on people: TQM, service quality, and human resources' *Personnel Review*, 24/7:25–40.

Cressey, P. (1998) 'European works councils in practice' *Human Resource Management Journal*, 8/1:67–79.

Cressey, P. and Scott, P. (1992) 'Employment, technology and industrial relations in the UK clearing banks: is the honeymoon over?' *New Technology, Work and Employment*, 7/2:83–96.

Cressey, P. and Scott, P. (1993) 'Careers and industrial action in banking: reply to a comment' *New Technology, Work and Employment*, 8/1:72–73.

Crompton. R. (1976) 'Approaches to the study of white-collar unionism' *Sociology*, 10/3:407–426.

Crompton, R. (1979) 'Trade unionism and the insurance clerk' *Sociology*, 13/3:403–426.

Crompton, R. (1989) 'Women in banking: continuity and change since the Second World War' *Work, Employment and Society*, 3/2:141–156.

Crompton, R. and Jones, G. (1984) *White Collar Proletariat: deskilling and gender in clerical work*, Macmillan, Basingstoke.

Cully, M., Woodland, S., O'Reilly, A. and Dix, G. (1999) *Britain at Work: as depicted by the 1998 Workplace Employee Relations Survey*, Routledge, London.

Danford, A., Richardson, M. and Upchurch, M. (2003) *New Unions, New Workplaces: a study of union resilience in the restructured workplace*, Routledge, London.

Deery, S. and Walsh, J. (1999) 'The decline of collectivism? A comparative study of white-collar employees in Britain and Australia' *British Journal of Industrial Relations*, 37/2:245–269.

Dickens, L. (1975) 'Staff association and the Industrial Relations Act: the effect on union growth' *Industrial Relations Journal*, 6/3:29–41.

Dolvik, J. and Waddington, J. (2002) 'Private sector services: challenges to European trade unions' *Transfer*, 3/2:356–376.

Dolvik, J. and Waddington (2005) 'Can trade unions meet the challenge? Unionisation in marketised services' in Bosch, G. and Lehndorff, S. (eds) *Working in the Service Sector: a tale from different worlds*, Routledge, Abingdon, pp280–296.

Donovan Report (1968) *The Royal Commission on Trade Unions and Employers' Associations 1965–1968,* HMSO, Cmnd 3623, London.

Earls, J. (2002) 'From adversarialism to aspirational – a new agenda for trade unions?' Unions21, London.

Eaton, J. and Gill, C. (1981) *The Trade Union Directory*, Pluto, London.

Edwards, P. (1983) 'The pattern of collective action' in Bain, G. (ed.) *Industrial Relations in Britain*, Blackwell, Oxford, pp209–236.

Edwards, P. (1986) *Conflict at Work: a materialist analysis of workplace relations*, Basil Blackwell, Oxford.

Edwards, P. (1995) 'Strikes and industrial conflict' in Edwards, P. (ed.) *Industrial Relations - theory and practice in Britain*, Blackwell, Oxford, pp434–460.

Edwards, P., Belanger, J. and Wright, M. (2006) 'The bases of compromise in the workplace: a theoretical framework' *British Journal of Industrial Relations*, 44/1:125–145.

Egan, A. (1982) 'Women in banking: a study in inequality' *Industrial Relations Journal*, 13/3:20–31.

European Foundation for the Improvement of Living and Working Conditions (2001) *Developments in the financial services sector*, Eurofound, Dublin.

European Monitoring Centre on Change (2003) *European Restructuring Monitoring Quarterly*, 3, Dublin.

European Monitoring Centre on Change (2004) *Financial services sector: what future?*, Dublin.

Fairbrother, P. (1989) *Workplace unionism in the 1980s: a process of renewal*, Workers' Educational Association, London.

Fairbrother, P. (2000) *Trade unions at the crossroads*, Mansell, London.

Farnham, D. and Giles, L. (1995) 'Trade unions in the UK: trends and counter-trends since 1979' *Employee Relations*, 17/2:5–22.

Financial Services Skills Council (2006) *UK Financial Services: five years forward*, FSSC, London.

Flanders, A. (1970) 'Collective bargaining: prescriptions for change' in Flanders, A. (ed.) *Management and Unions: the theory and reform of industrial relations*, Faber and Faber, London, pp.155–221.

Freeman, M. (1984) *Taking Control – a handbook for trade unionists*, Junius, London.

Fosh, P. and Cohen, S. (1990) 'Local trade unionists in action: patterns of union democracy' in Fosh, P. and Heery, E. (eds) *Trade Unions and their Members*, Macmillan, Basingstoke, pp107–146.

Gall, G. (1993) 'Industrial relations in UK clearing banks: a comment on Cressey and Scott' *New Technology, Work and Employment*, 8/1:67–71.

Gall, G. (1997) 'Developments in trade unionism in the finance sector in Britain' *Work, Employment and Society*, 11/2:219–235.

Gall, G. (1999) 'The changing nature of industrial relations and trade unionism in Britain; the case of workers and their unions in the banking industry' in Upchurch, M., (ed.) *State, Labour and Capital; comparative dynamics of national economies,* Mansell, London, pp113–140.

Gall, G. (2001) 'From adversarialism to partnership? Industrial relations in the finance sector in Britain' *Employee Relations*, 23/4:353–375.

Gall, G. (2003) *The Meaning of Militancy? Postal workers and industrial relations*, Ashgate, Aldershot.

Gall, G. (2004) 'Trade union recognition in Britain, 1995–2002: turning a corner?' *Industrial Relations Journal*, 35/3:249–270.

Gall, G. (2005a) 'Organising non-union workers as trade unionists in the 'New Economy' in Britain' *Economic and Industrial Democracy*, 26/1:43–65.

Gall, G. (2005b) 'Union organising in the 'new economy' in Britain' *Employee Relations*, 27/2:208–225.

Gall, G. (2005c) *The Political Economy of Scotland: Red Scotland? Radical Scotland?*, University of Wales Press, Cardiff.

Gall, G. (2005d) 'The Fruits of Labour? The bargaining and organising outcomes of the new recognition agreements' British Universities Industrial Relations Association Conference, July 2005, University of Northumbria, Newcastle.

Gall, G. (2007) 'Trade union recognition in Britain: a crisis of union capacity?' *Economic and Industrial Democracy*, 2007, 28/1:83–114.

Gall, G. (forthcoming) 'Labour union responses to participation' in Wilkinson, A., Gollan, P., Marchington, M. and Lewin, D. (eds), *The Oxford Handbook of Participation in Organisations*, Oxford University Press, Oxford.

Gall, G. and Hebdon, R. (2008) 'Conflict at work' in Bacon, N., Blyton, P., Fiorito, J. and Heery, E. (eds) *Sage Handbook of Employment and Industrial Relations*, Sage, London, pp588–605.

Gall, G and McKay, S. (1994) 'Trade union derecognition in Britain, 1988–1994' *British Journal of Industrial Relations*, 32/3:433–448.

Gall, G. and McKay, S. (1999) 'Developments in union recognition and derecognition in Britain, 1994–1998' *British Journal of Industrial Relations*, 37/4:601–614.

Geary, J. and Trif, A. (2008) 'Who gains from partnership? The distribution of benefits from workplace partnership in Irish retail banking' Paper presented to 26th annual International Labour Process Conference, Dublin, Eire.

Haipeter, T. (2002) 'Banking and finance in France and Germany - new regulations of work and working time: a challenge for the trade unions?' *Transfer*, 3/2:493–503.

Haipeter, T. and Pernod-Lemattre, M. (2005) 'Lean banking: direct and retail banking in France and Germany' in Bosch, G. and Lehndorff, S. (eds) *Working in the Service Sector: a tale from different worlds*, Routledge, Abingdon, pp213–231.

Hall, M. (2003) 'Consultation – union only arrangements' *IPA case study*, number 3, series 4.

Hall, M. (2004) 'Informing and consulting your workforce – union based arrangements at Abbey' *IPA case study*, number 6, series 4.

Harrington, J. (2001) 'Sisters' organising – the future for trade unions?' Critical Management Conference, University of Manchester, Manchester.

Harrington, J. (2003) 'Gender and women's union participation' International Labour Process Conference, University of West of England, Bristol.

Harrington, J. (2005) 'Women's employment and the experience of local trade union activity' in Stewart, P. (ed.) *Employment, Trade Union Renewal and the Future of Work: the experience of work and organisational change*, Palgrave Macmillan, Basingstoke, pp118–142.

Hartley, J, (1996) 'The 'new' service sector: employment status, ideology and trade union participation in the UK' in Pasture, P., Verbeckmoes, J., and de Witte, H. (eds) *The Lost Perspective? Trade union between ideology and social action in the new Europe: volume 2 significance of ideology in European trade unionism,* Avebury, Aldershot, pp326–352.

Haynes, P. and Allen, M. (2001) 'Partnership as union strategy: a preliminary evaluation' *Employee Relations*, 23/2:164–187.

Heery, E. (1997a) 'Performance-related pay and trade union de-recognition' *Employee Relations*, 19/3:208–221.

Heery, E. (1997b) 'Performance-related pay and trade union membership' *Employee Relations*, 19/5:430–442.

Heery, E. and Kelly, J. (1989) "A Cracking Job for a Woman' – a profile of women trade union officers' *Industrial Relations Journal*, 20/3:192–202.

Heery, E. and Kelly, J. (1994) 'Professional, participative and managerial unionism: an interpretation of change in trade unions' *Work, Employment and Society* 8/1:1–22.

Holden, L. (1999) 'The perception gap in employee empowerment: a comparative study of banks in Sweden and Britain' *Personnel Review*, 28/3:222–241.

Hyman, R. (1983) 'White collar workers and theories of class' in Hyman, R. and Price, R. (eds) *The New Working Class? White-collar workers and their organisations*, Macmillan, London, pp3–45.

Hyman, R. (1989) *Strikes*, fourth edition, Macmillan, London.

Incomes Data Services (1996) *Partnership Agreements, IDS Study* 656.

Income Data Services (1998a) 'Pay in financial services' *Report*, 773:9–17.

Incomes Data Services (1998b) *Pay and Conditions in Call Centres*, IDS, London.

Incomes Data Services (1998c) 'Barclays bank: introducing performance related pay' *IDS Report*, 757:25–28.

Income Data Services (1999a) 'Pay in finance' *Report*, 797:9–18.

Incomes Data Services (1999b) *Pay and Conditions in Call Centres*, IDS, London.

Income Data Services (2000a) 'Pay in banking and finance' *Report*, 822:12–19.

Incomes Data Services (2000b) *Pay and Conditions in Call Centres*, IDS, London.

Industrial Participation Association (1996) *Towards Industrial Partnership: a new approach to relationships at work*, IPA, London.

Industrial Relations Services (1991) 'Negotiating for change: restructuring at TSB retail bank' *IRS Employment Trends* 495:11–14.

Industrial Relations Services (1993) 'Militancy of bank staff underestimated, claims report' *IRS Employment Trends* 533:6.

Industrial Relations Services (1995a) 'Staff associations: independent unions or employer-led bodies?' *IRS Employment Trends*, 575:6–11.

Industrial Relations Services (1995b) 'UNiFI is launched to meet 'age of uncertainty' in finance' *IRS Employment Trends*, 582:3–4.

Industrial Relations Services (1995c) 'Dealing with redundancy and job loss: a union response' *IRS Employment Trends*, 582:5–12.

Industrial Relations Services (1996) 'Turning the tide: new unionism in finance' *IRS Employment Trends*, 619:12–16.

Industrial Relations Services (1997) 'New pay drive hard bargaining' *IRS Employment Trends*, 640:7–16.

Industrial Relations Services (1999d) 'European works councils: an account at Midland bank' *IRS Employment Trends*, 682:12–16.

Industrial Relations Services (1999b) 'United we stand' *IRS Employment Trends*, 691:6–11.

Industrial Relations Services (1999c) 'One big union' *IRS Employment Trends*, 691:11–16.

Industrial Relations Services (1999d) 'Pay Reports: Finance' *IRS Pay and Benefits Bulletin*, 472:8–12.

Industrial Relations Services (2000) 'Life after merger: managing change at Lloyds TSB' *IRS Employment Trends*, 709:11–16.

Industrial Relations Services (2004) 'No small change: industrial relations in the finance sector' *IRS Employment Trends*, 797:21–23.

Industrial Relations Services (2005) 'AXA EWC agrees restructuring principals' *European Works Council Bulletin*, 58.

Involvement and Participation Association (2002) 'How partnership is maintaining employment at Abbey National' *IPA Bulletin*, Number 16, May.

Jacks, D., Pullinger, D. and Reilly, P. (2000) 'Keep watching' *People Management*, 14 September.

Jefferys, S. and Contrepois, S. (1999) 'French and British bank union activist ideologies and identities' Unpublished paper, University of Keele.

Jefferys, S. and Contrepois, S. (2001) 'French and British bank union activist ideologies' Unpublished paper, University of North London.

Jenkins, C. (1990) *Against the Collar: struggles of a white-collar union leader*, Methuen, London.

Jenkins, C. and Sherman, B. (1979) *White Collar Unionism: the rebellious salariat*, Routledge, London.

Kelly, J. (1996) 'Union militancy and social partnership' in Ackers, P., Smith, C. and Smith, P. (eds) *The New Workplace and Trade Unionism: critical perspectives on work and organisation*, Routledge, London.

Kelly, J. (1998) *Rethinking Industrial Relations: mobilization, collectivism and long waves*, Routledge, London.

Kelly, J. (1999) 'Social partnership in Britain – good for profits, bad for jobs and unions' *Communist Review*, 30:3–10.

Kelly, J. (2004) 'Social partnership agreements in Britain: labor co-operation and compliance' *Industrial Relations*, 43/1:267–92.

Kelly, J. (2005) 'Social partnership agreement in Britain' in Stuart, M. and Martinez Lucio, M. (eds) *Partnership and Modernisation in Employment Relations*, Routledge, London, pp188–209.

Kelly, J. and Heery, E. (1994) *Working for the Union: British trade union officers*, C.U.P., Cambridge.

Kersley, B., Alpin, C., Forth, J., Bryson, A., Bewley, H., Dix, G. and Oxenbridge, S. (2006) *Inside the Workplace: findings from the 200 Workplace Employment Relations Survey*, Routledge, London.

Kessler, S. and Palmer, G. (1996) 'The Commission on Industrial Relations in Britain 1969–1974: a retrospective and a prospective evaluation' *Employee Relations*, 18/4:6–96.

Knights, D. and McCabe, D (1997) 'How would you measure something like that? Quality in a retail bank' *Journal of Management Studies*, 34/3:371–388.

Knights, D. and McCabe, D. (1998a) 'The times they are a' changing': transformative organizational innovations in financial services' *International Journal of Human Resource Management*, 9/1:168–184.

Knights, D. and McCabe, D (1998b) 'What happens when the phone goes wild? BPR, stress and the worker' *Journal of Management Studies*, 35/2:163–194.

Knights, D. and McCabe, D. (1999c) 'There are no limits to authority? TQM and organizational power relations' *Organization Studies,* 20/2:197–224.

Knights, D. and McCabe, D. (1998d) 'Dreams and designs on strategy: a critical analysis of TQM and management control' *Work, Employment and Society*, 12/3:433–56

Knights, D. and McCabe, D. (1998e) 'When 'Life is But a Dream': obliterating politics through business process reengineering, *Human Relations*, 51/6:761–789.

Knights, D. and McCabe, D (2000) "Ain't misbehavin'? Opportunities for resistance under new forms of 'quality' management' *Sociology*, 34/3:421–436.

Labour Relations Commission (2005a) 'Our changing voluntary system of industrial relations' *LRC Review*, 5/2:2–6.

Labour Relations Commission (2005b) 'Unions can deliver change quickly says IBOA leader' *LRC Review*, 5/2:25–27.

Labour Research Department (1992) 'Banking on workers to pay with jobs' *Labour Research*, 81/6:15–16.

Labour Research Department (1997) *Report on banking for BIFU*, Labour Research Department, London.

Lawler, T. and Serrano del Rosal, R. (1999) 'Banking' Rigby, M., Smith, R. and Lawler, T. (eds) *European Trade unions – change and response*, Routledge, London, pp139–180.

Lockwood, D. (1958) *The Black Coated Workers*, Allen and Unwin, London.

Lumley, R. (1973) *White-Collar Unionism in Britain: a study of the present position*, Methuen, London.

Luton, G. (2001) 'Trade union density in the European banking sector' in Jefferys, S., Beyer, F. and Thornqvist, C. (eds) *European Working Lives: continuities and change in management and industrial relations in France, Scandinavia and the UK*, Edward Elgar, Cheltenham, pp230–247.

Lynch, R. (1998) 'No stopping bank staff- when they know they can win' in Cohen, S. (ed.) *What's Happening? The truth about work and the myth of partnership*, Trade Union Forum, London.

MacInnes, J. (1988) 'New technology in Scotbank: gender, class and work' in Hyman, R. and Streeck, W. (eds) *New Technology and Industrial Relations*, Blackwell, Oxford, pp128–140.

Malcolm, C. (n.d.) *The Bank of Scotland, 1695–1945*, R. and R. Clark, Edinburgh.

Maksymiw, W., Eaton, J. and Gill, C. (1990) *The British Trade Union Directory*, Longman, London.

Marchington, M., Goodman, J., Wilkinson, A. and Ackers, P. (1992) *New Developments in Employee Involvement*, Employment Department, Sheffield.

Marginson, P. (1999) 'Employment security in banking: the case of the Co-operative bank' *EIROnline*, European Foundation for the Improvement of Living and Working Conditions, Dublin.

Marsh, A. and Ryan, V. (1980) *Historical Directory of Trade Unions: volume 1 non-manual unions*, Gower, Farnborough.

Martinez Lucio, M. and Stuart, M. (2005) 'Suspicious minds? Partnership, trade union strategy and the politics of contemporary employment relations' in Stewart, P. (ed.) *Employment, Trade Union Renewal and the Future of Work: The Experience of Work and Organisational Change*, Palgrave, Basingstoke, pp212–230.

Melling, J. (2004) 'Leading the white-collar union: Clive Jenkins, the management of trade union officers and the British labour movement' *International Review of Social History*, 49/1:71–102.

McCabe,D. (2000) 'The swings and roundabouts of innovating for quality in UK financial services' *Service Industries Journal, 20/4:1–20.*

McCabe,D. (2004) 'A land of milk and honey'? Reengineering the 'past and the 'present' in a call centre' *Management Studies, 41/5:827–856.*

McCabe, D. (2007) *Power at Work: how employees reproduce the corporate machine*, Routledge, London.

McCabe, D., Knights, D., Kerfoot, D., Morgan, G. and Willmott, H. (1998) 'Making sense of 'quality'? Towards a review and critique of quality initiatives in financial services' *Human Relations*, 51/3:389–411.

McCracken, M. and Sanderson, M. (2004) 'Trade union recruitment: strategic options?' *Employee Relations*, 26/3:274–291.

Morgan, G. and Sturdy, A. (2000) *Beyond Organisational Change: structure, discourse and power in UK financial services*, Macmillan, Basingstoke.

Morris. T. (1986a) *Innovations in Banking: Business Strategies and Employee Relations*, Croom Helm, London.

Morris, T. (1986b) 'Trade union mergers and competition in British banking' Industrial Relations Journal, 17/2:129–140.

Morris, T. and Willman, P. (1994) 'The union of the future and the future of unions' *Employee Relations*, 16/2:100–108.

Morris, T., Storey, J. Wilkinson, A. and Cressey, P. (2001) 'Industry change and union mergers in British retail finance' *British Journal of Industrial Relations*, 39/2:237–256.

Mueller, M. (1997) 'Institutional resilience in a changing world economy? The case of German banking and chemical industries' *British Journal of Industrial Relations*, 35/4:609–626.

Müller-Jentsch, W. (1985) 'Trade unions as intermediary organisations' *Economic and Industrial Democracy*, 6/1:3–33.

Munn, C. (1982) *Banking in Scotland*, Scottish Banking Practice series, second edition, Institute of Bankers in Scotland, Edinburgh.

Munn, C. (1988) *Clydesdale Bank: the first one hundred and fifty years*, Collins, Glasgow.

MSF (1999) *Achieving Employability in the Insurance Industry*, Manufacturing, Science and Finance Union, London.

Offe, C. and Wisenthal, H. (1985) 'Two logics of collective action' in C. Offe, (ed.) *Disorganised.*

*capitalism: contemporary transformation of work and politics*, Polity Press, Cambridge. pp. 170–220.

Oxenbridge, S. and Brown, W. (2002) 'The two faces of partnership? An assessment of partnership and co-operative employer/trade union relationships' *Employee Relations*, 24/3:262–276.

Oxenbridge, S. and Brown, W. (2004) 'Achieving a new equilibrium? The stability of cooperative employer-union relationships' *Industrial Relations Journal*, 35/5:388–402.

Oxenbridge, S. and Brown, W. (2005) 'Developing partnership relationship: a case of leveraging power' in Stuart, M. and Martinez Lucio, M. (eds) *Partnership and Modernisation in Employment Relations*, Routledge, London, pp83–100.

Parker, J. (2005) 'The many faces of eve: women's groups, diversity and democracy in British unions' *Warwick Papers in Industrial Relations*, No. 76, IRRU, Warwick University.

Poynter, G. (2000) *Restructuring in the Service Industries: management reform and workplace relations in the UK service sector*, Mansell, London.

Prandy, K., Stewart, A. and Blackburn, R. (1974) 'Concepts and measures: the example of unionateness' *Sociology*, 8/3:427–446.

Prandy, K., Stewart, A. and Blackburn, R. (1983) *White-Collar Unionism*, Macmillan, London.

Pritchard, T. (2006) *Amicus – the union: a history of the union in badges*, Amicus, London.

Pugh, P. (1998) *The Strength of Change – transforming a business for the 21st Century*, Penguin, London.

Purcell, J. (1984) 'Industrial relations in building societies' *Employee Relations*, 6/1:1–5.

Ramsay, H. (1977) 'Cycles of control: worker participation in sociological and historical perspective' *Sociology*, 11/3:481–506.

Redman, T., Wilkinson, A. and Snape, E. (1997) 'Stuck in the middle? Managers in building societies' *Work, Employment and Society*, 11/1:101–114.

Regini, M., Kitay, J. and Baethge, M. (eds) (1999) *From Tellers to Sellers – changing employment relations in banks*, MIT Press, London.

Robinson, O. (1969) 'Representation of the white-collar worker: the bank staff associations in Britain' *British Journal of Industrial Relations*, 7/1:19–41.

Rose, E. (2002) 'The labour process and union commitment within a banking services call centre' *Journal of Industrial Relations*, 44/1:40–61.

Samuel, P. (2005) 'Partnership working and the cultivated activist' *Industrial Relations Journal*, 36:1/59–76.

Samuel, P. (2007) 'Partnership consultation and employer domination in two British life and pensions firms' *Work, Employment and Society*, 21/3:459–477.

Saville, R. (1996) *Bank of Scotland – a history 1695–1995*, Edinburgh University Press, Edinburgh.

Sherman, B. (1986) *The State of the Unions*, Wiley, Chichester.

Smith, D. (1986) 'Organisational culture and management development in building societies' *Personnel Review*, 15/3:15–19.

Snape, E. (1994) 'Union organising in Britain: the views of local full-time officials' *Employee Relations*, 16/8:48–62.

Snape, E., Redman, T. and Wilkinson, A. (1993) 'Human resource management in building societies: making the transformation?' *Human Resource Management Journal*, 3/3:24–43.

Sparrow, P. (1996) 'Transitions in the psychological contract: some evidence from the banking sector' *Human Resource Management Journal*, 6/4:75–92.

Storey, J. (1995) 'Employment policies and practices in UK clearing banks: an overview' *Human Resource Management Journal*, 5/4:24–43.

Storey, J., Cressey, P., Morris, T. and Wilkinson, A. (1997) 'Changing employment practices in UK banking; cases studies' *Personnel Review*, 26/1–2:24–42.

Storey, J., Wilkinson, A., Cressey, P. and Morris, T. (1999) 'Employment relations in UK banking' in Regini, M., Kitay, J. and Baethge, M, (eds) *From Tellers to Sellers: Changing Employment Relations in Banks*, MIT Press, London, pp129–157.

Stuart, M. and Martinez Lucio, M. (2005) 'Building labour-management cooperation in the UK insurance sector: varieties of partnership in an environment of uncertainty' British Academy of Management HRM Special Interest Group Conference, Nottingham University Business School, Nottingham.

Stuart, M. and Martinez Lucio, M. (2008) 'Employment relations in the UK finance sector: between globalisation and re-regulation' Unpublished paper, University of Leeds, Leeds.

Stuart, M. Charlwood, A., Martinez Lucio, M. and Wallis, E. (2007) *Trade Union Modernisation Fund – Stage B: interim reports of projects in progress,* University of Leeds, Leeds

Swabe, A. (1989) 'Performance-related pay: a case study' *Employee Relations*, 11/2:17–23.

Swabe, A. and Price, P. (1984a) 'Building a permanent association? The development of staff associations in the building societies' *British Journal of Industrial Relations*, 22/2:195–204.

Swabe, A. and Price, P. (1984b) 'White-collar unionism in building societies' *Employee Relations*, 6/3:8–12.

Tailby, S, Richardson, M. Upchurch, M. Danford, A. and Stewart, P. (2007) 'Partnership with and without trade unions in the UK financial services: filling or fuelling the representation gap?' *Industrial Relations Journal*, 38/3:210–228.

Taylor, P. and Bain, P. (1999a) 'An assembly-line in the head': work and employee relations in the call centre' *Industrial Relations Journal*, 30/2:101–117.

Taylor, P. and Bain, P. (1999b) *Trade unions and call centres,* MSF, London.

Taylor, P. and Bain, P. (2001) 'Trade unions, workers' rights and the frontier of control in UK call centres' *Economic and Industrial Democracy,* 22/1: 39–66.

Taylor, P. and Bain, P. (2003) *Call centres in Scotland and outsourced competition from India*, Scotecon, University of Stirling, Stirling.

Taylor, P. and Bain, P. (2004) 'Call centre offshoring to India: the revenge of history?' *Labour and Industry*, 14/3:15–38.

Taylor, P. and Bain, P. (2005) 'India calling to the far away towns: The call centre labour process and globalization' *Work, Employment and Society*, 19/2: 261–282.

Taylor, P. and Bain, P. (2007) 'Trade union responses to call centre offshoring' in Cumbers, A. and Whittam, G. (eds) *Reclaiming the Economy: Alternatives to Market Fundamentalism in Scotland and Beyond*, Scottish Left Review Press, Biggar, pp80–95.

Taylor, P., Gall, G., Bain, P. and Baldry, C. (2005) 'Organisational turbulence and workplace relations' in Stewart, P. (ed.), *Employment, Trade Union Renewal and the Future of Work: the experience of work and organisational change*, Macmillan-Palgrave, Basingstoke, pp20–40.

Taylor, R. (1978) *The Fifth Estate – Britain's unions in the modern world*, Pan, London.

Terry, M. (1983) 'Shop steward development and managerial strategies' in Bain, G. (ed.) *Industrial Relations in Britain*, Blackwell, Oxford, pp67–94.

Terry, M. (1995) 'Trade unions; shop stewards and the workplace' in Edwards, P. (ed.) *Industrial Relations – theory and practice in Britain*, Blackwell, Oxford, pp203–226.

Terry, M. and Newell, H. (1996) 'Workers' participation in work organisation: the banking industry in the United Kingdom' *Economic and Labour Relations Review*, 7/1:46–66.

Thornley, C., Contrepois, S. and Jeffreys, S. (1997) 'Trade unions, restructuring and individualisation in French and British banks' *European Journal of Industrial Relations*, 3/1:83–105.

TUC (1999a) *Partnership – the way forward*, Trades Union Congress, London.

TUC (1999b) *Partner for progress*, Trades Union Congress, London.

Tuckman, A. and Snook, J. (2006) 'Cracking Egg: representation, employee representatives and voice at an online financial services provider' Paper presented to British Universities' Industrial Relations Association annual conference, Galway, Eire.

Tuckman, A. and Snook, J. (2008) 'Employee autonomy or organisational closure? Non-union employee voice in the new economy' Paper presented to 26th annual International Labour Process Conference, Dublin, Eire.

Undy, R., Ellis, V., McCarthy, W. and Halmos, A. (1981) *Change in Trade Unions: the development of UK unions since the 1960s*, Hutchinson, London.

Undy, R., Fosh, P., Morris, H., Smith, P., and Martin, R. (1996) *Managing the unions: the impact of legislation on trade unions' behaviour*, Clarendon Press, Oxford.

Unifi (2000a) 'Conference 2000 – General Secretary's speech' *Unifi News*, 23 May.

Unifi (2000b) *unifi@work/barclays*, March, Unifi, London.

Unifi (2001) 'Striking a balance' *Fusion*, February/March, Unifi, London, pp18–19.

Unifi (2002) *Unifi members survey 2001 report*, Unifi, London.

Unions21 (n.d.) 'A new generation' available at http://www.unions21.org.uk/newgen/UNIFI.htm.

Unite (2007) *Pay Bargaining in Unite Finance Sector: executive summary*, Unite, London.

Upchurch, M. and Danford, A. (2001) 'Industrial restructuring, 'globalisation' and the trade union response: a study of MSF in the south west of England' *New Technology, Work and Employment*, 16/2:100–117.

Upchurch, M. Richardson, M. Tailby, S. Danford A. and Stewart, P. (2006) 'Employee representation and partnership in the non-union sector: A paradox of intention?' *Human Resource Management Journal*, 16/4:393–410.

Upchurch, M., Danford, A., Tailby, S., Richardson, M. and Stewart, P. (2008) *The Realities of Partnership at Work*, Palgrave, Basingstoke.

Waddington, J. (1995) *The Politics of Bargaining: The merger process and British trade union structural development, 1892–1987*, Mansell, London.

Waddington, J. (2004) 'Why do members leave? The importance of retention to trade union renewal', mimeo, University of Manchester, Manchester.

Waddington, J. and Whitson, C. (1996) 'Collectivism in a changing context; union joining and bargaining preferences amongst white collar staff' in Leisink, P., van Leemput, J., and Vilrokx, J. (eds) *The Challenge to Trade Unions in Europe: innovation or adaptation,* Edward Elgar, Cheltenham, pp153–167.

Waddington, J. and Whitson, C. (1997) 'Why do people join unions in a period of membership decline?' *British Journal of Industrial Relations*, 35/4:515–546.

Weekes, B., Mellish, M., Dickens, L and Lloyd, J. (1975) *Industrial Relations and the Limits of the Law: The industrial effects of the Industrial Relations Act, 1971*, Basil Blackwell, Oxford.

Wilkinson, A. (1995) 'Towards HRM? A case study from banking' *Research and Practice in Human Resource Management*, 3/1:97–115.

Wilkinson, A. and Holden, L. (2001) 'Long term patterns in strategic human resource management: a case study from financial services' *International Journal of Employment Studies*, 9/2:1–27.

Wilkinson, A., Redman, T. and Snape, E. (1998) 'Employee involvement in the financial services sector: problems and pitfalls' *Journal of Retailing and Consumer Services*, 5/1:45–54.

Willman, P. (1986) *Technological Change, Collective Bargaining and Industrial Efficiency*, Clarendon Press, Oxford.

Willman, P. (1989) 'The logic of 'market share' trade unionism: is membership decline inevitable?' *Industrial Relations Journal*, 20/4:260–270.

Willman, P. (2005) 'Circling the wagons: endogeneity in union decline' in Fernie, S. and Metcalf, D. (eds) *Trade Unions: resurgence or demise?*, Routledge, Abingdon, pp45–61.

Willman, P., Morris, T. and Aston, B. (1993) *Union Business: trade union organisation and financial reform in the Thatcher years*, Cambridge University Press, Cambridge.

Wills, J. (1996) 'Uneven reserves: geographies of banking trade unionism' *Regional Studies*, 30/4:359–372.

Wills, J. (2004) 'Trade unionism and partnership: evidence from the Barclays-Unifi agreement' *Industrial Relations Journal*, 35:4/329–343.

Winterton, J. and Winterton, R. (1982) 'Employee representation in building societies' *Employee Relations*, 4/2:11–16.

# Index